Deterrence

Deterrence

Rising Powers, Rogue Regimes, and Terrorism in the Twenty-First Century

Edited by
Adam B. Lowther

DETERRENCE
Copyright © Adam B. Lowther, 2012.

All rights reserved.

First published in 2012 by
PALGRAVE MACMILLAN®
in the United States—a division of St. Martin's Press LLC,
175 Fifth Avenue, New York, NY 10010.

Where this book is distributed in the UK, Europe and the rest of the
World, this is by Palgrave Macmillan, a division of Macmillan Publishers
Limited, registered in England, company number 785998, of Houndmills,
Basingstoke, Hampshire RG21 6XS.

Palgrave Macmillan is the global academic imprint of the above
companies and has companies and representatives throughout the world.

Palgrave® and Macmillan® are registered trademarks in the United
States, the United Kingdom, Europe and other countries.

ISBN: 978–1–137–28979–7

Library of Congress Cataloging-in-Publication Data

Deterrence : rising powers, rogue regimes, and terrorism in the
    twenty-first century / edited by Adam B. Lowther.
      p. cm.
   ISBN 978–1–137–28979–7 (hardback)
   1. Deterrence (Strategy)   2. United States—Military policy.
   I. Lowther, Adam.
   U162.6.D487 2012
   355.02'17—dc23   2012024484

A catalogue record of the book is available from the British Library.

Design by Integra Software Services

First edition: December 2012

10 9 8 7 6 5 4 3 2 1

Transferred to Digital Printing in 2013

To our spouses and children. We work for the nation's defense so they may live in a peaceful world.

Contents

List of Figures and Tables ... ix

Foreword by Major General William A. Chambers ... xi

Acknowledgments ... xv

1 Introduction: How Has Deterrence Evolved? ... 1
 Adam B. Lowther

I Deterrence in Cyberspace

2 Can an Operationally Responsive Cyberspace Play a Critical Role in the Strategic Deterrence Equation? ... 17
 Kevin R. Beeker, Robert F. Mills, Michael R. Grimaila, and Michael W. Haas

3 Does the United States Need a New Model for Cyber Deterrence? ... 33
 Kamaal T. Jabbour and E. Paul Ratazzi

II Nuclear Deterrence

4 Is Nuclear Deterrence Still Relevant? ... 49
 Elbridge Colby

5 Can Tailored Deterrence and Smart Power Succeed Against the Long-Term Nuclear Proliferation Challenge? ... 75
 Jonathan Trexel

6 Is a New Focus on Nuclear Weapons Research and Development Necessary? ... 97
 Anne Fitzpatrick

7 Missile Defenses and Nuclear Arms Reductions: Can Deterrence Withstand the Attention? ... 117
 Stephen J. Cimbala

III Nontraditional Deterrence

8 Are Rogue Regimes Deterrable?   135
   Gary Schaub Jr.

9 How Can the United States Deter Nonstate Actors?   163
   Adam B. Lowther

10 Is Space Deterrence Science Fiction?   183
   Dale Hayden

11 Can Unmanned Aerial Systems Contribute to
   Deterrence?   215
   James D. Perry

Notes on Contributors   237

Index   241

FIGURES AND TABLES

FIGURES

5.1	Strategic deterrence model	77
5.2	Long-term deterrence scenarios and strategies	80
5.3	Strategy options	81
5.4	Campaigning and bargaining	86
5.5	Bargaining early	88
7.1	US-Russia arriving retaliatory weapons, 1100 deployment limit	125
7.2	US-Russia arriving retaliatory weapons, 1100 deployment limit, random defense penetration	126
7.3	US-Russia, arriving retaliatory weapons, 800 deployment limit	126
7.4	US-Russia, surviving and retaliating warheads, 800 deployment limit, random defense penetration	127
7.5	US-Russia, arriving retaliatory weapons, 400 deployment limit	127
7.6	US-Russia, arriving retaliatory weapons, 400 deployment limit, random defense penetration	128

TABLES

2.1	Comparison of ORS to ORC	22
3.1	The AF's strategic imperatives are enabled by nine primary technical capabilities	35

3.2	Cyberspace differs fundamentally from other domains	39
5.1	Long-term deterrence strategy overview	83
11.1	Manned vs. unmanned aircraft	221
11.2	Hours on station per sortie for manned and unmanned aircraft at a given range	222
11.3	Number of persistent orbits a force of 100 aircraft generates at a given range	222

Foreword

We are in the post-post–Cold War era and the strategic environment continues to shift before our very eyes. The US National Military Strategy notes that "ongoing shifts in relative power and increasing interconnectedness in the international order indicate a strategic inflection point." The landscape at this inflection point is a mix of the familiar and the foreign.

The United States remains the world's preeminent power, and nation-states play the primary role in the globalized world they created. However, there are nation-states of increasing influence that were not coauthors of the existing rule sets and international norms. Many have a regional perspective, not a global perspective, but their regional interests cannot be pursued without global effect. We do not yet know for certain how they will adapt and where they will challenge current structures.

Instant global reach is a defining characteristic of the twenty-first century. It reinforces our interconnectedness and, at the same time, provides asymmetric opportunity to nonstate actors. Even now, there remain non-status-quo states that keep their populaces in the dark or subject them to information manipulation.

Nuclear weapons and deterrence remain characteristics of the post-post–Cold War. On April 5, 2009, in Prague, President Obama stated that "the United States will take concrete steps towards a world without nuclear weapons. To put an end to Cold War thinking, we will reduce the role of nuclear weapons in our national security strategy, and urge others to do the same. Make no mistake: As long as these weapons exist, the United States will maintain a safe, secure and effective arsenal to deter any adversary, and guarantee that defense to our allies."

These few words capture many of the challenges facing those who study and conduct deterrence in the twenty-first century, with multiple nuclear-armed states, rising regional non-status-quo powers, nonstate actors, and an intertwined network of allies and partners. There are regions where multiple states possess nuclear weapons for divergent reasons with conflicting doctrines and beliefs regarding their efficacy, and where geography and operational reach shape, or shake, stability.

The United States remains the sole power able to reach and influence every one of these regions, but our own historical and cultural values are manifest in offshore hesitancy, which sometimes produces a distinct lag in the development of both grand strategy and operational concepts. We will find ourselves in situations simultaneously conducting deterrence (to prevent a power from considering harm against us), extending deterrence (to protect allies and partners), and underwriting assurance (to maintain security relationships and support nonproliferation). Tailoring twentieth-century platforms and weapon systems to such a problem set requires fresh thinking.

To transcend Cold War thinking, we need to move beyond reliance solely on deterrence through imposition of costs, to integrate denial of benefits and methods to encourage restraint. To do this sort of thinking requires diversity in our analytical tool kits. We should retain effective classic methodologies (e.g., game theory) and at the same time integrate newer behavioral approaches outside a *rational* state-based actor construct.

It also requires an understanding that reductions in arsenal sizes change the problem itself and do so in a nonlinear manner. The combination of smaller arsenals and multiple nuclear-armed states is not a matter of arithmetic.

We will see continued efforts to decrease our and our allies' military expenditures. This demands that we increase rigor behind our analysis of the capabilities needed to deter and the platforms, personnel, and concepts sufficient to generate those capabilities. While we require sufficiency, we have little room for overcapacity.

A major challenge of deterrence in the twenty-first century lies in understanding the contribution of nonnuclear capabilities and proper integration of defensive systems. Success will also require the right mix of specific capabilities across air, cyber, and space domains that influence adversaries' decision calculus. Employing conventional and nuclear force structures, postures, and doctrines to create synergistic effect across these domains will require innovation. The freedom to maneuver in these domains will not only provide the president valuable options for influencing an adversary's decision-making process, but is a prerequisite to successfully reducing our reliance on nuclear weapons.

Perhaps it is counterintuitive, but as we "reduce the role of nuclear weapons in our national security strategy, and urge others to do the same," we must increase our commitment to improving expertise and modernizing our forces. With smaller arsenals, we can afford less risk in either systems or personnel. The illusionary, but logical, tension between decreasing the role of nuclear weapons, while at the same time strengthening deterrence, means that it will remain challenging to recruit and retain the best. An encouraging sign is the number of young academics conducting new analysis and openly debating and publishing on nuclear issues and twenty-first-century deterrence.

As we continue the work of reducing the size of the world's nuclear arsenals, and as we analyze the rich complexity of our current strategic setting, efforts such as this volume are welcome additions to the much needed discussion and debate of deterrence concepts. This work provides much for the serious student of deterrence to contemplate and poses several ideas and methods to meet the challenges of deterrence in the twenty-first century.

William A. Chambers, Maj. Gen., USAF
Assistant Chief of Staff, Strategic Deterrence & Nuclear Integration

Acknowledgments

Without the support of the Air Force Research Institute (AFRI), this work would not be possible. Gen. John Shaud, PhD (Ret.), and Dr. Dale Hayden were particularly helpful in providing the time needed to complete this volume. My contributors also deserve special thanks. Without their patience in the midst of a long process, this work would not have such excellent chapters. The editorial staff at Palgrave Macmillan has also been a pleasure to work with. Finally, I would like to thank my wife for editing each chapter in the midst of a busy schedule.

CHAPTER 1

Introduction: How Has Deterrence Evolved?

Adam B. Lowther

Rapidly evolving strategic challenges, difficult fiscal conditions, and a desire to refashion national security policy are giving new life to an old concept—deterrence. While two decades of constant military operations in Iraq, Afghanistan, and elsewhere are largely responsible for American decision makers focusing on present conflicts, scholars and strategists are beginning to undertake a long-overdue reexamination of Washington's approach to national security. This renaissance in strategic thinking is leading many to reconsider deterrence theory and practice. According to *Joint Publication 1–02, Department of Defense Dictionary of Military and Associated Terms*, deterrence is defined as "The prevention from action by fear of the consequences. Deterrence is a state of mind brought about by the existence of a credible threat of unacceptable counteraction." From this definition it is easy to see that deterrence can incorporate a wide range of means that are focused on an equally wide array of actors. Unfortunately for deterrence thinking, the concept was often seen as synonymous with the nation's Cold War nuclear strategy, which played a major role in post–Cold War stagnation. Efforts are now under way to expand the context in which deterrence may prove useful in defending national interests against a host of new and developing threats.

During the half-century-long Cold War the United States and Soviet Union maintained an uneasy peace largely because each country relied on a deterrence theory and policies that focused on preventing nuclear war. Theorists, such as Bernard Brodie, Herman Kahn, and Thomas Schelling, clearly emphasized that conventional conflict could escalate into nuclear war, thus requiring careful attention on the part of statesmen.[1] The special circumstances of the Cold War kept attention focused on *preventing* nuclear war rather than analyzing the continuities between nuclear and "lesser included" conflicts.

The watershed events represented by the end of the Cold War and the terrorist attacks of September 11, 2001, called into question the relevance of deterrence as a strategic approach. Falling out of favor soon after the Soviet Union's collapse, democratization, globalization, and a focus on second and third world economic development displaced the decades-long focus on hard power.[2] Nuclear operations seemed less relevant in a world characterized by diverse challenges such as failed states, humanitarian disaster, genocidal conflict, counter/nonproliferation, terrorism, and asymmetric conflict. Amid this changing strategic milieu, few sought to adapt deterrence's central premise—altering an ally's or adversary's behavior—to remain a relevant strategic approach. Instead, a new paradigm was needed for a "New World Order."[3]

A generation later, optimism has faded as conflict and strife has proven as persistent as ever. Thus, a new opportunity for deterrence is presenting itself. However, if deterrence is to be relevant, it must move well beyond the vestiges of its Cold War past and focus on linking efforts to desired effects—regardless of the actor being deterred. In other words, states that adopt deterrence as part of a comprehensive strategy should be able to determine, with a fair degree of certainty, that the policies and initiatives intended to deter some behavior actually achieve their objective. The difficulty in establishing such causation, however, makes the success of deterrence difficult to determine.

While theorists and practitioners agree that, at its core, deterrence is about convincing adversaries and allies that the costs of an undesirable action are greater than the rewards, demonstrating success remains so elusive that a number of policy makers are reluctant to invest in new deterrence concepts and strategies. As in the past, moving deterrence forward will require an understanding of an adversary's motives, decision-making processes, and objectives.[4] While the Cold War structure may have evolved to give strategists some degree of confidence that American capability, force structure, and alliances deterred the principal adversary, today's diversity of challenges increases the complexity of formulating successful deterrence strategies.[5] In fact, not all adversaries may be deterrable. This may be particularly true of some nonstate actors.

Several analysts postulate that globalization has fundamentally transformed the security environment, making unilateral state action impractical and ineffective.[6] Those who adopt this perspective often argue that the threat-based nature of deterrence creates a diplomatic and military environment that precludes constructive conflict resolution.[7] Others claim that the fiscal costs of developing and maintaining the military platforms necessary to sustain a credible deterrent are prohibitively expensive and ineffectively consume limited resources that could be more efficiently used to better humanity.[8] Others see the primary utility of deterrence in deterring nuclear weapons and their potential to prevent or cause major conflicts.

The lack of a post–Cold War "school of thought" has produced a situation in which the understanding of deterrence has stagnated. Thus, deterrence is receiving woefully inadequate consideration as a potential approach to the defense of the nation's vital, major, and peripheral interests. Ultimately, this could lead to policies that do not consider the full range of available options. Preventing such an outcome by encouraging deterrence thinking is the objective of this volume. Before turning to the specific chapters, which take a more granular look at specific aspects of deterrence, addressing four broad questions may serve to set the baseline for understanding.

What Is Twenty-First Century Deterrence?

When it comes to deterrence, there are more questions than answers. Those who expect quick, concise, and immediate answers are destined to be frustrated by the highly theoretical nature of deterrence thinking. Those who would like to move deterrence into new areas may experience similar frustration as the conversation quickly becomes constrained to notions of nuclear deterrence, arms control, and counter- or nonproliferation. There are, however, several insights that can inform policy discussions.

First, deterrence may not work in all situations. Some adversaries are simply unlikely to be deterred by the means available to the state. When such an adversary arises, containment or eradication may be the only viable options. However, understanding the culture, interests, and objectives of an adversary has the potential to decrease the number of adversaries who cannot be deterred.[9] Possessing a value system that differs from Western norms does not make an adversary irrational. It requires greater knowledge and understanding on the part of the United States and its allies, if deterrence is to be successful.

For instances in which statecraft does apply, situations can and should be shaped without resorting to the threats inherent in deterrence interactions. This suggests that states develop coherent and comprehensive approaches that are applicable to the global security environment and that they deliberately employ all instruments of power to achieve preferred objectives. In such a context, states would focus and tailor their strategies according to the demands of the threat.[10]

In situations where deterrence may apply, policy makers must determine the appropriate instruments ensuring that they effectively communicate the desired state of affairs (status quo) and that the target audience accepts it. Additionally, the success of deterrence depends on the ability to understand an adversary's behavior and possible countermoves. In the absence of such assessment, deterrence will remain a theoretical construct with little relation to actual conditions as they actually exist.

Second, although it may not be possible to deter all nonstate actors, it may be possible to deter many.[11] This is an area requiring further research aimed at developing an understanding of these actors' objectives and values. Only by understanding a nonstate actor can the United States and its allies target what it values most. While it is often said that Islamic fundamentalists are undeterrable, they do seek to achieve tangible worldly objectives.[12] This presents an opportunity to develop an effective set of deterrence policies that may include all aspects of diplomacy, information, military, and economics. To the extent that criminals, insurgents, terrorists, and other groups represent challenges to state and international security, they operate outside the accepted laws of conflict out of weakness, not an inherent preference for the "tactics of the weak." To suggest that nonstate actors are—by nature—irrational would be a grave mistake.[13]

Finally, as long as states possess nuclear weapons and as long as there are those willing to share weapons of mass destruction (WMD) information and technology, deterrence remains a valid strategic approach. Where states have acquired such capabilities, deterrence is the primary approach that provides a foundation for governing interaction with adversaries. For states that seek to acquire WMD, deterrence provides an approach that states can use to counter the proliferation threat.

What Means Are Available for Deterrence?

During the Cold War, the means of deterrence would not have generated significant interest. They were simple, straightforward, and well understood. However, the collapse of the Soviet Union on Christmas Day 1991, followed a decade later by the 9/11 terrorist attacks on the United States, left many within the academic and policy communities searching for new solutions to current problems. Most importantly, these events undermined the foundation on which Cold War deterrence was built. Before December 25, 1991, it was widely understood that deterrence and nuclear weapons went hand in hand and were reliable partners. The end of the Cold War decoupled the two.

During the 1990s, globalization and democratization filled the void left by the Cold War's end. Although the United States experienced terrorist attacks on more than a few occasions before 9/11, it was not until the attacks on New York City and Washington, DC, that national security policy focused on the defeat of violent Islamic fundamentalism. Nonstate actors became the primary threat to American security. The elimination of al Qaeda and other terrorist networks rose to preeminence among foreign policy and military objectives. Kinetic force became the primary instrument of power.

The mood of Washington did, however, change when a new administration took office in January 2009. This presented an opportunity to examine the usefulness of deterrence in an international system where the primary threats to security and stability are, and will remain, rogue regimes and nonstate actors—with the potential for a peer competitor down the line.[14] For deterrence to once again play a prominent role in defense policy, the instruments of deterrence must be applicable to current threats.

Unlike the Cold War, violent Islamic fundamentalism does not pose an existential threat to the United States. However, this does not mean that the United States should not maintain its capabilities (means) at all levels of conflict.

Nuclear deterrence will remain the capstone of defense policy for many years to come. Determining the correct number of weapons and the proper mix of delivery platforms is a critical challenge for maintaining credible nuclear deterrence. While the threat of nuclear conflict is greatly diminished from its Cold War height, disarmament would allow and encourage adversaries operating at the lower end of the conflict spectrum to seek equality with the United States. Thus, it may be possible to deter nuclear proliferation by maintaining a credible nuclear deterrent.

With a wide variety of threats to security and stability in the international system, a new set of "red lines" that effectively communicate boundaries to potential adversaries are required. Not only do rogue regimes and nonstate actors pose a significant threat to American interests, but their tactics (terrorism and cyber attack) are among the more difficult to deter. These adversaries operate from a rationale that is difficult for Americans to understand and develop effective deterrence policies to counter.[15]

Thinking in terms of weapons of "mass effect" rather than weapons of mass destruction may be a better approach. In an era where cyberwarfare is becoming an increasingly important capability of state and nonstate actors—even as terrorism remains a key threat—the role of kinetic force is diminishing. Deterring current and future adversaries will require an expanded set of tools that rely more on the diplomatic, informational, and economic elements of national power.[16]

Intelligence will play an increasingly important role in supporting policies of dissuasion, denial, and deterrence. American Cold War strategists believed that they understood rational Soviet leaders. The same cannot be said of modern adversaries who do not operate within the same rational framework as their Western adversaries. Intelligence plays a vital role in providing the knowledge and understanding required to develop credible deterrence policies.

Strategic communication will play an important role in undermining an adversary's attempts to establish the narrative and capture the moral high ground—a key component of any deterrence strategy. Nonstate actors are experienced at manipulating media coverage to gain the sympathy that often accompanies coverage of the "underdog." They are also adept at maximizing the public relations benefits of mistakes made by stronger adversaries. Successful nonstate actors are masterful in articulating a set of grievances that draw support from target audiences. Effectively countering the communications and public relations efforts of nonstate actors has the potential to undermine their cause and deter their efforts.

Rather than allowing nonstate actors to deter states through superiority in information/communication operations, states must develop the capability to deter nonstate actors through similar advantages. This may prove particularly difficult for democracies that are often unwilling to develop effective propaganda capabilities.[17]

Modernizing the instruments of deterrence for an international security environment different from its Cold War predecessor is long overdue and may yield unanticipated benefits. Doing so does not, however, guarantee the success of deterrence. Like all strategies, deterrence is prone to shortcomings that require alternative courses of action. As the following section illustrates, deterrence is not a magic bullet.

WHY DOES DETERRENCE FAIL?

Actors operate within a strategic environment where incomplete information and sub-optimal choices are characteristic of decision making. Some scholars suggest that decision makers operate within a framework of bounded rationality where variables such as stress, fear, exhaustion, and imperfect information abound.[18] Decision makers can see their adversaries very differently than they actually are due to the importance of cultural, historical, linguistic, political, or religious difference. These limits in rationality and understanding can lead to a lack of situational awareness, poor signaling, misinformation, confusion, and the misreading of signals.[19]

Deterrence may fail because the United States, or any actor, does not understand its adversary. As mentioned earlier, American decision makers often operate without understanding an adversary's culture, history, language, politics, and religion. Mirror imaging frequently occurs, leading decision makers to develop deterrence policies that are less effective than potentially possible.[20] The war in Iraq is one example where a more complete understanding of these variables may have led to the development of policies that could have deterred a domestic-led or foreign-led insurgency.

There may also be a "credibility gap" between capability and will. Although the United States possesses unrivaled economic and military might, American decision makers, for many reasons, often respond to deterrence failures with insufficient punitive action to restore the status quo and credibility. This creates a gap between capability and will. Thus, future adversaries may not be deterred because of a history of unconvincing American action. For example, Osama bin Laden stated in a post-9/11 interview that weak American responses to previous al Qaeda attacks created an expectation that President Bush would respond in a limited fashion to the 9/11 attacks, as had previous administrations.[21]

While ambiguity is a necessary element of a deterrence strategy, communicating a message that is too ambiguous can mislead an adversary and suggest that the United States, for example, will accept a change in the status quo when it will not. Ambiguity has worked best when uncertainty surrounds the severity of a response, not the possibility of a response. One of the most widely used examples of too great a degree of ambiguity is the July 25, 1990, comments of the US ambassador to Iraq April Glaspie. She stated to Saddam Hussein that the United States had "no opinion" on the conflict between Iraq and Kuwait. This opened the door for the Iraqi dictator's invasion of his neighbor.

One scholarly study suggests that approximately 30 percent of conflicts are initiated by the weak with an attack on the strong.[22] Despite the probability of defeat or annihilation, strong states frequently fail to deter weaker adversaries because the weaker state is highly motivated (asymmetry of interests), misperceives the probable response, and seeks to take advantage of an acute military vulnerability. Although risks often outweigh rewards, weaker states frequently feel risks more acutely.[23] The Japanese attack on Pearl Harbor is the most familiar example of a weaker state attacking a much stronger adversary despite an admittedly low probability of winning a prolonged conflict. For the Japanese, the risks of not attacking far outweighed the risks of an American response.[24] This was the result of clear misperception of American will by the Japanese High Command.

Often deterrence fails because of a combination of the above points. Rarely is it one variable that causes an adversary to seek a change in the status quo, despite an articulated deterrence policy. It is, however, clear that the United States and others can reduce deterrence failures by more effectively communicating with an adversary. Successfully deterring current and future adversaries will depend on these variables.

What Impacts a Deterrence Strategy?

Undoubtedly, answering this final question is the most difficult of the four. The breadth of the question allows for varying interpretations of its meaning, which is useful in making three final points.

First, decision makers (political and military) in democracies are particularly guilty of focusing almost solely on current threats, rather than long-term strategic interests. Deterrence, on the other hand, is dependent on developing effective policies well in advance of an adversary's attempt to alter the status quo. This condition requires decision makers to devise a tailored strategy and policy, effectively communicate objectives, and respond to potential threats well in advance of any adversary taking action.[25]

Second, the nuclear umbrella and extended deterrence remain a critical component of American foreign policy. As Japan remains committed to a nonnuclear defense posture—despite growing threats—the credibility of deterrence that the United States extends weighs heavily in the strategic calculations of the nuclear umbrella's beneficiaries. Further reduction in the operationally deployed strategic nuclear force is of great concern to the Japanese, for example, and risks encouraging proliferation should extended deterrence lose credibility. Japan and other allies have the potential to rapidly join the nuclear club should perceived threats and a lack of American commitment warrant such a response.

Third, public debate of deterrence concepts, policy, and strategy is a difficult task that often devolves into emotion-laden arguments. During the Cold War, the respected nuclear strategist Herman Kahn advocated a policy that would have enabled the United States to survive and win a nuclear conflict with the Soviet Union. His frank and calculating approach led policy makers, journalists, and scholars to dismiss his ideas. Today, it is equally difficult to discuss deterrence in public venues. The often-unpleasant policy choices that are required lead policy makers, journalists, academics, and the American public to reject the entire discussion.

Although Herman Kahn found fostering a public debate on nuclear strategy difficult, there was at least some interest in the topic by the public at large. Today, nuclear issues are passé and often seen as a relic of the Cold War. As in the past, today's threats require that decision makers contemplate unseemly options, which the public find at odds with American values. In part, this volume seeks to further an often stagnant debate.

FORMAT

To shed new light on deterrence—moving beyond the Cold War—the contributors to this work were asked to address specific questions relating to one or more of deterrence's many applications or characteristics. While there is a broad consensus among the contributors that deterrence will remain relevant throughout the twenty-first century, there are differences in perspective when it comes to the prospects of successfully deterring peer competitors, rogue regimes, and nonstate actors across all domains with conventional and nuclear forces. Each chapter focuses on addressing a contemporary question that is relevant to the current debate and assumes at least some knowledge of deterrence.

The work is divided into three sections that address

1. the prospects for deterrence in cyberspace,
2. the relevance of nuclear deterrence in the twenty-first century, and
3. new approaches to conventional deterrence.

Section I begins with "Can an Operationally Responsive Cyberspace Deter Adversaries?" Kevin R. Beeker, Robert F. Mills, Michael R. Grimaila, and Michael W. Haas suggest that deterrence in cyberspace is possible and that it should look much like the current approach to deterrence in space. They argue for the creation of an operationally responsive cyberspace capability that brings government and private-sector cyber assets together to focus on a three-tiered approach. Tier 1 centers on the employment of capabilities, Tier 2 focuses on reconstitution efforts, and Tier 3 incorporates efforts to develop new capabilities. In all, the authors suggest that cyber deterrence is possible, if the right actions are taken.

"Does the United States Need a New Model for Cyber Deterrence?" begins by examining the distinct differences between the cyber domain and those of air, land, sea, and space. Kamaal T. Jabbour and E. Paul Ratazzi point out how some of the differences in fundamental characteristics make traditional approaches to deterrence unlikely to succeed. They offer alternatives that are more likely to succeed given the current state of technology and understanding.

Section II begins with "Is Nuclear Deterrence Still Relevant?" Elbridge Colby argues that those who posit a fundamentally different strategic environment in which major war is no longer possible are mistaken. Liberal values, economic globalization, and the international community have not changed the nature of conflict. Colby argues that human nature has not changed, making fear, honor, and interest no less drivers of human action today than they were in the time of Thucydides. Thus, nuclear deterrence and the nuclear arsenal remain as relevant today as they were during the Cold War.

In "Can Tailored Deterrence and Smart Power Succeed against the Long-Term Nuclear Proliferation Challenge?" Jonathan Trexel moves beyond the strict limitations of nuclear deterrence to suggest that a new approach to long-term deterrence is necessary. In keeping with the approach laid out in the 2006 *Deterrence Joint-Operating Concept*, Trexel seeks to move deterrence beyond its Cold War roots, making it a concept that can be employed against a wide array of actors that challenge US interests. One particular challenge he is concerned with is the proliferation of nuclear weapons in the years and decades ahead.

Anne Fitzpatrick asks, "Is a New Focus on Nuclear Weapons Research and Development Necessary?" In addressing this question, she examines the changing nature of knowledge in nuclear weapons science and research, development, test, and evaluation (RDT&E) since the end of underground testing. She focuses on the nuclear weapons enterprise and stockpile stewardship programs and explores recent developments in knowledge generation.

The final chapter in this section asks, "Missile Defenses and Nuclear Arms Reductions: Can Deterrence Withstand the Attention?" Here, Stephen Cimbala examines the planned US-NATO missile shield in an effort to determine whether it may destabilize nuclear deterrence between the US and Russia and how it may affect further reductions in the two country's nuclear arsenals. With Russian leaders expressing concern that US-NATO missile defense may make an attempted Russian retaliatory strike ineffective, Cimbala examines a pertinent issue of strategic consequence.

Section III incorporates a number of chapters that examine deterrence in relation to nontraditional actors and tools. It begins with Gary Shaub's "Are Rogue Regimes Deterrable?" He examines the deterrence literature highlighting the fact that it often explains adversary intent from the perspective of one of two frameworks: strategic intent or internal logic. Actors were either motivated by a desire to change the status quo to mitigate external threats or because they sought to influence an internal audience. Schaub suggests that both have explanatory power and are incorporated into the US Strategic Command's *Deterrence Operations Joint Operating Concept*. This, he argues, is the right approach.

Adam Lowther takes on the challenge of deterring nonstate actors in "How Can the United States Deter Nonstate Actors?" He suggests that a layered approach to deterrence is required. Addressing the threat posed by nonstate actors at the international, domestic, and individual levels is necessary. And, at each level, policies that employ dissuasion, denial, and threat are critical to ensuring that deterrence does not fail if one particular effort is unsuccessful. By creating a layered approach to deterrence that employs multiple methods, deterrence has a greater chance to succeed.

In "Is Space Deterrence Science Fiction?" Dale Hayden argues that the Cold War approach to deterrence is insufficient for the challenges posed by space. With the United States committed to keeping space weapons-free, Hayden suggests that a new approach to deterring adversaries from attacking US space assets is required. He proposes creating a space force that is resilient, responsive, and cost effective. If successful, the United States will deter adversaries by demonstrating that the United States can rapidly reconstitute any loss of space-based capabilities.

The final chapter examines innovative approaches to ensuring the success of conventional deterrence. "Can Unmanned Aerial Systems Contribute to Deterrence?" takes an innovative look at the role of unmanned aerial systems (UAS) in a conventional deterrence strategy. James Perry suggests that they can serve as strike and intelligence, surveillance, and reconnaissance (ISR) platforms, which can be employed against peer-competitors, rogue regimes, and nonstate actors. UASs can play an important role in holding that which an adversary values at risk. Because these systems are unmanned, the United States can take much greater risks with these assets—a fact that may improve the effectiveness of a conventional deterrence strategy.

In the end, the central theme of this work is simple. Deterrence remains relevant. Those who think about deterrence are not stuck in the Cold War. In fact, in difficult fiscal circumstances, deterrence may be more relevant than ever. The liberal dream held by neo-conservatives and internationalists alike is an expensive one that the United States may no longer have the resources to fulfill. If this is true, expending greater energy on often cost-effective deterrence strategies may be the best approach for the United States.

NOTES

1. See Bernard Brodie, *Strategy in the Missile Age* (Princeton, NJ: Princeton University Press, 1959); Herman Kahn, *On Thermonuclear War* (New Brunswick, NJ: Transaction, 1960); and Thomas Schelling, *Arms and Influence* (New Haven, CT: Yale University Press, 1966).

2. John Lewis Gaddis, "Toward the Post–Cold War World," *Foreign Affairs* 70, no. 2 (Spring 1991): 102–122.
3. Walter Russell Meade, "The Bush Administration and the New World Order," *World Policy Journal* 8, no. 3 (Summer 1991): 375–420.
4. Robert Jervis, Richard Ned Lebow, and Janice Gross Stein, *Psychology and Deterrence* (Baltimore, MD: Johns Hopkins University Press, 1985).
5. Lawrence Freedman, *The Evolution of Nuclear Strategy* (New York: St. Martin's Press, 1989).
6. Charlene Haddock Siegfried, "The Dangers of Unilateralism," *NWSA Journal* 18, no. 3 (Fall 2006): 20–32.
7. Fotios Moustakis and Rudra Chaudhuri, "The Rumsfeld Doctrine and the Cost of US Unilateralism: Lessons Learned," *Defence Studies* 7, no. 3 (November 2007): 358–375.
8. Lawrence J. Korb, Alex Rothman, and Laura Conley, "Defensible Budget Cuts," Center for American Progress, April 13, 2011.
9. Alexander George, "The Need for Influence Theory and Actor-Specific Behavioral Models of Adversaries," *Comparative Strategy* 22, no. 5 (December 2003): 463–487.
10. Schelling, ch. 1; and Lawrence Freedman, *Deterrence* (Malden, MA: Polity Press, 2004), 76–80.
11. Gary Geipel, "Urban Terrorists in Continental Europe after 1970: Implications for Deterrence and Defeat of Violent Nonstate Actors," *Comparative Strategy* 26, no. 5 (October 2007): 439–467.
12. Kristopher K. Robinson, Edward M. Crenshaw, and J. Craig Jenkins, "Ideologies of Violence: The Social Origins of Islamist and Leftist Transnational Terrorism," *Social Forces* 84, no. 4 (June 2006): 2009–2026.
13. Lee Dutter and Ofira Seliktar, "To Martyr or Not to Martyr: Jihad Is the Question, What Policy Is the Answer?" *Studies in Conflict and Terrorism* 30, no. 5 (May 2007): 429–443.
14. Directorate of Strategic Planning, Headquarters, United States Air Force, *Strategic Environmental Assessment* (Washington, DC: US Air Force, 2011), 11–15.
15. Bruce Hoffman, "A Counterterrorism Strategy for the Obama Administration," *Terrorism and Political Violence* 21, no. 3 (July 2009): 359–377.
16. Robert Gates, *Quadrennial Defense Review Report* (Washington, DC: Department of Defense, 2010), 57–69.
17. Shireen Burki, "Ceding the Ideological Battlefield to al Qaeda: The Absence of an Effective US Information Warfare Strategy," *Comparative Strategy* 28, no. 4 (September/October 2009): 349–366.
18. Behrooz Kalantari, "Herbert A. Simon on Making Decisions: Enduring Insights and Bounded Rationality," *Journal of Management History* 16, no. 4 (September 2010): 509–520.
19. Dan Lindley and Ryan Schildkraut, "Is War Rational? The Extent of Miscalculation and Misperception as Causes of War," *Conference Papers—International Studies Association* (Tucson, AZ: International Studies Association, 2006).

20. Marc Reuel Gerecht, "Mirror-Imaging the Mullahs: Our Islamic Interlocutors," *World Affairs* 170, no. 3 (Winter 2008): 91–100.
21. See Bruce Lawrence, ed., *Message to the World: The Statements of Osama bin Laden* (New York: Verso Press, 2005), 155–156.
22. Barry Wolf, *When the Weak Attack the Strong: Failures of Deterrence* (Santa Monica, CA: RAND Publishing, 1991), ch. 2.
23. Ibid., 11.
24. Michael Slackman, *Target: Pearl Harbor* (Honolulu: University of Hawaii Press, 1990), ch. 1.
25. Freedman, *Deterrence*, ch. 3.

SECTION 1

DETERRENCE IN CYBERSPACE

CHAPTER 2

CAN AN OPERATIONALLY RESPONSIVE CYBERSPACE PLAY A CRITICAL ROLE IN THE STRATEGIC DETERRENCE EQUATION?

KEVIN R. BEEKER, ROBERT F. MILLS, MICHAEL R. GRIMAILA, AND MICHAEL W. HAAS

> The views expressed in this article are those of the authors and do not reflect the official policy or position of the United States Air Force, Department of Defense, or the United States Government.
>
> Cyber superiority ensures freedom of action in all domains (and denies freedom of action to adversaries) ... predicate to all military and national security ops.
>
> Lt. Gen. Robert L. Elder[1]

INTRODUCTION

Superiority does not imply complete dominance in a warfighting domain; if superiority in any domain were easily gained, there would be little need for our military to deter an adversary from conducting attacks against the United States and its interests, both at home and abroad. In Operation

Desert Storm, the Iraqi Air Force flew 122 aircraft to Iran to avoid destruction by coalition air forces.[2] This operation demonstrates a successful deterrent strategy on our part, because the Iraqis knew full well that the cost of attacking the coalition's air forces would be far higher than any benefit that could be gained by having them fight directly. Granted, those 122 aircraft did not comprise the entire Iraqi air defense capability; Iraq retained and employed other air defense capabilities, resulting in the loss of 37 fixed-wing aircraft and 5 helicopters on the part of the United States and its allies.[3]

At a micro level, the coalition's loss of these aircraft might represent a "prohibitive interference" for accomplishment of tactical missions, but at a macro level, most would accept that the coalition had achieved air superiority and was not prohibitively restricted from accomplishing its goals. Going into the conflict, we knew that there would be opposition, and we were prepared to operate in a contested environment. Air superiority had to be established in varying degrees in different geographical areas to ensure overall mission accomplishment.

As we mature our understanding of military operations in cyberspace, a number of questions arise. For example, what does cyberspace superiority really mean, and how is it achieved? How can and should we deter attacks in and through cyberspace against our national interests? Assuming that deterrence fails, how do we conduct operations ("fight through") in a contested cyberspace environment? What lessons can we learn from deterrence concepts in other domains that might shed some light on cyberspace "fight-through"? The purpose of this chapter is to examine some of these concepts as they relate to cyberspace. First, we discuss a deterrence strategy that is based on denying benefits to adversaries for their actions. This strategy is highly applicable to the cyberspace environment because it avoids some of the problems associated with attribution and instead focuses on mission assurance. Next, we discuss what the space community has done in terms of developing a mission assurance strategy, the cornerstone of which is called operationally responsive space, or ORS. We then show how many of the problems and challenges of cyberspace deterrence and security are actually quite similar to space and then describe how far an operationally responsive cyberspace (ORC) capability will go in addressing many of our deterrence needs.

DETERRENCE STRATEGY: DENIAL OF BENEFITS

Deterrence is all about convincing an adversary to not do something undesirable. A useful framework for developing a deterrence strategy is the Department of Defense (DOD) *Deterrence Operations Joint Operating*

Concept (DO JOC), which provides the military's doctrinal foundation for deterrence operations. The central idea of the *DO JOC* is "to decisively influence the adversary's decision-making calculus in order to prevent hostile actions against US vital interests."[4] The *DO JOC* seeks to accomplish this deterrence through a combination of strategies such as denying benefits, imposing costs, and encouraging restraint.[5] The actor seeking to deter attempts to view each effort from the adversary's point of view, because it is in the adversary's mind that the decision to commit the act is made. Deterrence is successful when the perceived costs incurred by an adversary outweigh the perceived benefits in regard to the consequences of restraint. Deterrence fails if an adversary perceives that a benefit of taking an action outweighs any associated costs, and then commits those actions.

Beeker et al.[6] provide a more detailed discussion of how the *DO JOC* model can apply in cyberspace. For the remainder of this chapter, we will focus primarily on the denial of benefits. A prime example of how denying benefits can support deterrence and mission assurance is our approach to chemical or biological weapons. The US military equips its forces with mission-oriented protective posture (MOPP) gear and trains its members to carry out their missions despite the potential use of biological and chemical weapons on the battlefield. This preparation demonstrates to enemies that while their use of such weapons may make it more inconvenient for us to conduct our mission, *we will get it done*. In other words, the adversaries will be denied whatever reward they seek by employing such weapons and would hopefully decide not to use them in the first place. If they are not deterred from using those weapons, then our training and exercising will ensure that our forces can operate safely and continue the mission with minimal casualties.

Similarly, our cyberspace deterrence strategies should seek to deny benefits to adversaries from their actions against us in and through cyberspace. Exercising and proving capabilities to operate while under duress or to fight through cyberspace attacks will contribute to cyberspace deterrence. The United States must be able to fight through attacks in cyberspace, including being able to bring the fight to adversaries when required. This in turn will deny them benefits should they desire to attack. Demonstrating an ability to operate in a contested network environment will help influence any adversaries not to conduct cyberspace attacks against the United States, because there will be little permanent or lasting effect. The ability to recover from and generate a quick, effective, and overwhelming response to an attack in cyberspace is an important factor in deterring an adversary's initiation of attack.

Domain Comparison: Space versus Cyberspace

While examining deterrence within cyberspace, it is useful to examine the common ground between space and cyberspace strategies. Space and cyberspace are "utility domains" in that they enable operations in other domains. It is difficult to imagine trying to conduct operations in the air, on land, and at sea without space and cyberspace capabilities. A Government Accountability Office (GAO) report on military space operations recognized that space systems play an "increasingly important role in DoD's overall warfighting capability as well as the economy and the nation's critical infrastructure" and that "this growing dependence, however, is also making commercial and military space systems attractive targets for adversarial attacks."[7] Similarly, President Obama, in his remarks on securing the nation's information technology (IT) infrastructure, said:

> From now on, our digital infrastructure—the networks and computers we depend on every day—will be treated as they should be: as a strategic national asset. Protecting this infrastructure will be a national security priority. We will ensure that these networks are secure, trustworthy and resilient. We will deter, prevent, detect, and defend against attacks and recover quickly from any disruptions or damage.[8]

But space and cyberspace are also warfighting domains in their own right—contested domains at that. Military commanders realize that space dominance can no longer be assumed. Consequently, on March 30, 2009, Admiral Mullen, the chairman of the Joint Chiefs of Staff, introduced a new special area of emphasis, titled "Space as a Contested Environment." Space systems are vulnerable to a variety of attack vectors, including electronic jamming, dazzling, and debris fields causing kinetic destruction. Cyberspace is similar, and perhaps even more complicated, because the cost of entry for a cyberspace actor is much lower than for space. Costs include gaining the required technical expertise, the ability to command and control attacks, and the time to develop attack capabilities as well as the monetary costs to participate in the given domain. The interdependency between space and cyberspace is significant. Barriers to entry in the form of costs are traditionally higher in space, and it becomes much easier for someone to attack our space capabilities through the cyberspace domain, which fundamentally changes the deterrence equation. Deterrence strategies must recognize and address these cross-domain attacks; further, space and cyberspace planners must work together to explore and understand these issues.

To help ensure that we have unfettered access to space, United States Strategic Command (USSTRATCOM) created an ORS capability that uses activities in three tiers to improve robustness and enhance our deterrence posture. Conceptually, Tier 1 involves leveraging existing capabilities (employment) to meet the needs of a joint force commander (JFC); an example might be adjusting a satellite orbit to provide better coverage in a warfighting region. Tier 2 involves replacing a damaged satellite or providing capability via small launchers within weeks (launch/deploy). Finally, Tier 3 addresses rapid development and deployment, such as deploying a new satellite to fill a capability gap within months. USSTRATCOM works closely with all of the combatant commands and JFCs to identify requirement gaps in the space infrastructure and prioritize requests for space capabilities.

A key element of the Tier 2 ORS strategy is the Rapid Response Space Center (RRSC), or the Chile Works.[9] The RRSC should be fully operational in 2015, and its purpose is to use pre-built components, solar arrays, power sources, and control mechanisms to attach to payloads (such as imagery and communications), in order to rapidly field a satellite in a matter of days. While establishing an ORS office to develop contingency plans may better position the United States in the space domain and to some extent affect an adversary's decision making, building and funding a project like the Chile Works sends a much stronger message by demonstrating our resolve and ability to sustain capabilities in a contested environment.

A rapid satellite development and launch capability communicates to our adversaries that despite their efforts to destroy or degrade our space capabilities, we have the resolve and wherewithal to replace those space assets if needed. The benefit portion of the deterrence calculation of adversaries is reduced by the fact that satellite destruction or disruption will not achieve their desired ends. This affects the decision to attempt satellite destruction or degradation; it might even deter them from pursuing a destructive anti-satellite program in the first place.

THE UNITED STATES NEEDS AN OPERATIONALLY RESPONSIVE CYBERSPACE CAPABILITY

Given our nation's heavy dependence on cyberspace infrastructure, one might ask how we are posturing ourselves to continue operating given that cyberspace is a contested domain. Cyberspace is perhaps more contested than is space because of the much lower cost of entry into the domain. Do we have a cyberspace equivalent of ORS? In the same way that the ORS office is designed to provide quick reconstitution upon the destruction of our space assets, is there anything that can be done in cyberspace to quickly reconstitute after the destruction or compromise

Table 2.1 Comparison of ORS to ORC

Tier	Operationally Responsive Space	Operationally Responsive Cyberspace
1	Re-tasking a remote-sensing satellite to provide reconnaissance photos	Reallocating satellite or "backbone" network bandwidth toward urgent communications need
	Requesting additional bandwidth from civilian communications satellites	Assigning extra computing processors across organizational boundaries
2	Building a new satellite with off-the-shelf components in weeks or days	Developing robust cyber infrastructure continuity of operations plans to recover and reconstitute quickly Using virtual servers and desktop thin clients Using data storage backup sites to improve redundancy Implementing the "Net Force Maneuver" concept
3	Transitioning a new capability to operational use in less than one year	Continually transitioning new cyber reconstitution/recovery technologies to operational use

of key cyberspace infrastructure? Creating an ORC capability would be a step in the right direction.

ORC would be based on similar principles to ORS (see table 2.1), but it would likely not operate in the exact same capacity. For example, ORS includes the ability to build and deploy satellites within weeks to replace damaged assets or provide new capabilities. It is unlikely that an ORC office would "build" equipment or software that is commonly associated with cyberspace infrastructure (for example, routers and computer operating systems). This is primarily due to the much more widely pervasive and varying nature of cyberspace, to include large diversity in applications, information databases, network layouts, and actual hardware.

Instead, ORC would contribute more in the areas of providing leadership and focus for cyberspace operations and capability development. Cyberspace is a created domain—created by governments, businesses, organizations, and individuals—which represents another significant difference between the domains of space and cyberspace. Within the DOD alone, many entities are responsible for creating, sustaining, and defending the cyberspace domain, including the services, combatant commands, and combat support agencies. Defending and sustaining the domain is a shared responsibility, and focusing the capability to reconstitute our cyber infrastructure in a single ORC office, even in a limited sense, would be problematic. That said, we need to think about how ORC principles could be achieved. If the network or key services are not available, whether because of an attack, accident, or self-induced maintenance action, the response to such events should not be to send people home until the "IT guys" can figure out workarounds at the local level. The ability to fight through such events is critical.

While there may not be a direct one-to-one comparison between ORC and ORS functionality, an ORC office can still be modeled on similar principles. It could still have the same three-tier focus, but instead of being directly involved in recovery and reconstitution efforts, the ORC office would be a focal point for coordinating and encouraging activities and providing guidance throughout government and our national critical infrastructure sectors. The ORC office would also advocate policy and priorities to ensure that activities in each of the tiers requiring national level attention and investment are pursued. These activities would include developing principles, lessons learned, and best practices (for example, doctrine) to better help the nation prepare and respond to attacks in and through cyberspace. As these principles are implemented, exercised, and promoted, they will have an increasing deterrent effect on adversaries' desire to attack the nation's cyberspace infrastructure. The objective is to convince our adversaries that any attempt to attack our systems would be a wasted effort because of the demonstrated ability to quickly reconstitute affected cyber resources.

Although ORC in this context is centralized at the national level, the concept can—and probably should—be decentralized in its application. USSTRATCOM oversees space reconstitution and recovery efforts for the DOD; the United States Cyber Command (USCYBERCOM) could fulfill a similar role in reconstituting DOD cyber capabilities to a certain extent without intruding upon the military services' organize, train, and equip responsibilities. In this instance, ORC looks very similar to ORS. Reconstitution and recovery capabilities must be pushed beyond and below the USCYBERCOM commander and should conceptually be constituted at the lowest possible levels. Examples abound and include backup servers for information and cyber-specific Continuity of Operations Planning (COOP). Some thoughts and ideas related to activities that could be pursued in each of the tiers are discussed below.

Tier 1

As with ORS, ORC Tier 1 focuses on how to employ existing capabilities to achieve a desired effect. For example, a particular organization may need additional bandwidth across satellite communication networks for a period of time to support a task requiring increased data rates. Or an organization may need additional computer processors beyond its current capability to complete a modeling and simulation run and may require processors from other organizations to accomplish the task.

Both of these examples would contribute to our deterrence posture. Cyberspace is a malleable, constructed domain, and the ability to change the domain quickly—whether in response to an attack or to meet near-term mission requirements—demonstrates a high degree of agility and adaptability. Re-tasking cyber infrastructure assets can be extremely complicated because of highly shared resources and the intertwined nature of cyberspace. Cyberspace assets, such as satellite communications and Internet "backbone" pipes, are used by a variety of customers that cross organizational boundaries. In these instances, there is rarely a single authority or process that can reallocate resources quickly to support emergency requests. An ORC-type office could have the responsibility to establish procedures and define authorities for making decisions to reallocate or re-task cyber infrastructure assets across organizational boundaries at the national level (for example, government versus private sector or DOD versus Department of Homeland Security). At lower levels, single authorities may be easier to identify, such as in the DOD, where USCYBERCOM has been given the responsibility for securing and defending the Global Information Grid (GIG). Even then, however, the authority to secure and defend the GIG may not provide the authority to reallocate assets within the GIG. As a result, a similar ORC reallocation function may be required at lower organizational levels as well.

Tier 2

With ORS, Tier 2 focuses on deployment, to include the ability to rapidly launch new satellite capabilities. In a similar way, we must be prepared to reconstitute our cyberspace capabilities to prove and demonstrate to an adversary our ability to fight through an attack with little or no degradation in capability. To do this, ORC must focus on all elements of the cyberspace infrastructure. This includes not only the network links over which information flows and the hardware/computers that process the information, but also the information itself stored in various databases and computer systems.

Significant strides have already been made in handling reconstitution of equipment, software, and data. Best practices for network operations include automatic failover, hot swappable storage devices, mirroring of databases and websites, and off-site storage of critical data, just to name a few. For example, if information at a primary operations center is destroyed or compromised, a backup copy of the information can be retrieved from an off-site location. In a worst-case scenario where the primary operations center is physically destroyed or needs to be moved because of a high-threat environment, backup sites can even function as alternate operations centers. Private companies such as Carbonite,[10] DriveHeadquarters,[11] and others are providing similar data storage backup capabilities to both individuals and organizations.

A vast majority of the IT professionals at all levels (unit, major command, service, and USCYBERCOM, etc.) are primarily concerned with keeping the network operational—keeping the bits and packets flowing. This activity is necessary but not sufficient for cyberspace fight through. There is a dichotomy in the perception between network defenders and operations personnel in military operations.[12] Network defenders are typically focused on ensuring the health of the networked information infrastructure and have a limited view of the operational importance of the missions supported. In contrast, operations personnel tend to be focused on their own missions and have limited understanding of how the missions depend on the cyberspace infrastructure. These communities are inherently linked, because while network operations personnel focus on maintaining the health and safety of the network and information systems, the mission operations personnel, who inherently rely on the network and information systems, focus on assuring mission operations through command decision-making. Since the network exists to support organizational missions, there needs to be a stronger focus on mission assurance and mission situational awareness.[13]

The DOD defined "mission assurance" for the first time in DOD Directive 3020.40, titled *DoD Policy and Responsibility for Critical Infrastructure*:

> A process to ensure that assigned tasks or duties can be performed in accordance with the intended purpose or plan. It is a summation of the activities and measures taken to ensure that required capabilities and all supporting infrastructures are available to the Department of Defense to carry out the National Military Strategy. It links numerous risk management program activities and security-related functions, such as force protection; antiterrorism; critical infrastructure protection; IA continuity of operations; chemical, biological, radiological, nuclear, and high explosive defense; readiness; and installation preparedness to create the synergy required for the Department of Defense to mobilize, deploy, support, and sustain military operations throughout the continuum of operations.[14]

While this definition is broad and focuses on all critical infrastructure, it clearly identifies that the ability to perform operations is what is being protected, not just the information and communications infrastructure. While this sounds like a trivial difference, it is not because its understanding requires a much stronger link between the operations and communications communities. This is one of many reasons behind the creation of the cyber operations career field within the United States Air Force (USAF).[15] This increased mission focus represents a significant culture change from traditional communications and IT support.

An often overlooked part of the mission assurance puzzle is business continuity planning (BCP), or continuity of operations planning (COOP). The purpose of BCP is to mitigate operational risks and help organizations stay in business when they are confronted with disasters, fire, data loss, cyber attacks, or other serious events. Effective mission assurance planning requires significant introspection by the end users. We must not forget that the whole point of building cyberspace is to enable information sharing among diverse and distributed users, and only they understand the context of the information being transmitted through the network.

BCP planning should be nothing new for most organizations in the DOD and should be included in any organization's continuity plans, especially those dealing with critical infrastructure. The Center for Strategic and International Studies (CSIS) Commission on Cybersecurity for the 44th Presidency summarizes the philosophy of COOP: "We will never be fully secure in cyberspace, but much can be done to reduce risk, increase resiliency, and gain new strengths."[16] The 2009 *National Infrastructure Protection Plan*, along with the underlying plans that focus on the nation's critical infrastructure sectors, also states the need for COOP and resiliency plans. However, the primary emphasis in these documents continues to be on *protection* of cyber assets, not *recovery*.[17] As a result, these documents contain little detail or guidance for generating robust COOPs that adequately meet cyber infrastructure requirements.

A strategically focused ORC office would be an ideal location to develop appropriate COOP guidance for the DOD and national critical infrastructure and provide experts to assist governmental and private organizations in developing such plans. The need for an ORC office to provide this functionality is highlighted by the fact that often COOP is not robust in cyber infrastructure.[18] A classic example of inadequate cyberspace infrastructure BCP planning came to light in the aftermath of Hurricane Katrina, during which emergency response efforts were crippled by a lack of communications: companies were unable to contact their employees to coordinate a response, and municipal websites normally used to disseminate disaster recovery and other information were unavailable for weeks.[19] It is in these areas where an ORC office could provide the needed expertise and assistance to organizations and governmental entities to ensure that their COOP plans sufficiently provide for reconstituting cyber infrastructure following attacks or other events. Further, the ORC could take on the role of developing curriculum and training for cyber infrastructure disaster recovery. This would help solve the lack of cyber infrastructure disaster recovery material within most IT curricula[20] and help ensure that personnel entering the IT career fields are able to assist their employers with robust cyber COOP plans. As robust cyber infrastructure COOPs are implemented, exercised, and updated, they will assist in creating a deterrent effect by demonstrating our will, resolve, and ability to continue operations in the face of determined opposition. These efforts will frustrate attacks by adversaries and call into question their judgment for initiating such attacks.

In addition to continuity planning, the ORC could also take a lead role in leveraging new technologies that enable rapid reconstitution and service restoral. One example would be encouraging the use of virtual servers. Virtual servers can help provide quick recovery, because if a server has a hardware failure, it can be replaced with a spare and reimaged in a matter of minutes. Thin clients can provide the same type of recovery capability to desktops. Within the USAF, the Combat Information Transport System (CITS) is designed to provide these technologies and capabilities throughout much of the USAF's cyberspace infrastructure.[21] An ORC office could take lessons learned and successes from efforts such as CITS and provide insights and advice to other governmental and private organizations on how to implement similar systems. As implementation of these technologies becomes more ingrained within the United States, our ability to respond and reconstitute quickly from cyber attacks will improve.

The previous discussion refers to reconstitution of cyberspace infrastructure and data; that is, protection of the data at rest. Another significant issue is the ability to fight through attacks that degrade or deny our communication links. Since more and more of our communication capabilities are becoming IP based (the Internet), our critical infrastructure has become less redundant and has fewer alternatives for passing information in the event that IP-based networks fail. Also, unlike data backups and computer hardware, it is difficult (and expensive) for organizations to quickly deploy new physical network infrastructure. Further, creating redundant network links, especially at the backbone level, is unlikely since the companies that run and maintain the current links operate on thin margins that do not justify significant investment to build redundant links. This is where an ORC office could advocate for funding and developing policy to assist in establishing redundant links and improved capability. Without government investment, it is unlikely that redundant links at the backbone level will ever be built. Private companies are unlikely to provide significant investment in redundant links based only on "proposed" scenarios that have yet to occur. The ORC's role would be to identify the most critical points where redundant links are needed and to ensure that they are appropriately resourced.

Finally, the ORC could assist in identifying and implementing strategies for building resiliency in organizational networks. An interesting concept is "Net Force Maneuver,"[22] which is based on the idea of polymorphic networks. The objective is to provide adversaries a confusing picture of our cyberspace infrastructure, thereby causing them to have an incorrect notion of how portions of our cyberspace infrastructure tie to certain missions and operational tasks. The adversaries' network reconnaissance and attacks will then be directed at the wrong points owing to misperception of our network operations, resulting in a diminishing return for hostile efforts. Hence, adversaries see their cost portion of the deterrence calculation increase, so that a situation is created where they are less likely to attack our critical cyber infrastructure.

Typically, maneuver warfare is seen as "a warfighting philosophy that seeks to shatter the enemy's cohesion through a variety of rapid, focused, and unexpected actions which create a turbulent and rapidly deteriorating situation with which the enemy cannot cope."[23] In the traditional warfighting perspective, offensive maneuver is used to arrange conflict at the most advantageous time and location. However, from a cyberspace perspective, maneuver can be used in a defensive manner to frustrate the attacker's ability to identify and successfully attack the right resources. Different strategies for conducting this deception could be pursued. For example, fake (but realistic) operating environments could be created to alter the adversary's perception of key network operations and the location or existence of important data. These fake environments, also known as honeypots or honeynets, could be placed on alternative links, upon which the main operations do not rely. In this case, the adversary could be led to attack the wrong targets, with little or no effect on main operations. Another potential strategy could be virtually maneuvering between different links, networks, and databases, et cetera, to make the enemy uncertain as to where the real cyber operations are occurring at any given time. The ORC office could be responsible for maturing these types of strategies and developing new techniques for Net Force Maneuver, as well as developing a doctrine for employment.

Tier 3

The focus of Tier 3 ORS capabilities is the rapid transition of new space capabilities from development to delivery in a time frame of months versus years. A Tier 3 capability in cyberspace is even more critical because of the quick-changing technology throughout the cyberspace domain. Governmental reviews continue to highlight the need for research and innovation, including President Obama's recent 60-day cyberspace policy review, which has, as part of its near-term action plan, the following:

> Develop a framework for research and development strategies that focus on game-changing technologies that have the potential to enhance the security, reliability, resilience, and trustworthiness of digital infrastructure; provide the research community access to event data to facilitate developing tools, testing theories, and identifying workable solutions.[24]

It is important to note that "resiliency" is included in the research efforts, to mean "developing options for additional services the Federal government could acquire or direct investments the government could make to enhance the survivability of communications during a time of natural disaster, crisis or conflict."[25] Also, an action to "coordinate with international partners and standards bodies to support next-generation national security/emergency preparedness communications capabilities in a globally distributed next-generation environment"[26] is included.

It is encouraging to see an increased focus on cyber infrastructure resiliency and recovery efforts, in addition to the usual heavy emphasis on network protection. However, there are several foundational research themes that must be addressed in depth to support the implementation of ORC. A significant challenge is to fully understand the cause-and-effect relationship between a given action to be undertaken and the adversary's subsequent "decision-making calculus." The cyberspace domain has many more nation-states, nongovernmental organizations, and ad hoc groups interconnected than does the space domain; there are exponentially more interrelated responses that could be triggered by any single action or set of actions. In addition, it is not beyond the realm of possibility that a set of actions could induce one or more of these interrelated nation-states, nongovernmental organizations, or ad hoc groups to move from a neutral mindset to an adversarial mindset adding complexity, and potentially deepening a conflict. This is true of either defensive or offensive actions, if made public.

Effects caused by offensive cyber actions can be classified as affecting the physical domain and the cognitive domain. Physical domain effects of a cyber action can be evaluated on test hardware and software that replicates, as closely as possible, the hardware and software environment being targeted. It is much more difficult to predict, or even forecast, how future cyber actions will affect the cognitive domain. In addition, uncertainty exists regarding cascading effects in the cognitive domain—that is, subsequent (higher order) effects caused by cognitive domain effects that are directly attributable to the initial cyber actions. Cognitive domain effects are a function of many variables, such as culture; perceived conditions of one's environment; the perceived target of the attack; level of belief in the knowledge of the attacker's identity; content of any present internal media coverage; and reaction by governmental, secular, or religious leaders.

Development of a robust understanding of the cause-and-effect link between defensive and offensive cyber actions undertaken for deterrence and resultant influence on potential adversaries must be accelerated and maintained at a high level to keep pace with rapid advances in cyberspace technology. This increased understanding of cause-and-effect links within the cognitive domain will reduce the potential of deepening future conflicts by presenting combatant commanders with a more predictable set of cognitive effects achievable through the use of offensive and defensive cyber actions. In essence, the increased understanding of achievable cognitive domain effects associated with a particular set of cyber actions increases the level of security by increasing the assurance that the desired cognitive domain effects will be achieved and by reducing the risk of generating unwanted initial or cascading cognitive domain effects, as discussed earlier. An ORC office would take the lead in increasing the emphasis on research into cyber infrastructure recovery and reconstitution, and transitioning new technologies, capabilities, and processes to both governmental and private sectors. Through these efforts, the ORC could fulfill Tier 3-type activities and contribute to deterrence by proving to our adversaries our commitment to recovery and reconstitution capabilities and mission accomplishment. A comparison of efforts within each tier across the space and cyberspace domains was presented in table 2.1 as an enabling concept.

CONCLUSION

The domains of space and cyberspace have such great similarities that when policy makers, leaders, and strategists develop deterrence policies, they should consider how they can complement and support each other. Deterrence efforts impose costs, deny benefits, and encourage adversary restraint. In space, USSTRATCOM's Operationally Responsive Space office contributes to deterrence by denying the adversary the benefits of a space attack. ORS efforts signal to others that attacks against our satellites and space assets will be less effective, because these attacks can be mitigated using a three-tiered approach to developing, deploying, and employing space capabilities.

An Operationally Responsive Cyberspace construct affords much the same result for our nation in cyberspace. ORC would contribute to denying benefit to potential adversaries through a combination of robust cyber infrastructure continuity of operation plans, focused research and development of new recovery and reconstitution technologies, exercises that demonstrate and advance Net Force Maneuver and related concepts, and dedicated research efforts focused on cyber infrastructure recovery. The establishment of a national ORC office (within USCYBERCOM perhaps) would be a positive first step that would contribute to a strategic cyberspace deterrence strategy in a very real way. Organizing to fight through cyber attacks not only prepares the United States to operate under duress, but sends a strong deterrence message to potential adversaries that the United States aims to deny the benefit derived from an adversary's cyberspace attacks.

Notes

1. R. Elder, *National Defense Industrial Association 2007 Defense Industrial Base Infrastructure Protection Symposium*, April 11, 2007, http://proceedings.ndia.org/7030/Elder.pdf.
2. US Air Force, "Air Force Fact Sheets—Airpower in Operation Desert Storm," About.com. http://usmilitary.about.com/library/milinfo/affacts/blairpowerinoperationdesertstorm.htm.
3. American Forces Press Service, "The Operation Desert Shield/Desert Storm Timeline," US Department of Defense, http://www.defenselink.mil/news/newsarticle.aspx?id=45404.
4. US Department of Defense, *Deterrence Operations Joint Operating Concept*, Version 2.0, December 2006, http://www.dtic.mil/futurejointwarfare/concepts/do_joc_v20.doc.
5. H. Okey, *Strategic Deterrence (SD) Joint Operating Concept (JOC) Version 2.0*, http://www.dtic.mil/futurejointwarfare/strategic/sd_joc.ppt.
6. K. R. Beeker, R. F. Mills, and M. R. Grimaila, "Applying Deterrence in Cyberspace," *IO Journal* (February 2010), 21–27.
7. Okey, *Strategic Deterrence (SD) Joint Operating Concept (JOC) Version 2.0.*
8. B. Obama, "Remarks by the President on Securing our Nation's Cyber Infrastructure," The White House, May 29, 2009, http://www.whitehouse.gov/the_press_office/Remarks-by-the-President-on-Securing-Our-Nations-Cyber-Infrastructure/.

9. E. Holmes, "Lab to build special order satellites in days," *Air Force Times*, February 20, 2009, http://www.airforcetimes.com/news/2009/02/af_satellites_space_022009/.
10. Carbonite, "Online Backup," http://www.carbonite.com.
11. DriveHeadquarters Website, "Online Backup Files & Emails," http://www.drivehq.com/.
12. L. S. Tinnel, O. S. Saydjari, and J. W. Haines, "An Integrated Cyber Panel System," Proceedings of the 2003 DARPA Information Survivability Conference and Exposition, Vol. 2, 32–34.
13. B. Hale, M. R. Grimaila, R. F. Mills, M. Haas, and P. Maynard, "Communicating Potential Mission Impact Using Shared Mission Representations," Proceedings of the 2010 International Conference on Information Warfare and Security, WPAFB, OH, April 8–9, 2010.
14. "DoD Policy and Responsibility for Critical Infrastructure," Department of Defense Directive 3020.40, January 14, 2010.
15. US Air Force Public Affairs, "Communications Airmen meet to discuss career field's transformation," June 9, 2009, http://www.af.mil/news/story.asp?id=123153203.
16. CSIS Commission on Cybersecurity for the 44th Presidency, *Securing Cyberspace for the 44th Presidency*, Center for Strategic and International Studies, December 2008, http://www.carlisle.army.mil/DIME/documents/CSISCyber%20Report%20Final.pdf.
17. Department of Homeland Security, *National Infrastructure Protection Plan: Partnering to Enhance Protection and Resiliency*, 2009, http://www.dhs.gov/xlibrary/assets/NIPP_Plan.pdf.
18. J. Vijayan, "Data Security Risks Missing from Disaster Recovery Plans," *Computer World* 39, no.41 (October 10, 2005); US Government Accountability Office, *Internet Infrastructure—Challenges in Developing a Public/Private Recovery Plan*, GAO-06-1100T, September 13, 2006.
19. B. J. L. Landry and S. M. Koger, "Dispelling 10 Common Disaster Recovery Myths: Lessons Learned from Hurricane Katrina and Other Disasters," *ACM Journal on Educational Resources in Computing* 6, no. 4 (December 2006).
20. Ibid.
21. C. Paone, "CITS Key to Air Force Cyber Superiority Goal," 66th Air Base Wing Public Affairs, May 28, 2009, http://www.af.mil/news/story.asp?id=123151424.
22. C. Hunt, J. R. Bowes, and D. Gardner, "Net Force Maneuver," *Proceedings of the 2005 IEEE Workshop on Information Assurance and Security*, United States Military Academy, West Point, NY, 2005.
23. Marine Corps Doctrinal Publication 1, *Warfighting*, 1997.
24. The White House, "Cyberspace Policy Review: Assuring a Trusted and Resilient Information and Communications Infrastructure," 2009.
25. Ibid.
26. Ibid.

CHAPTER 3

Does the United States Need a New Model for Cyber Deterrence?

Kamaal T. Jabbour and E. Paul Ratazzi

> History teaches that wars begin when governments believe the price of aggression is cheap.
> —President Ronald Reagan, Address to the Nation, January 16, 1984

Introduction to Cyberspace

Joint Publication 1–02, Department of Defense (DoD) Dictionary of Military and Associated Terms,[1] defines

> *Cyberspace* as a global domain within the information environment consisting of the interdependent networks of information technology infrastructures, including the Internet, telecommunications networks, computer systems, and embedded processors and controllers,

and

> *Cyberspace operations* as the employment of cyber capabilities where the primary purpose is to achieve military objectives or effects in or through cyberspace. Such operations include computer network operations and activities to operate and defend the Global Information Grid.

We view cyberspace first and foremost as a foundational domain that enables US military superiority and secondarily as another warfighting domain in its own right, where specific effects can be achieved through cyberspace operations. In the past, cyberspace has been viewed as a largely *uncontested* environment.[2] However, a recent Air Force Scientific Advisory Board (SAB) study[3] concluded that during a conflict, the nature and availability of this environment can and will change dramatically. Furthermore, there exists mounting evidence that our national approach to security in this domain is not keeping pace with the threat,[4] our military networks have widespread vulnerabilities,[5] and the strategy to protect our national interests in this new environment has been largely unsuccessful.[6]

A new strategy for securing cyberspace must employ new technical solutions that implement many of the warfighting concepts that have served us well in other domains. Presumably, deterrence, as the first line of defense[7] and a fundamental element of defensive strategy,[8] must be explored as the foundation for this new strategy. Unfortunately, traditional notions of separate offensive and defensive cyber forces serve to artificially limit the full potential of a deterrence strategy in cyberspace. Since both red and blue forces can simultaneously occupy various areas of cyberspace, offensive and defensive operations must likewise occur simultaneously and in concert, and not be treated as separate endeavors. A framework for integration of offense and defense is thus required to go beyond a Maginot line model.[9]

Cyber Operations Vision

In 2009, we developed a science and technology (S&T)-based vision for cyberspace operations.[10] This vision identified nine key technical capabilities that form an enabling framework for the Air Force's strategic imperatives of Global Vigilance, Global Power, and Global Reach, as shown in table 3.1.

One feature of this new framework is that it blends offense and defense within each imperative, and thus optimizes the use of both capabilities in support of cyberspace operations. Several of the nine technical capabilities directly support deterrence strategy. Specifically, assurance and avoidance technologies can significantly raise the costs of attacks while simultaneously lowering the probability of success.

Assurance

A credible fighting force does not conduct warfare with unreliable, untrustworthy, and untested weapons that fail under adversary attack. Assurance in cyberspace demands building warfighting systems that ensure the success of specific missions, even in a contested environment,

Table 3.1 The AF's strategic imperatives are enabled by nine primary technical capabilities

Global vigilance is the ability to keep an unblinking eye on any entity—to provide warning on capabilities and intentions, as well as identify needs and opportunities.*			**Global power** is the ability to move, supply, and position assets—with unrivaled velocity and precision anywhere.*			**Global reach** is the ability to hold at risk or strike any target, anywhere, and project swift, frequently decisive, precise effects.*		
Situational awareness	Assurance	Avoidance	Access	Survival	Cross-domain operations	Precision effects	Effects assessment	Response action

*Gen. Norton A. Schwartz (ret.), "Fly, Fight and Win," CSAF's Vector, September 2008.

using formal requirements-driven systems engineering processes. When performed properly, assurance results in systems that guarantee the ability to execute mission-essential functions (MEFs), even under conditions where the adversary is attempting to deny our use of cyberspace. Warfighting systems developed with this approach will be inherently more difficult and costly to attack, likewise decreasing the benefits of attempting attacks.

Avoidance

Unlike a traditional cyber defense mindset that assumes the extent of the attack surface to be fixed and that addresses risks with additional intrusion and attack detection mechanisms, avoidance seeks to create a *strategic* advantage in cyberspace by eluding threats altogether. Threat avoidance reduces or eliminates the need to fight, increases the difficulty of attacking, and lowers the probability of a successful attack. Threat avoidance may be accomplished by way of three interrelated approaches: reducing target system cross-section, increasing agility, and implementing deterrence methodologies.[11]

In reducing target system cross-section, we make many threats irrelevant by eliminating vulnerabilities and their exposure beforehand. As with assurance, vulnerabilities can be "designed out" through a systematic, requirements-based process. However, mission dynamics and ever-changing threats dictate that these secure configurations be constantly and automatically maintained to ensure minimum exposure and responsiveness to system-level mission requirements.[12] Furthermore, legacy protocols and architectures can be replaced with those that favor defense and support defensive prerequisites that are standard in other domains. When nonrepudiation is deemed important, protocols that guarantee attribution and facilitate geolocation must be employed. Likewise, if broad classes of threats exploit stored-program computer architectures, then architectures using physically separate memories must be considered. In effect, many "laws" that govern cyberspace operations consist of manmade protocols, interfaces, devices, and architectures that can be redesigned to avoid attacks by ensuring a defensive advantage through "threat non-interoperability."

Agility in cyberspace implies maneuverability and the capability to evade attacks. With agility, attacks are avoided by denying the adversary the advantage of time and the benefit of previously collected intelligence. A study of activities across the life cycle of an attack showed that an attacker spent up to 95 percent of the time in *preparation* for executing the actual attack.[13] A conclusion based on this estimate asserts that mechanisms designed to frustrate the intelligence-gathering and preparation phases of an attack are highly effective in increasing the probability that the attack will never occur.[14] Real-time agility is accomplished through the use of polymorphic techniques at multiple points within the system and network architecture to present an agile, evasive "moving target" that forces an attacker to spend 100 percent of the time in the "find" state of the kill chain.[15] As an example,[16] rapid Internet protocol (IP) address and port hopping among peers across untrustworthy networks can thwart an attacker's ability to find, fix, track, and target key systems, and allow a system to deploy escape tactics when faced with a viable threat.

The third element of threat avoidance, cyber deterrence, is the subject of this chapter. Although assurance and threat avoidance contribute to deterrence by way of increased cost and decreased benefit, deterrence is arguably more complex and more difficult to implement than these purely technological means. This is because deterrence includes considerations beyond those that are strictly technological, such as expressed intent[17] and political will.[18] Furthermore, fundamental differences between cyberspace and other domains add to this complexity and render many assumptions of traditional deterrence theory invalid. As such, a brief examination of the properties of cyberspace is warranted.

PROPERTIES OF CYBERSPACE

As a warfighting domain, cyberspace is fundamentally different from other domains. An understanding of these differences is an important prerequisite to developing approaches to cyber deterrence; several of them have a significant impact on the underlying assumptions of traditional deterrence theory.

CYBERSPACE IS UNBOUNDED AND CHANGES RAPIDLY

Unlike air, space, sea, and ground that are essentially fixed in size, cyberspace is a technological domain that changes and expands every time it is touched. Although limited by physical laws, cyberspace operations become useful through the protocols, devices, and architectures that harness them. It is through these designs that we connect, communicate, process, store, attack, and defend in cyberspace.

These "laws" of cyberspace operations dictate how we interface systems, how links and nodes behave, and what works and what does not work. This is analogous to how we harness the physical laws of other domains for the conduct of warfare. However, unlike in other domains, the laws of cyberspace operations change as technology changes.

The result of this evolution is that the threat environment and the means for defense are constantly changing. A zero-day attack executed 30 years ago against an IBM System/360 via malicious punch cards would not be effective today for the same reason Windows malware propagated via a USB thumb drive would not have been effective 30 years ago. While the laws of physics have not changed in 30 years, their technical applications have changed. In cyberspace, technological change brings new capabilities and threats at the same time it obsoletes current ones.

Cyberspace Is Nongeographic

Possibly, the aspect of cyberspace most challenging for the application of traditional concepts is that cyberspace has no geographic dimensions or boundaries. For millennia, nearly all aspects of warfare have been intimately tied to geography. Strategic advantage, doctrine, success, failure, the element of surprise, and many other characteristics and results of warfare have depended on geographic features. Like space, cyberspace has no defined range of operations of areas or responsibility.[19] However, unlike even space, cyberspace has none of the geographic dimensions that we are so familiar with in other domains. The frames of reference that do exist in cyberspace (e.g., logical connectivity) are highly dynamic.

Cyberspace Is Jurisdictionally Complex

Determining jurisdictional boundaries in cyberspace is complicated and not yet well defined. On the one hand, it has been argued that cyberspace is an international space (i.e., global commons) that lacks territorial jurisdiction and that its jurisdiction should be based on nationality, much like the high seas or outer space.[20] On the other hand, because cyberspace exists only where technology exists, every piece is privately owned and operated and subject to the owners' laws, regulations, and terms of service, and so forth. On this premise, jurisdiction would be determined on the basis of the owner of a given piece of cyberspace.

Cyberspace Is Non-attributional

Many aspects of current cyberspace operations lack attribution and favor anonymity, although these are not its inherent traits. Moreover, an overall global move toward technology that would provide a high degree of nonrepudiation in cyberspace is unlikely, because of cyberspace's status as a global commons and increasing trends toward digital anonymity.[21]

THE UNITED STATES IS ASYMMETRICALLY DEPENDENT ON CYBERSPACE

Another difference lies in our dependence on cyberspace. Our increasing reliance on cyberspace, usually viewed as an indicator of technological superiority, has become a vulnerability.[22] The United States is target rich in cyberspace, while many of our adversaries are not.

CYBERSPACE HAS A LOW COST OF ENTRY

Vast arsenals, costly, complex delivery systems, and a standing army are not required for an entity to threaten or attack others in cyberspace. In addition, anonymity is virtually guaranteed, further lessening the non-monetary costs of launching attacks.[23] Finally, there is no significant cost to the adversary for maintaining a sustained attack or if an attack fails.

Table 3.2 contains a summary of this comparison.

CYBER DETERRENCE

Traditional approaches to deterrence include the following:

1. Deterrence through threat of retaliation
2. Deterrence through assured mutual destruction
3. Deterrence by denial
4. Deterrence through increased cost to the adversary
5. Deterrence through decreased benefits for the adversary

The inherent characteristics of cyberspace, as well as the ways in which cyberspace is currently implemented, will have a significant impact on the viability of these strategies if they are simply borrowed from tradition

Table 3.2 Cyberspace differs fundamentally from other domains

	Cyberspace	Air, space, sea, ground
Size	Unbounded	Essentially fixed
Rate of change	High	Low
Governed by	Technology	Physical laws
Ownership and jurisdiction	Private	Sovereign and international
Cost of entry	Low	High
Attribution	Difficult or impossible as currently implemented	High due to physical evidence
Dimension	Connectivity	Geographic
Cost of attack	Little or none	Expended munitions

without revisiting the assumptions behind each. Many of these traditional approaches, especially deterrence through threat of retaliation, have serious shortcomings in the cyber domain because of the fundamental differences outlined previously and summarized here:

1. Lack of attribution
2. Low cost of aggression with high payoff for success
3. Inconsequentiality (due to conflicting, impeding, or nonexistent laws)
4. Low probability of detection
5. Probability of losing more than the adversary
6. Ability of new technology to instantly "change the game" and invalidate basic assumptions

In addition, many criticisms of deterrence strategy are based on weaknesses that are only amplified in the cyber domain. Assumptions about the identity, intent, nature, or rationality of a typical cyber adversary can be readily called into question when forming the basis for retaliation.

With all these potential pitfalls, is cyber deterrence worth pursuing or even possible at all? Obviously, if it can be realized, the foundation for deterrence in cyberspace will be much different than for other domains. The basic theory must be reestablished from the ground up, and many of the fundamental assumptions that have been the hallmark of deterrence in the nuclear era will have to be reevaluated. Policy and national strategy must be created and clarified so that adversaries have a basis for decision making and consequence evaluation. Finally, specific technologies must be developed and implemented in critical portions of cyberspace to enable cyber deterrence.

Beginning with an evaluation of the basic theory, we analyze each of these traditional approaches.

DETERRENCE THROUGH THREAT OF RETALIATION

The current Joint definition of deterrence is as follows:

> The prevention from action by fear of the consequences. Deterrence is a state of mind brought about by the existence of a credible threat of unacceptable counteraction.[24]

This somewhat narrow view of deterrence has its roots in the Cold War. Especially for those with childhood memories of fallout shelters and duck and cover drills, it conjures up images of a nuclear Armageddon and a doctrine of deterrence through massive retaliation and mutually assured destruction. From this definition, which focuses only on consequences through counteraction, one might conclude that deterrence can only be achieved through a threatened counteraction.

Some have argued that the geographic and attribution ambiguities in cyberspace make this form of deterrence largely unachievable in cyberspace. These domain characteristics lead to several key difficulties:[25]

1. No actionable basis for deterrence
2. Lack of high-confidence, rapid attribution
3. Lack of a credible and demonstrated capability for response

Although these problems may indeed preclude effective deterrence of an attacking cyber adversary, this form of deterrence is actually employed routinely and effectively in cyberspace. Every day, millions of DOD and corporate computer users are deterred from violating organizational policy concerning their use of cyberspace. Penalties for misuse are understood and displayed at every login, attribution is virtually certain by way of access credentials, and retribution can be swift and severe. Therefore, deterrence by threat of retaliation does exist in cyberspace, but only against users who have a tangible risk and fear certain retaliation. These are the authorized users, not the adversary.

Before concluding that deterrence of the adversary by these means is not possible because of the difficulties outlined above, recall from the previous section that cyberspace is a technological domain. In this domain, cyberspace operations must obey "laws" that are derived from the design of the technology. Because of this, it should be possible to design cyber infrastructure that enables this type of deterrence against even the adversary. Just as authorized users are deterred from misusing corporate resources because of technological means that enable retribution, a properly designed cyberspace would allow unauthorized users to be similarly held at risk.

ASSURED MUTUAL SELF-DESTRUCTION

More and more, cyberspace is becoming interconnected with many of its users dependent on the proper functioning of shared resources. Cloud computing, for example, offers the ability for any individual or organization to have access to vast computing and storage resources without the added baggage of owning and maintaining the resources. Companies and governments are outsourcing their enterprise applications and storage needs to providers such as Google, Amazon, and Microsoft. The "black box" nature of these services makes it difficult, if not impossible, to know where a particular application is executed or a particular file is stored within the cloud. Even precision attacks against these services may likely have widespread unintended effects, possibly against an attacker's interests. Similar to the way in which we and our adversaries are mutually dependent on the financial stability of world markets, actors in cyberspace are increasingly dependent on the proper functioning and availability of cyber infrastructure. This mutual dependence translates into a deterrent force if MEFs are carefully and securely placed alongside collateral activities that would be disadvantageous for the adversary to disrupt or destroy.

Deterrence by Denial

Deterrence by denial relies on the buildup of defensive technologies to neutralize or mitigate attacks.[26] Deterrence by denial works well in a "defense-dominant" environment, such as missile defense, where the denial of attack success costs more than the expected benefits.[27] Unfortunately, in cyberspace an adversary incurs very little cost when an attack fails, and is usually free to keep trying without incurring additional costs. Thus, deterrence by denial is not currently feasible in cyberspace. However, the fact that there is no cost for attempting and failing an attack is simply a result of how cyberspace is currently implemented. If cyberspace were implemented in such a way that attack detection was certain and attribution was rapid and reliable, the cost for failure may begin to outweigh the expected benefit for some attackers. For example, if a critical function was isolated physically or logically from the rest of cyberspace, the added effort required of an attacker may become prohibitive and expose the attack, thereby providing a deterrent. Similarly, selective substitution of hardware for software in critical systems denies an attacker the ease of remote modification of a target.

Deterrence Through Increased Cost to the Adversary

Increasing the cost to attack to the point where an adversary decides it is no longer worth it relies on an understanding of the adversary's cost model and level of relative expertise. Agile cyber systems that break attack planning cycles and render an attacker's knowledge base worthless may increase the cost and difficulty of an attack enough to deter. In addition, if the adversary's perception of costs can be manipulated by how our defenses are presented, it will also serve to deter. For example, prepositioning an application on thousands of dissimilar systems across cyberspace increases disproportionately the cost to an adversary.

Deterrence Through Decreased Benefits for the Adversary

In an environment where there will always be some level of vulnerability, deterrence through decreased benefits involves ensuring that successful attacks do not result in significant payoffs for the adversary. Assuming that an attack is detected, this approach might involve deceptive techniques to lure attackers into honeypots or into exfiltrating bogus information. Attackers who perceive (whether true or not) that their costly attacks are producing useless results may be deterred from continuing.

This type of deterrence can also be realized by way of highly resilient systems—systems that have an innate ability to adapt to unexpected inputs, such as those likely presented by an attacker, and continue operating in spite of the attack. An example of this includes genetic algorithms that allow a software system to evolve when new negative test cases are discovered during operation.

Summary and Conclusion

A fundamental element of defensive strategy, deterrence has been the foundation of US military strategy for decades. With cyberspace now recognized as both an enabling domain, as well as a warfighting domain in its own right, it is understandable how warfighters and policy makers wish to extend deterrence concepts to cyberspace. Going forward, we must recognize that deterrence models will be unique for every domain, including cyberspace. Much of the current theory and approach has been built within the context of nuclear deterrence. Blind application of this framework will fail because the context and very properties of the domain are completely different.

Based on an analysis of the properties of cyberspace, we conclude that there are several opportunities for applying new deterrence theory in cyberspace. The threat of assured mutual self-destruction of cyberspace assets and approaches that manipulate the adversary's cost-benefit equation seem to hold the most promise. Realization of these will require fundamental technological changes to the cyberspace domain, as well as a new set of rational policies that are scientifically sound and enforceable by way of the technical characteristics of the domain.

Notes

1. Department of Defense, *Dictionary of Military and Associated Terms*, Joint Publication (JP) 1–02, April 12, 2001 (as amended through August 19, 2009), 141.
2. Gen. John A. Shaud (ret.), "In Service to the Nation... Air Force Research Institute Strategic Concept for 2018–2023," *Strategic Studies Quarterly* 2, no. 4 (Winter 2008): 35.
3. USAF Scientific Advisory Board, *Defending and Operating in a Contested Cyber Domain*, SAB-TR-08-01, August 2008, 2.
4. The White House, *Cyberspace Policy Review: Assuring a Trusted and Resilient Information and Communications Infrastructure*, May 2009, v.
5. Defense Science Board, *Challenges to Military Operations in Support of US Interests*, vol. 2, December 2008, 320.
6. Center for Strategic and International Studies, *Securing Cyberspace for the 44th Presidency: A Report of the CSIS Commison on Cybersecurity for the 44th Presidency*, December 2008, 12.
7. David S. Alberts, *Defensive Information Warfare* (Washington, DC: National Defense University Press, 1996), 59.
8. Walt Tirenin and Don Faatz, *A Concept for Strategic Cyber Defense*, Military Communications (MILCOM) Conference Proceedings, 1999, 458–463.
9. William A. Wulf, *Cyber Security: Beyond the Maginot Line*, statement before the House Science Committee, US House of Representatives, October 10, 2001, http://www.nae.edu/News/SpeechesandRemarks/CyberSecurityBeyondtheMaginotLine.aspx.
10. Kamal Jabbour, "The Science and Technology of Cyber Operations," *High Frontier* 5, no. 3 (May 2009): 11–15.
11. Air Force Research Laboratory Information Directorate, *Integrated Cyber Defense & Support Technologies*, BAA-08-08-RIKA, October 14, 2008.
12. Sanjay Narain, Gary Levin, Sharad Malik, and Vikram Kaul, "Declarative Infrastructure Configuration Synthesis and Debugging," *Journal of Network and Systems Management* 16, no. 3 (September 2008): 235–258.
13. J. Lowry, "An Initial Foray into Understanding Adversary Planning and Courses of Action," *DARPA Information Survivability Conference & Exposition II, 2001 (DISCEX'01) Proceedings*, vol. 1, June 2001, 123–133.
14. Air Force Research Laboratory, *Proactive and Predictive Cyber Indications and Warnings (P2CIW)*, AFRL-IF-RS-TR-2006-226, contract no. F30602-03-C-0232 (final technical report), July 2006, 82–83.
15. Based on the Air Force-centric definition of the kill chain: (1) find; (2) fix; (3) track; (4) target; (5) engage; and (6) assess (F2T2EA).
16. Polymorphic Cyber Defense-Active Repositioning in Cyberspace (award notice), March 13, 2009, https://www.fbo.gov/spg/USAF/AFMC/AFRLRRS/Awards/FA875009C0051.html.
17. W. W. Kaufmann, *The Evolution of Deterrence 1945–1958* (Santa Monica, CA: RAND, 1958).

18. Lt Col Lorina A. Frederick, "Deterrence and Space-Based Missile Defense," *Air & Space Power Journal* 23, no. 3 (Fall 2009): 107–118.
19. Gen Kevin P. Chilton, "Cyberspace Leadership: Toward New Culture, Conduct, and Capabilities," *Air & Space Power Journal* 23, no. 3 (Fall 2009): 5–10.
20. Darrel Menthe, "Jurisdiction in Cyberspace: A Theory of International Spaces," *Mich. Telecomm. Tech.L. Rev.* 69 (1998), July 15, 2010, http://www.mttlr.org/volfour/menthe.html.
21. Martin C. Libicki, "Deterrence in Cyberspace," *High Frontier* 5, no. 3 (May 2009): 11–15.
22. Shaud, "In Service to the Nation . . . Air Force Research Institute Strategic Concept for 2018–2023."
23. Ibid., 36.
24. Department of Defense, JP 1–02, 161.
25. Libicki, "Deterrence in Cyberspace"; Tirenin and Faatz, *A Concept for Strategic Cyber Defense.*
26. Wikipedia, "Deterrence theory," http://en.wikipedia.org/wiki/Deterrence_theory.
27. Richard J. Harknett, "To Deter or Not to Deter, That is the Cyber Dilemma," presentation, AFEI Strategic Cyber Deterrence Conference, Washington, DC, November 1–2, 2007.

Section II

Nuclear Deterrence

CHAPTER 4

Is Nuclear Deterrence Still Relevant?

ELBRIDGE COLBY

IS NUCLEAR DETERRENCE STILL RELEVANT TO US POLICY?[1] Compared with the heights of its prominence in the depths of the Cold War, nuclear deterrence has fallen into relative obscurity. Given the nature of the conflicts in which the United States is engaged, attention today in defense circles focuses on counterinsurgency, counterterrorism, and high-level conventional conflict. So stark has the shift been that a blue-ribbon panel, appointed in the wake of embarrassing incidents within the US nuclear bomber force, found "a serious erosion of focus, expertise, mission readiness, resources, and discipline in the nuclear weapons enterprise within the Air Force" and a general lack of interest in nuclear matters within the Defense Department as a whole.[2] The broader intellectual climate has been even less favorable than the neglect suffered within the defense community. Indeed, much of the focus that nuclear deterrence has received in recent years has been generated by the well-publicized effort to eliminate nuclear weapons, an effort that in one way or another has received the endorsement of President Obama and his Republican 2008 rival Senator John McCain, legions of former senior officials, as well as countless cultural, religious, and other influential figures. Someone not steeped in the intricacies of nuclear deterrence might be forgiven for thinking that the broader military's lack of interest in nuclear deterrence and the testimonies against its necessity by its former high priests and practitioners, like Henry Kissinger, constitute pretty powerful evidence that nuclear deterrence is no longer relevant—or even needed.

There is an element of truth to this view. The obsessive, at times almost maniacal, focus of the Cold War years on nuclear weapons has passed, and has passed on good grounds. For a variety of reasons, the intense competition between the United States and the Soviet Union in the years between 1945 and the denouement of the USSR in the 1980s led to, above all, a nuclear weapons arms race. Each side sought to develop and deploy nuclear weapons that could gain for it what each perceived to be an advantage—not only in military terms but also in the geopolitical perceptual test of strength. This dynamic had the effect of pushing the two superpowers to field forces whose unimaginable destructive capabilities, well beyond the bounds of any rational strategic goal, simply demanded the creation of the peculiar neologism "overkill." With each side possessing tens of thousands of thermonuclear weapons, both had the power to annihilate not only the other, but perhaps even civilized life on earth. Accompanying this arsenal were fervent efforts to develop strategies for their use. Some of these efforts were reasonable attempts to grapple with the contorting challenge of seeking to satisfy political objectives with weapons whose destructiveness transcended the boundaries of the politically sensible; others, however, seemed so untethered from a sensible grasp of the weapons' catastrophic power that they imbued nuclear deterrence as a whole with an air of unreality, if not morbid insouciance, perhaps best captured by Stanley Kubrick's *Dr. Strangelove*.[3]

The dissolution of the Soviet Empire and the consequent relaxation of tensions between West and East, the disappearance of a credible alternative to socially minded liberal market systems, and the overweening dominance of the United States in the post–Cold War era, however, have ushered in a radically different perspective on the salience of nuclear deterrence. From being a central concern of geopolitics and, indeed, of humanity, nuclear deterrence suddenly has become marginal and, to many, unnecessary. The chief virtue claimed for it during the dark days of the Cold War had been the prevention of major war, but, in the wake of the demise of the great challenger to the free market's ascendancy, such war no longer seems, to many, to be a serious possibility. Indeed, some analysts have gone so far as to claim that war is, in fact, obsolete, a residual vestige of more primitive eras.[4] And one cannot but observe that the rate of wars has declined substantially over the past centuries. This development has been seen as stemming from a variety of roots. Some have emphasized the triumph of pacifying liberal democracy and the eclipse of rival ideologies.[5] Others have stressed the role of a softening of once-belligerent social mores and intellectual attitudes and the correlative development of strong "norms" against war.[6] Still others have pointed to the declining economic rationality of war, noting that, in an age of relatively open and free trade, the advantages of territorial conquest in a Malthusian world no longer apply.[7] Such arguments for why major war is no longer a serious possibility may be synthesized into two main thrusts: humanity has moved beyond war and war no longer pays.

If this view is correct, then it surely follows that nuclear deterrence is indeed irrelevant—and, worse than that, dangerous, given the ever-present chances of accident or miscalculation.[8] A world in which, even without nuclear weapons, great war is impossible or perhaps even just extremely unlikely would also be a world in which nuclear weapons would serve no rational purpose, for the only justification for maintaining and threatening to use arms of such apocalyptic destructiveness is whether they are effective at restraining Mars in the first place. But is it true that major war is no longer possible?

DOES WAR PAY?

Let us first consider the narrower claim for war's obsolescence—that it no longer pays. According to this argument, traceable back to the school of Adam Smith, the long-term gains to be had from trade outweigh those held out by aggressive war. Nations, and interest groups within nations, profit more from the liberal path of specialization and free commerce, which propels the broad enrichment of all parties, than from conquest or subordination.[9] Moreover, especially in a world of highly destructive nonnuclear weaponry and in which nations can mass their populations into great armies, the costs of war are also potentially very high, even without nuclear weapons entering into the equation.

There is much truth to this argument. In a post-Malthusian world in which primarily productivity rather than the exploitation of the land equates to prosperity, it does pay to orient society toward the cultivation of productive and efficient labor rather than military might. Beyond the requirements of defense and the stabilization of the overarching order, it does not really make sense to use the military instrument to extract wealth, even for an order's hegemon, because such use is likely to undermine the free-market system itself by spurring countervailing responses by the exploited or those fearing exploitation and by undermining confidence in the stability and market rationality of the order. Even within a country, exploitation may lead to ultimately counterproductive distortions in the economy.[10]

But vesting too much confidence in this argument for the passing of major war risks is akin to confusing the *telos* of a system with the actual dynamics of its workings. Capitalism, taken to its fullest logical conclusions, would presumably involve the abolition of restraints on the free hiring and firing of labor, the dissipation of international constraints on the movement of persons and goods, and, indeed, even the retirement of the concept of nationhood and citizenship themselves. Yet, is there any reason to think such developments likely, let alone desirable? Are human societies straining to approximate the capitalist ideal of a perfectly rational allocation of capital and effort, in the pursuit of the best aggregate outcome even at the expense of the unproductive? The answer must be a clear no. Quite to the contrary, human beings seem keen to maintain themselves in groupings of one kind or another, above all the nation-state, designed to shield individuals and social groups from a too perfect market rationality and to improve their advantages relative to others.[11] The persistence of this behavior indicates that states and other entities still seek economic protection and advantage from noneconomic sources and thus may still seek to wrest economic prosperity or shelter through military force, including through coercion rather than pure brute force—even if such advantages are less impressive than the absolute gains they might garner in a perfect international market system.[12] This suggests that market suboptimal "errors," ranging from Saddam Hussein's brazen attempt to gain Kuwait's oil riches to variants of the more subtle "Finlandization" feared for West Germany during the 1970s, are still possible.

Nor is the danger of war in liberal capitalism confined to suboptimal "errors." For instance, observers of international political economy have emphasized that the liberal market system is not reliably self-generating but rather may be best sustained by a hegemonic power prepared to enforce the rules of the system through both economic measures and military force.[13] Yet the exertions of such hegemons tend to sow the seeds of their own demise, leading to the weakening of the system, perilous instability, and, ultimately, the hegemons' breakup.[14] The absence of an effective hegemon can, in turn, lead to the balkanization of economic relations and thus to inefficiencies and distortions in the economic system that appear invidious to some members. Even if neither the hegemon nor the system's participants saw the advantages of waging war during the hegemon's ascendancy, the same might not hold true for periods of a hegemon's wane, let alone when there is no hegemon at all. In simple terms, states may often simply have to make do in a world that is not optimally organized on liberal trade principles, a world in which the use of military force might not, from a purely economic point of view, be the per se suboptimal option.

But there is a deeper problem with the argument that war no longer pays—for wars have been waged for reasons other than material gain, and indeed in some cases with the assessment that war would likely result in material loss rather than gain, as in the case of Japan in 1941.[15] In many instances nations have made war because of the often tragic nature of the structure of international politics, in which states may feel most secure in costly domination or the weakness of their rivals and neighbors rather than in a more prosperous but insecure peace.[16] France's policy of seeking to cripple Germany in the interwar years out of fear of its resurgence stands as a classic example of this. The policy no doubt was economically suboptimal, but Paris saw it as the safer option, the loss of wealth be damned. If nations still feel insecure in a competitive and anarchic international environment, then there is little reason to see why these classical impulsions to war no longer operate.

Nor is the structure of the international environment the only generator of war. Pride, honor, the *libido dominandi*, the thrill of warfare and conquest, and the like are also primal drivers of human interaction and have historically played important, if not at times dominant, roles in fostering war.[17] The ambitions of Hitler, Mussolini, Napoleon, Genghis Khan, Attila the Hun, Julius Caesar, and Alexander the Great—as well as the armies and peoples they led—simply cannot be understood without reference to the salience of pride, honor, the allure of power and domination, and glory. While calculations of advantage clearly factored into the considerations of leaders and their citizenry, demonstrating that exploitative war is not as profitable as a free-market peace only tinkers at the edges of the calculations of those for whom comfortable prosperity is only one good among others. For Communists, Fascists, and steppe barbarians, it was a secondary concern or even an object of disdain.

The proposition that war does not pay, then, may be generally true, but, given the incomplete scope of its applicability and the verity that wars do not stem solely from the pursuit of material gain, it is surely far too narrow a base to conclude that war is passé.

PROGRESS BEYOND WAR? THE ISSUE OF SECURITY COMMUNITIES

But what if deeper forces are at work in making war no longer possible, even in a nuclear weapons-free world? Indeed, some argue that not only does war no longer pay, but international politics does not need to generate the insecurities that can lead to war and that the nature of society and societal mores have so fundamentally changed in advanced liberal democratic systems that great war is no longer a serious option (at least within certain circumstances).

Rather than vainly seeking to survey a vast and variegated literature on this question, it may be more appropriate to focus on a synthesis of these arguments, which Robert Jervis offers in his book *American Foreign Policy in a New Era*. Jervis is not only one of the foremost international relations scholars of the era, but he is also highly respected for his judiciousness, wisdom, and immunity to faddishness. Moreover, he is generally identified as a "realist" in political science terms, and so taking on his argument for the obsolescence of major war is to take on the argument in its most careful, sophisticated, and resilient form. His arguments for the proposition that "war among the leading great powers—the most developed states of the United States, Western Europe, and Japan—will not occur in the future, and indeed is no longer a source of concern for them," can thus reasonably be taken as a champion for the set of arguments as a whole.[18]

Jervis's basic argument is that war can, and within certain conditions has, become a thing of the past. Drawing from the work of "constructivist" and liberal as well as realist analysts and scholars, he argues that a "security community" in which war is no longer plausible has emerged as a result of "the destructiveness of war, the benefits of peace, and the changes in values" among the participant nations, which more or less correlate with the North Atlantic community and Japan.[19] The outcome has been that, within this community, "neither the publics nor the political elites nor even the military establishments expect war with each other."[20] Indeed, these developments "have ma[de] war unthinkable" within the precincts of the security community.[21]

Jervis sees this transcendence of the serious possibility of war as stemming from several factors. Culling from the constructivist school, he first argues that the norms, values, ideas, attitudes, and the like that are used to impel nations and peoples to war have been replaced within the security community by those that render war against fellow security community members not only anathema, but unthinkable—simply not a genuine policy option. As he puts it, "Although war is still seen as necessary when imposed on states by extreme circumstances . . . no one talks about the importance of honor, which sparked many wars in the past, or sees wars as a way to satisfy national or individual quests for glory. States with these outlooks will not fight each other."[22] Moreover, these changes in values are "self-reinforcing," constituting "a benign cycle of behavior, beliefs, and expectations" that allows nations under its influence to get out of the cycle of anxiety and distrust that characterizes states in the suspicious anarchy of realist thought.[23]

The second strand of argument that Jervis draws upon is the liberal one, emphasizing the importance of democratization, economic interdependence, and, to a lesser degree, the role of inter- and supranational organizations. Jervis is more skeptical of the role of these factors, noting that multiple conditions invariably attach to arguments for the salience of democracy and economic interdependence and dismissing the role of international organizations as "slight."[24] Nonetheless, he contends that the gains brought by peaceful coexistence and the habits of democracy, when operating together with other factors, such as the softening of mores, have contributed to making war implausible within the community.[25]

Finally, Jervis points to the critical importance of the traditional realist influences of power and fear. Indeed, Jervis's argument is not that nuclear weapons have made no difference. Rather, he judges that "a necessary condition" of great power peace "is the belief that conquest is difficult and war is terribly costly" and that it is nuclear weapons in particular have made it "hard for anyone to believe that war could make sense."[26] Yet, while Jervis holds that the presence of nuclear weapons *was* essential for the creation and consolidation of the security community of pacific nations, he argues that the progress of "the Community is path-dependent . . . [that] forms of cooperation [have] set off positive feedback and are now self-sustaining."[27] Given that he argues that war among the participants in the community is "unthinkable," a word variously defined as deeming something impossible to conceive or imagine or not capable of being grasped by the mind, it stands to reason that nuclear weapons either are or will become irrelevant and presumably unnecessary among them—and so the same would hold true if the security community were to expand.

Jervis is careful to note that this "community" is composed only of those states that have been subject to the relevant influences, but they are also those states that represent the vanguard of history.[28] Given that Jervis argues that the security community is self-sustaining in part because its system is superior in delivering value to its members, it stands to reason that the model will expand in one way or another as the rest of the world develops.[29] This is especially so because Jervis emphasizes the critical pacifying importance of nuclear deterrence in making war too costly, a realization that changes in values and then works upon to cement the obsolescence of war. Jervis also cautions that war is still possible between members of the security community and outsiders, such as China and Russia (as well as smaller nations), but argues that, even here, such disputes are "not like those that characterized great-power conflicts over the past three centuries." Rather than contests for supremacy, he sees these tensions as stemming from advocacy for "milieu goals," and so as presumably more amenable to amelioration and eventual transcendence.[30]

The upshot of Jervis's argument, which synthesizes a vast literature and captures the spirit of a prominent contemporary intellectual attitude, is that the maturation of mores and the progress of democracy and free trade, when combined with the lessons learned from the costliness of war and its limited value, have created a self-sustaining and self-propagating community of nations and peoples for which war is simply unthinkable, as foreign to political and social life as dueling is to interpersonal relations.[31] To this view, while war is still with us as a matter of fact, this is a contingent rather than a necessary aspect of human social interaction. Indeed, the direction of history indicates that it is a passing characteristic; its salience is inversely correlated to the increasing development of human society. Needless to say, a world in which war is simply unimaginable, beyond the pale, is also a world in which nuclear weapons would be unnecessary.

THE ESSENTIAL IMPORTANCE OF POWER

But this is not in fact the world in which we live, or the one in which we can expect to live in the future. The root flaw in Jervis's argument, and in the arguments of those who contend that war is passé, is a conception of history and of human political and social development that markedly overestimates the durability of historically contingent value systems while seriously downplaying the enduring centrality of competition, fear, uncertainty, and power. Jervis is right in marveling at the creation of a pacific community of nations and peoples, and at the stark changes in mores and attitudes that have helped propel and cement this community.[32] He is even right in emphasizing that such a community has considerable resilience. But is he right that the basic nature of human politico-social interaction—and to some degree human nature itself—has changed, or is capable of changing so deeply through the alteration of value systems? The answer is that it has not; nor is it capable of such change. Even as conditions and mores have changed, the same basic competitive dynamics that Hobbes boldly outlined three and a half centuries ago (and that Darwin sketched out in the animal kingdom) remain active today and will continue to remain so as long as human beings are constituted as they have been for millennia.[33] Because of this enduring reality, we must always be acutely aware that war is possible and thinkable, and that the most reliable method for minimizing its appearance is through the prudent manipulation of fear and interest.

Let us first examine the particular case of the "security community" of Europe, for it is within this security community that Jervis makes his claims of war's impossibility. Jervis is right that Europe has become a continent in which war among its major nations is undesired and indeed implausible. But this is not at its root due to the changes in values of the Europeans, but rather to developments in the European power structure, developments that have not removed the possibility of war as such but rather transferred them to a different plane. The most important factors in explaining the current implausibility of war in Europe are the combination of the essential irrelevance of European state power since the end of World War II and the concurrent rise of American power. These factors have combined to make serious war between European states pointless, exceptionally difficult to mount, and unnecessary, not to mention unattractive—pointless because such wars would not directly affect the primary, relevant power balance, difficult because European states have not had the power to go to war without American assistance and authorization, and unnecessary because European security has been guaranteed by the regional hegemon, the United States.

What has happened? Wars throughout history, and particularly major wars in modern Europe, have been driven primarily by the desire to dominate a given state system or to stave off such domination by another.[34] Indeed, all the major wars in modern European history have been attempts to dominate the interstate system or to prevent its domination by another. The Thirty Years' War was a struggle by the Habsburg Empire to assert its dominance over Europe and by the Protestant powers and France to resist such domination. The wars of Louis XIV represented successive attempts by France to achieve supremacy over Western Europe. The wars of the French Revolution and especially Napoleon were the apotheosis of this attempt. Finally, World Wars I and II represented efforts by Germany to dominate Europe. Each of these conflicts directly affected the European power balance, was necessary in that the independence or autonomy of the states could not, it was believed, be protected without going to war, and could be initiated at will by any of the major parties to the war. Throughout the modern period, and well before it, state policies on war and peace have been primarily driven by such considerations. Great Britain's historical policy of intervening on behalf of the weaker coalition in order to prevent the consolidation of power on the continent stands as a prime example of this, as do France's policies seeking to counterbalance German power in the years before each of the world wars.

With the end of World War II, Europe had, however, essentially exhausted itself, leaving the field to the true victors, the giants America and Russia, whom Tocqueville as early as the 1830s had recognized would come to overawe and outclass Europe.[35] But the European powers were not simply conquered or garrisoned as a matter of contingency; rather, they had been "priced out of the market" of the great power contest.[36] For, after 1945, the European states simply could not stand in the same category as the superpowers militarily or economically. No individual European state or plausible combination of states could match either

American or, during the Cold War, Soviet power. Unlike the two superpowers, the states of Europe could not develop secure, effective, and discriminate strategic nuclear and adequate conventional forces and thus faced, at best, the deathly choice of "suicide or surrender" if abandoned by Washington to Soviet aggression. As with the princely states of the Holy Roman Empire after Napoleon or the American states in the wake of the Civil War, the European states had been transcended as politico-strategic units. Instead of a power balance among the European states, therefore, after 1945 there ensued first a bipolar structure between the United States and the USSR and then a hegemonic unipolar structure under US auspices, with the European states of Jervis's "security community" serving as allies, irritants, or neutrals, but not leading strategic actors of their own.

These developments, strengthened by the central role of the United States and the dollar in international economic stability, have meant that the contest for power and dominance over Europe since 1945 has taken place at a level beyond which individual European states have been able to play leading roles, a point that was driven home rather harshly by the United States and the Soviet Union during the Suez Crisis of 1956. So dependent on external protection and leadership have the European states been since 1945, and indeed increasingly over the course of the Cold War, that many astute analysts have regarded them as being part of an American "empire," albeit a special kind of liberal imperium.[37]

In any case, war between European states in the post-1945 world would, unlike those before 1945, have been irrelevant to determining the status of the European system, unnecessary for their preservation, and essentially impossible without US authorization. Neither the United States nor the Soviet Union during the term of its empire would have allowed its allies or client states to fight one another.[38] Indeed, most North Atlantic Treaty Organization (NATO) nation-states, and especially the most powerful European state, Germany, have been and are simply incapable of operating substantial military forces independent of US assistance, as evidenced in the 2011 Libyan operation.

This is not to deny the role of changes in values, liberal systems of government, and other factors in propelling and cementing the peace within the European community. Europeans have clearly become less martial (just as Americans have become considerably more martial after assuming a global security role), but this in some ways suits their role as security wards of the United States. And European democratic governments have not pushed for intra-European war and avoided (with the partial exception of France) directly challenging or excessively undermining the American-led security system. Meanwhile, economic growth has enabled Europeans to focus on prosperity and social welfare. These factors are of course important but they are secondary causes, aids to the underlying dynamic of the transcendence of the intra-European state balance.

Jervis is right, then, that war within the European security community is implausible under current circumstances. But *why* it is so does not support the proposition that such implausibility means that strategic competition and war can be pushed out of international politics. For the basic reason why Europe is a security community is that the relevant echelon for strategic interaction has risen above inter-European state boundaries to a level at which they cannot act autonomously without uniting. In this the once fiercely independent states of Europe resemble the once fractious states of the United States, the patchwork of princely fiefdoms and republics of the Holy Roman Empire, the city-states and principalities of pre-*risorgimento* Italy, the warring tribes of Italy before the Social War, and the proud *polises* of ancient Greece before Philip of Macedon. In each of these cases, political, social, or economic developments made once intransigent disputes among states irrelevant, and ultimately led to their forming, usually through compulsion, into a larger entity, which then directed those energies outward to some other opponent.[39] No one can imagine Virginia fighting Massachusetts and New York today, or Saxony Bavaria, but that is not because the *potential* for war has disappeared from human affairs, but rather because these political units cannot compete with more efficiently organized larger entities.

Indeed, it is instructive in this respect to note the progress toward the unification of Europe. For centuries, from Charlemagne through Charles V and Louis XIV on to Napoleon and Kaiser Wilhelm, Europeans have dreamed of unification of the states of Europe, but consistently failed. Only today has there been significant, stable progress toward such unification. Why? Clearly the increased fellow-feeling in Europe and the decline of militarism have played roles, but more determinative has been the compulsion to scale. Economically, increased unification through the abolition of trade barriers and synchronization of economic policies has allowed Europe to increase efficiency and thereby seek to compete in a globalized economy. Politically, it has allowed Europe to try to exercise some of its lost influence on the world stage. And, perhaps most revealingly, it has served as a way to begin to try to achieve some autonomy from and balance with the superpower, particularly through the potential for greater strength afforded by the euro. Though this unification represents a pacification of intra-European relations, it does not mean the end of strategic competition as such—rather it is in part an attempt to engage at that very strategic plane from which Europe has largely been excluded by its inability to achieve scale, to punch, in more colloquial terms, at the heavyweight level.

Europe's progress toward becoming a security community does not represent, then, a transcendence of war, but rather mainly war's displacement from its traditional arena among the states of Europe to a broader vista. For better or worse, the United States is Europe's security guarantor, and in key respects its benign imperial overseer, and the United States is engaged in strategic competition—with a rising China, with a recalcitrant Russia, with an ambitious Iran, and so forth. Europe's development cannot be seen, then, as a model for or an augury of the world's pacification. It is, rather, another chapter in the long history of the interaction of state power, technology, and strategic competition, one for which war continues to be supremely relevant. Strategic competition and the possibility of great war remain.

THE HISTORICAL CONTINGENCY OF EUROPE'S PEACEFULNESS

The pacific stability of postwar Europe stems primarily, then, from the obsolescence of the European state system and from the security patronage of the United States. Shifts in values and systems of government have helped, but they could not uphold such stability without a favorable power structure. But we would be remiss to reduce this story to power politics and liberalism alone and to dismiss more organic factors in explaining what has happened in Europe; for there may be deeper currents at work in reducing the probability of war within Europe.

Foremost is the possibility that Europe is in a civilizational phase of softening mores, introversion, and complacency. Organic conceptions of the rise, flourishing, and decline of nations and civilizations are woefully unfashionable in an empiricist age, but they have been central to explanations of history and international politics from antiquity until the twentieth century.[40] From Plato to Toynbee, thinkers have observed that powerful nations, peoples, cities, and the like appear to go through stages of development involving some variations of a vigorous and energetic rise, a proud flourishing, and a softening or stultifying decline. The Romans, whose martial prowess, stern discipline, and unwavering determination overpowered every rival in the ancient Mediterranean, became known in the late imperial period rather for their opulence and their unwillingness to shoulder the demands of civic virtue.[41] The Byzantines, who under

Justinian reconquered most of the Mediterranean and under Heraclius took on the Persian Empire, succumbed to the Arab invasions in large part because of exhaustion and internal discord. Machiavelli dedicated himself to understanding why the Italians had declined from the mastery of the Romans to the disunion and weakness of the city-states and principalities of the Renaissance.[42] Perhaps the best example in the early modern period is Spain, which became the premier power in Europe in the sixteenth century before exhausting itself in the confessional wars, debasing its economy, and yielding to a long decline. Outside Europe, Chinese imperial dynasties seemed to past observers to follow a pattern of vigorous conquest, flourishing, luxuriation, and finally overthrow. The Ming and the Manchu dynasties followed this pattern. In the Middle East, the stern and lean Arabs who rode out of the desert and conquered all before them eventually were seen to become lethargic and fell to the steppe Turkic peoples.

Europe's current, more pacific phase, then, might be seen as a stage in its civilizational development.[43] Throughout the history of post-antique Europe, war as a manifestation of vigorous interstate competition has been a constant, indeed perhaps a driving force in Europe's success in gaining world supremacy.[44] But the cataclysms of the two world wars, the declining influence of and confidence in the traditional sources of Western civilization, and the adoption of modernity by and consequent rise of non-European nations and peoples, among other factors, have contributed to what has to be seen as a decline in civilizational vigor, for lack of a better term, by the European peoples.[45] This might be particularly intensified by the marked aging of the European population. Europeans are not just less bellicose within Europe, within the "security community," they are also less bellicose in general. In earlier eras, such a civilization would likely have fallen prey to hungrier, more aggressive peoples or nations, as Rome fell to the Germanic barbarians, China to Mongols and Manchus, and Arabs to Mongols and Turks. Even during the Cold War, such a Europe left to its own devices almost certainly would have fallen under Soviet sway or outright dominion. But as Europe has been and is protected by the United States and by nuclear weapons, this did not come to pass. That Europe has entered into such a historical phase does not, then, mean that war is passé in general—Europe may be at the end of its run rather than at the end of history. Peoples and nations have many times before lost the appetite for war, but that has not meant that war, to paraphrase Trotsky, was not interested in them.

In point of fact, though, we should not take Europe's development as a one-way ratchet, for history may be sinusoidal rather than a bell curve.

The Chinese, who were bywords for the "sick men" of Asia in the nineteenth century, have clearly recovered a civilizational vigor that they had lost during the heyday of Western supremacy. Unsurprisingly, China in recent years has exhibited very clearly an appreciation for the military instrument, even as it promises to surpass Europe in economic success.[46] So we should be extremely cautious about assuming that Europe itself has abandoned its warlike ways for good.

Yet our caution about foretelling the demise of war should not be tied only to views of history, for there are wellsprings of human belligerence that go even deeper than the historical contingency of the security community of Europe.[47] Though the "realists" of neorealism are right that war is endemic to an anarchic state system, man is not driven toward war only by the structure of the international system, which is a relatively recent phenomenon in human development, but also by his deepest instincts and sentiments.[48] Pride, honor, biological necessity, the desire to dominate, the desire to feel "the passion of life to its top," ideological or religious obligations, et cetera, have all combined to drive men to go to war.[49] It would be inane to try to catalog fully the historical examples of those who have gone to war for more than pure reasons of state, but a few might include Alexander the Great, Julius Caesar, and Louis XIV, who pursued conquests for glory, and Napoleon and Hitler, whose wars sprang from combinations of vainglory, ideological zeal, and mania; the religious wars of the Arab Conquests, the Crusades, and the confessional wars, which, while they are certainly not reducible to religious motivations, can hardly be understood in their absence. Man is not, by nature, a pacific animal, as attested by the bloody example of early human history, in which a substantial fraction of deaths—perhaps even as high as a half—were caused by violence.[50] Nor must one see human beings as highly instinctive or emotional for war to take place. Hobbes envisioned man in his natural state acting purely out of self-interest and saw that a war of all against all would be the result in the absence of the Leviathan.[51] Changes in values and the application of power are epiphenomenal upon this enduring reality of humanity's native capacity for bellicosity. Unless our nature is decisively changed to one typified by a reliable selfless humility, which seems exceptionally unlikely, we will continue to have a propensity toward competition and war.

War remains, in brief, eminently possible, ever potential.[52] Deep structural shifts in power and in the nature of European civilization over the past half century, and particularly in the past twenty years, have obscured this reality, but it remains.

NUCLEAR WEAPONS AS PEACEMAKERS

Yet, thankfully, as the past sixty-five years demonstrates, great war is preventable. But its prevention begins precisely with the recognition that war is always possible, that it is always "thinkable." From this beginning, states can take actions to make war unlikely. Even with their bellicose instincts and incentives, men, and especially those who rise to positions of authority, are rarely madmen. Above all, they value survival and the preservation of what they have and love. Threatening these things, not least a potential adversary's life, can, then, serve to turn them away from war.[53] So also, albeit less reliably, can superior power.[54] Moreover, the *libido dominandi* and the other impulses that drive men toward war can, at least to some extent, be channeled into other, less destructive pursuits, especially when such attractions are coupled with a clear threat of devastation if the aggressive path is taken.[55] Thus a combination of the exploitation of fear and interest on the one hand and the redirection of warlike instincts toward other endeavors can combine to lessen substantially the probability of war. These are the core verities of deterrence and of enlightened statecraft.

In a nonnuclear world, this task was and would be a great and dubious challenge. Since conventional weapons effect damage at a scale readily cognizable by the human mind and are generally tolerable to a committed nation (excepting prodigies of effort available largely only to great states fully mobilized), war in a conventional world was and would be a matter of calculations of foreseeable risk and perceptible gains and losses. Deterring great war in such a world was and would be both very demanding and, in the long term, unreliable. This is because there would always be scenarios in which a state could often justifiably see the real possibility of gaining more through war than it would lose. While catastrophic wars, such as the Thirty Years' War, the Napoleonic Wars, and World War I, would always be possible and thus serve as deterrents, situations would continually arise in which decision makers could reasonably assess that their expected benefits would outweigh the possibility of such disaster. Nor would this necessarily be an unreasonable assessment. Throughout history, for every cataclysmic war, there were multiple smaller but still major wars that advanced the interests of a party—and, more importantly, multiple instances of the explicit or implicit threat to *go to* war that resulted in advantage for the threatening party and that decisively shaped the international environment. Bismarck unified Germany under Prussian control through a series of highly successful, contained wars against Denmark, Austria, independent German states like Bavaria, and France. Similarly, Sardinia and then Italy waged a series of advantageous wars to consolidate its control over the peninsula against other Italian states, Austria, and France. Wars of conquest would not pose the only danger, for war could break out as a product of attempts to ensure influence or dominance. Bismarck advised against Germany taking possession of Alsace and Lorraine, since he viewed the war against France as primarily a means to assert dominance and secure a unified Germany in Central Europe. Via its policy in Latin America, for instance, the United States long desired to ensure its own dominance over the region rather than territorial conquest, a policy that brought the United States close to war several times and into conflict with Spain. In a nonnuclear world, a rising power such as China might similarly pursue such dominance in its near abroad. Nor would all leaders be as reliably restrained as Bismarck. Leaders like Napoleon or Hitler who were fully prepared to countenance massive but still, compared with nuclear conflicts, limited wars could always arise.

In a nonnuclear world, then, war was and would be a potentially attractive policy option—indeed, it might often be the optimal choice, assuming that Christian or humanitarian impulses do not always prevail in strategic decision making. That implies that the only sure way to deter attack or coercion would be to be so strong as to resist and, ideally, overpower one's opponent, which, of course, has as its tragic corollary the "security dilemma"—that is, making it highly likely that one would be strong enough to molest the very powers that posed the threat in the first place.[56] In such a world, deterrence was and would be uncertain, as calculations of advantage for closely matched conventional conflicts would be speculative and "near run things"; unstable, as perturbations in the power balance, technological developments, and differential growth could determine the winner in a fight; and ultimately unreliable, as war was and would be effectively inevitable.[57]

This is why nuclear weapons remain as relevant today as they have ever been in the past, for nuclear weapons are by far the most effective method of deterring aggression. The prompt, sure devastation that a major nuclear attack can wreak on a targeted country is so catastrophic that the credible threat to initiate one is almost sure to dissuade any country from aggression. Considerations of state power and security, of glory and honor, of conquest and plunder, all pale in contest against the absolute destruction and defeat of all worldly ends that a major nuclear strike represents. Whereas in a nonnuclear world, aggression and war involve calculations of comparative advantage and calculable risks, great war is much less likely in a nuclear world because no worldly objective can justify the destruction that a large-scale nuclear attack would cause, destruction that in its prompt devastation is thousands of times greater than what conventional weapons can cause. Nuclear weapons cut through calculations of advantage to speak directly to man's most basic instincts of survival and preservation. In a sense, as Robert Jervis himself has pointed out, nuclear deterrence represents the negation of strategy, since it sunders military action from any plausibly commensurate political ends.[58] Needless to say, nuclear deterrence does not prevent every conflict or ensure against war—but when it is implicated, its cautionary pall makes war dramatically less likely.

It is this blunt reality that explains the post-1945 peace, not progressive values or liberalism or economic interdependence. Indeed, Europe's postwar history offers a more compelling testimony to the effectiveness of nuclear deterrence than any merely abstract argument can offer. Whereas Europe had suffered great wars from the first stirrings of civilization, it passed through a great and fearsome standoff in the Cold War as well as its aftermath without major conflict precisely because all have recognized the consequences of a full-scale war in a nuclear world. Nor was this achievement cheap or easy—to be effective nuclear deterrence must rely on real and fearsome capability and the genuine threat to use nuclear weapons. Thus the Cold War was an era of continual "imagined wars," with both sides again and again comparing how they would fare in a conflict, balancing each other's force developments, and working to strengthen their capabilities and make manifest their resolve.[59] The manifest seriousness of both sides, and the fear of what triggering the other's resolve would entail, led to the cold peace.

Yet the very success of nuclear weapons in making great war such an extremely perilous and unattractive endeavor has, paradoxically, made them seem irrelevant. They have, in a sense, been victims of their own success, which is so pacifying that they have made the peace seem independent of their influence. Countries spend and focus less on armaments and armies because they know how limited the gains are from such investments as long as nuclear weapons overhang. Yet this has the effect of making it seem like war is simply falling away of its own accord. But we should not confuse the effect with the cause. Nuclear weapons are what make great war unlikely, not new values or economic interdependence.

If nuclear weapons continue to play a salient role in world politics, we might expect this restraint to continue. But if they do not, as those who see the development of self-sustaining security communities presumably would argue, then war will tend to become more of a matter of calculable gains and losses, and thus is likely to become more salient again in human affairs. Needless to say, this would be a catastrophe.

THE ROLE OF NUCLEAR STRATEGY

To say that nuclear weapons remain relevant, indeed central, to peace and stability, however, is not quite to say that nuclear *strategy* is so central, or at least as central as it was during the Cold War. In those years, debates about nuclear strategy occupied center stage in deliberations about defense policy, and even about foreign policy more broadly. The deployment by the United States of the Pershing II intermediate-range ballistic and of BGM-109B ground-launched cruise missiles to Europe, for instance, was one of the highest-profile foreign policy issues of the late 1970s and early 1980s. Today, contrarily, the decision whether NATO will retain a nuclear capability of its own within Europe whatsoever is basically an issue mostly for those who till the fields of nuclear weapons or NATO for a living. More broadly, debates about the contours of our nuclear strategy, such as the varying pros and cons of counterforce targeting, the survivability of the land-based strategic force, and the role of tactical nuclear weapons, to name a few, have abated markedly.

This development is likely to endure and, moreover, is on balance a good thing. The strategic stability that preserves the peace is almost certainly less sensitive to changes in nuclear targeting doctrine and other finer aspects of nuclear strategy than was sometimes thought, at least in some quarters, during the Cold War.[60] Nuclear weapons deter above all through the promise of inflicting horrendous destruction. As long as the credible resolve to effect such devastation is firmly established, any additional superior military capability that nuclear weapons provide is effectively irrelevant, as meaningful victory in a true nuclear exchange is impossible. If so much of what one values is lost, it does not really matter if the other side loses more. Even so steely and determined an opponent as the Soviets seem to have understood this, despite what they said to the contrary.[61]

This is not to say that nuclear strategy is not still very important and relevant. Quite to the contrary—above all, for nuclear deterrence to be effective, it must rest on the credible threat to employ nuclear weapons. Thus nuclear capabilities and the plans to use them must bear some relation to the potential conflict. This means that defense planners and strategists will continue to need to grapple with the irreducibly complex, unpredictable, and changing issues of how to field, and if necessary employ, nuclear weapons in ways that most effectively deter major aggression and coercion.

The rise of China in particular will likely make nuclear strategy again more salient than it has been since 1991. Let us presume that China's rise will, at the very least, create great pressure on American hegemony in the

Western Pacific and the East Asian littoral. In such a situation, will the United States be able to continue to extend a credible nuclear umbrella over its allies and associates in East and Southeast Asia as China waxes in strength? Will Washington and these allies and associates want the United States to do so? If they do, what kind of military posture and strategy will be most effective and efficient in deterring Chinese aggression, coercion, or aggrandizement against US-protected states? If the Chinese manage to wrest superiority in conventional military terms away from the United States, which, after all, is located across the Pacific Ocean, will the United States find it attractive to place more reliance on nuclear weapons for extended deterrence purposes? What posture would this entail, with what kinds of weapons and delivery systems? Will US allies and associates be drawn (again) toward nuclear weapons programs of their own?[62] Would such "friendly" proliferation be more stabilizing than the attempt by the United States to maintain its hegemony? Similar, albeit less, stressing will continue to arise about Russia and about potentially nuclear-armed rogue states such as Iran and North Korea. Thus even as it is unlikely to dominate public consciousness as it did during the Cold War, nuclear strategy will remain relevant and indeed will probably become more important over the coming decades.

CONCLUSION

It is a remarkable fact that the mighty scourge of war has, to a degree only dreamt of by earlier ages, passed away. Countries and peoples that had waged and endured war from time immemorial have not suffered its direct effects for over half a century. Needless to say, this is a good to be cherished, and one whose preservation we are duty-bound to pursue. Thus we must search out why this peace has descended upon the advanced world and seek to extend its operation. But in so doing we must exercise the utmost caution when we infer gentle causes from pacific consequences, for we have seen that fear and interest provide a firm grounding for peace and that pacific mores and liberal values can build upon that grounding. But we have not seen, nor does history, biology, or philosophy give us a sturdy basis for believing, that we can safely entrust our security and the vitality of civilization solely to a vision of the new man formed by changes in values and attitudes, economic incentives, and democracy. Prevalent as these influences may be, they are not nearly dominating enough to persuade the prudent to abandon the tested method of deterrence. War remains eminently thinkable and possible and so it is best kept at bay through the threat of punishing force. Nuclear weapons and the deterrence they provide thus remain not only relevant but essential. No other weapons are so fearsome in their destructiveness, and thus in their effects so manifestly incommensurate with any worldly gain that would trigger its usage at any significant scale. War as the continuation of political advantage, war as an expression of man's animal nature, war as a manifestation of man's prideful and self-aggrandizing nature—all of these must be restrained in the face of the absolute weapon, for their pursuit is not merely illogical or misguided if it results in nuclear devastation, but actually mad, indeed completely incompatible with the most basic rationality. This is as secure a bind as we are likely to find. War, in a sense, is a caged animal. The beast may have been pacified by its years of confinement, but we would be most unwise to trust our lives to its good graces.

Notes

1. The author would like to thank Bruno Tertrais, George Quester, James Acton, and Robert Jervis for their helpful comments in preparing this manuscript. Professor Jervis was especially but characteristically generous in reviewing a chapter that takes aim at one of his own arguments.
2. "Report of the Secretary of Defense Task Force on DoD Nuclear Weapons Management, Phase II: Review of the DoD Nuclear Mission," September 2008, 1.
3. For a critique of this way of thinking, see Hans Morgenthau, "The Fallacy of Thinking Conventionally About Nuclear Weapons," in *Arms Control and Technological Innovation*, ed. David Carlton and Carlo Schaerf (New York: Wiley, 1976), 256–264. For a history of some of the more fervid theorizing (as well as the more solidly grounded), see Fred Kaplan, *The Wizards of Armageddon* (New York: Simon & Schuster, 1983).
4. John Mueller, *Retreat from Doomsday: The Obsolescence of Major War* (New York: Basic Books, 1989); and *The Remnants of War* (Ithaca, NY: Cornell University Press, 2004).
5. Francis Fukuyama, *The End of History and the Last Man* (New York: Avon Books, 1992).
6. Alexander Wendt, *Social Theory of International Politics* (Cambridge: Cambridge University Press, 1999); and James J. Sheehan, *Where Have All the Soldiers Gone? The Transformation of Modern Europe* (Boston: Houghton, Mifflin, 2008).
7. Richard Rosecrance, *The Rise of the Trading State* (New York: Basic Books, 1986). For the classic statement of the argument that commerce would make war impossible, see Norman Angell, *The Great Illusion* (New York and London: G. P. Putnam's Sons, 1913). See also Joseph Schumpeter, *Capitalism, Socialism, and Democracy* (New York: Harper Perennial, 1962); and "The Sociology of Imperialism," in *Imperialism and Social Classes* (Cleveland, OH: World Publishing, 1955), esp. 55–98.

8. Scott D. Sagan, *The Limits of Safety: Organizations, Accidents, and Nuclear Weapons* (Princeton, NJ: Princeton University Press, 1993).
9. For the classic argument along these lines, see Adam Smith, *An Inquiry into the Nature and Causes of the Wealth of Nations* (London: 1776). See also, inter alia, David Hume, *Essays Moral, Political, and Literary* (London: 1742), especially "Of the Jealousy of Trade"; and David Ricardo, *On the Principles of Political Economy and Taxation* (London: 1817).
10. For an example of the practical influence of this way of thinking, see Lee Kuan Yew, *From Third World to First—The Singapore Story: 1965-2000* (New York: HarperCollins, 2000), 481 and 612, inter alia. Lee recounts the central importance of free trade in allowing formerly aggrandizing countries such as Germany and Japan to "grow through trade and investments. They cooperated and competed with other nations and were able to prosper and flourish without wars." But Lee emphasizes that this beneficial development is contingent on the active maintenance of open markets and free trade. It is not a given.
11. For an analysis of this, see Samuel P. Huntington, "Why International Primacy Matters," *International Security* 17, no. 4 (Spring 1993): 71–82.
12. Peter Liberman, for instance, argued that "ruthless invaders can, in fact, successfully exploit industrial societies, at least for short periods of time. Control over industrial societies, moreover, can be maintained for longer periods of time at relatively low expense." Peter Liberman, *Does Conquest Pay: The Exploitation of Occupied Industrial Societies* (Princeton, NJ: Princeton University Press, 1996), 4.
13. See, e.g., Robert Gilpin, *Global Political Economy: Understanding the International Economic Order* (Princeton, NJ: Princeton University Press, 2001). As Gilpin summarized, "A liberal international order requires strong leadership and cooperation among the major economic powers. . . . American leadership and interstate cooperation constitute the only possible foundation for an open and stable global economy." 388. See also Charles P. Kindleberger, *The World in Depression, 1929–1939* (Berkeley, CA: University of California Press, 1986).
14. See, e.g., Robert Gilpin, *War and Change in World Politics* (Cambridge: Cambridge University Press, 1981), 156–157.
15. Ian Kershaw, *Fateful Choices: Ten Decisions That Changed the World, 1940–1941* (New York: Penguin, 2007), 331–381.
16. For explications of this view, see, e.g., Kenneth Waltz, *Theory of International Politics* (Reading, MA: Addison-Wesley, 1979); and John J. Mearsheimer, *The Tragedy of Great Power Politics* (New York: W. W. Norton & Company, 2001).
17. See, for instance, Thucydides, *The Peloponnesian War*, trans. Rex Warner (London: Penguin, 1972), esp. 80; and St. Augustine, *City of God*, trans. H. Bettenson (New York: Penguin, 1972), esp. 196–201 and 212–214.
18. Robert Jervis, *American Foreign Policy in a New Era* (New York: Routledge, 2005), 12. For another, similarly judicious argument akin to Jervis's, see

Paul W. Schroeder, "Does the History of International Politics Go Anywhere?" in *Systems, Stability, and Statecraft: Essays on the International History of Modern Europe*, ed. David Wetzel et al. (New York: Palgrave MacMillan, 2004), esp. 277–284. For the classic anticipation of this argument, see Immanuel Kant, *Perpetual Peace: A Philosophical Essay*, 1795. See also, inter alia, Abbe de Saint-Pierre, *A Project for Settling an Everlasting Peace in Europe*, 1712.
19. Jervis, *American Foreign Policy in a New Era*, 28. For more on the concept of the "security community," see Karl W. Deutsch et al., *Political Community and the North Atlantic Area: International Organization in the Light of Historical Experience* (Princeton, NJ: Princeton University Press, 1957); and Emanuel Adler and Michael Barnett, eds., *Security Communities* (Cambridge: Cambridge University Press, 1998).
20. Jervis, *American Foreign Policy in a New Era*, 12.
21. Ibid., 17
22. Ibid.,
23. Ibid., 16. For the classic description of states in anarchy, see Hans Morgenthau, *Politics Among Nations* (New York: Alfred A. Knopf, 1948).
24. Jervis, *American Foreign Policy in a New Era*, 18–24.
25. Ibid., 26–27.
26. Ibid., 26.
27. Ibid., 29.
28. Ibid., 29–32, inter alia. This argument resembles a variant of the Hegelian argument laid out by Francis Fukuyama in *The End of History*. While Jervis does not predict that all other nations will necessarily track the development of what he refers to as the "leading powers," it is clear that he sees the "leading powers" as representing the most advanced form of social organization. Fukuyama similarly argued that, while history would continue in the contests among nations and peoples, no other form of sociopolitical organization would supersede social liberal democracy and that the world would tend toward that form of organization over time. Fukuyama, *The End of History*, 64 and 311, inter alia. Hegel's original argument is laid out in Georg W. F. Hegel, *The Philosophy of History*, trans. J. Sibree (New York: Dover, 1953).
29. Jervis, *American Foreign Policy in a New Era*, 13–14. Jervis does note that backsliding is possible, but these cautionary remarks cannot be understood as essential, since, if so understood, they would entirely undermine his argument that "war is unthinkable." If backsliding to a situation in which war *is* thinkable is possible, then war itself is eminently possible and eminently thinkable. War cannot be both unthinkable and yet also plausible. As Jervis himself argues, "some of these changes may be irreversible" (28).
30. Ibid., 14.
31. Ibid., 28.
32. For a peerless description of this development, see Tony Judt, *Postwar: A History of Europe Since 1945* (New York: Penguin, 2005).

33. Thomas Hobbes, *Leviathan* (Harmondsworth: Penguin, 1986); and Charles Darwin, *The Origin of Species* (New York: New American Library, 1958).
34. See, for instance, Thucydides, *The Peloponnesian War*, esp. 49; and Polybius, *The Rise of the Roman Empire* (London: Penguin, 1979), esp. 535.
35. Alexis de Tocqueville, *Democracy in America*, trans. Harvey C. Mansfield and Delba Winthrop (Chicago: University of Chicago Press, 2000), 395–396.
36. For an exceptionally insightful analysis on this point, emphasizing the implications of the military revolution brought on by World War II and the nuclear age for European autonomy, see James R. Schlesinger, *European Security and the Nuclear Threat Since 1945* (Santa Monica, CA: RAND Corporation, 1967), P-3574. Schlesinger observed that Europe had been "hopelessly priced out of the game" by the need for sophisticated strategic forces and that the result after 1945 had been an increasing dependence on the United States (10). This, he saw, had led to the "ultimate strategic dominance of the United States and the Soviet Union" (25).
37. William E. Odom and Robert Dujarric, *America's Inadvertent Empire* (New Haven, CT: Yale University Press, 2004).
38. As Tony Judt put it, "Western Europeans owed their newfound well-being to the uncertainties of the Cold War. The internationalization of political confrontations, and the consequent engagement of the United States, helped draw the sting from domestic political conflicts. Political issues that in an earlier age would almost certainly have led to violence and war—the unresolved problem of Germany, territorial conflicts between Yugoslavia and Italy, the future of occupied Austria—were all contained, and would in due course be addressed, within the context of Great Power confrontations and negotiations over which Europeans had very little say" (Judt, *Postwar*, 242).
39. For a historical analysis of this development, see Martin Van Creveld, *The Rise and Decline of the State* (Cambridge: Cambridge University Press, 1999); and Robert Gilpin, *War and Change in World Politics*.
40. See, for instance, Plato, *The Republic*, trans. T. Griffith (Cambridge: Cambridge University Press, 2000), Book VIII; Edward Gibbon, *The Decline and Fall of the Roman Empire* (London: Penguin, 1994); Montesquieu, *Considerations on the Causes of the Greatness of the Romans and Their Decline*, trans. D. Lowenthal (Indianapolis, IN: Hackett, 1965); and Arnold J. Toynbee, *A Study of History* (Oxford: Oxford University Press, 1934–1961). For a more recent influential example, see Paul Kennedy, *The Rise and Fall of the Great Powers* (New York: Vintage, 1987).
41. Gibbon, *Decline and Fall of the Roman Empire*.
42. Niccolo Machiavelli, *The Discourses*, trans. L. J. Walker (London: Penguin, 1970).
43. For a more recent example of this perspective, see Samuel P. Huntington, *The Clash of Civilizations and the Remaking of World Order* (New York: Simon & Schuster, 1996), 301–303.
44. Geoffrey Parker, *The Cambridge Illustrated History of Warfare* (Cambridge: Cambridge University Press, 2008).

45. For a recent assessment of this dynamic, see Christopher Caldwell, *Reflections on the Revolution in Europe: Immigration, Islam, and the West* (New York: Doubleday, 2009).
46. See, for instance, Department of Defense, *Annual Report to Congress: Military and Security Developments Involving the People's Republic of China*, 2010, http://www.defense.gov/pubs/pdfs/2010_CMPR_Final.pdf (July 24, 2012).
47. For an analysis of the multiple causes of war, see Jack S. Levy and William R. Thompson, *Causes of War* (Chichester, UK: Wiley Blackwell, 2010), who conclude in their analytical survey of explanations of the causes of war that "there are multiple causal paths through which war can occur" (213).
48. See, for instance, Hans Morgenthau, *Politics Among Nations* (New York: Knopf, 1948). For a classic statement of neorealism, see Kenneth Waltz, *Theory of International Politics* (Reading, PA: Addison-Wesley, 1979).
49. See, for example, John Keegan, *A History of Warfare* (New York: Alfred A. Knopf, 1993), esp. 3–12; and Martin van Creveld, *The Culture of War* (New York: Ballantine Books, 2008). For "the passion of life to its top," see Oliver Wendell Holmes, Jr., "Memorial Day Speech," May 30, 1895.
50. Lawrence H. Keeley, *War Before Civilization: The Myth of the Peaceful Savage* (Oxford: Oxford University Press, 1996), 88–90. See also Nicholas Wade, *Before the Dawn: Recovering the Lost History of Our Ancestors* (New York: Penguin, 2006), 9.
51. Thomas Hobbes, *Leviathan*, chapter 13, 183–188.
52. For a similar assessment on the end of war, see Samuel P. Huntington, "No Exit: The Errors of Endism," *The National Interest* no. 17 (Fall 1989): 3–11. As Huntington pithily but sagely advised, "To hope for the benign end of history is human. To expect it to happen is unrealistic. To plan on it happening is disastrous."
53. Thomas Schelling, *Arms and Influence* (New Haven, CT: Yale University Press, 1966), inter alia.
54. Glenn Snyder, *Deterrence and Defense: Toward a Theory of National Security* (Princeton, NJ: Princeton University Press, 1961), 14–16.
55. Such ideas were central to the whole thrust of Enlightenment thought on the free market, represented above all in Adam Smith's *Wealth of Nations*. See, for instance, Bernard Mandeville, "The Fable of the Bees," in *The Fable of the Bees and Other Writings* (Indianapolis, IN: Hackett, 1997). For a modern appraisal, see Albert O. Hirschman, *The Passions and the Interests: Political Arguments for Capitalism Before Its Triumph* (Princeton, NJ: Princeton University Press, 1977). A very clear example along different lines is the militaristic Society of Jesus, founded by the ex-soldier Ignatius of Loyola on the military model and commanding perfect obedience from its members to its Superior General and its ultimate commander, the Pope.
56. John H. Herz, "Idealist Internationalism and Security Dilemma," *World Politics* 2 (1950): 157–158.

57. For an analysis of the role of differential growth rates in causing great power conflicts, see Dale C. Copeland, *The Origins of Major War* (Ithaca, NY: Cornell University Press, 2000).
58. Robert Jervis, *The Illogic of American Nuclear Strategy* (Ithaca, NY: Cornell University Press, 1984).
59. See, for instance, Robert D. Blackwill and Jeffrey W. Legro, "Constraining Ground Force Exercises of NATO and the Warsaw Pact," *International Security* 13, no. 3 (Winter 1989–1990): 68–98.
60. For a similar assessment, see Lawrence Freedman, *The Evolution of Nuclear Strategy*, 3rd ed. (Houndsmills, UK, 2003), especially the Conclusion. 458–464.
61. See interviews of former Soviet officials in John G. Hines et al., *Soviet Intentions 1965-1985* (McLean, VA: BDM Federal, 1995).
62. For a history of some earlier moves toward nuclear weapons by US allies, see Kurt M. Campbell et al., eds., *The Nuclear Tipping Point: Why States Reconsider Their Nuclear Choices* (Washington, DC: Brookings Institution Press, 2004).

CHAPTER 5

CAN TAILORED DETERRENCE AND SMART POWER SUCCEED AGAINST THE LONG-TERM NUCLEAR PROLIFERATION CHALLENGE?

JONATHAN TREXEL

INTRODUCTION

There are many strategic deterrence challenges facing the United States now and over the long term. For example, one might want to deter aggression, or deter an adversary from using weapons of mass destruction (WMD) once a conflict has begun, or deter cyberspace or counterspace attacks in a crisis. But a recurring and mounting challenge for the United States, and one that will likely recur (possibly several times) in the coming years, is stemming nuclear weapons proliferation among potential adversaries.

As we consider various ways to support the president's emphasis on addressing nuclear nonproliferation, there is a role for strategic deterrence. But when one considers this problem, a conceptual bridge is needed to help us think about such challenges with a long-term perspective. Strategic deterrence concepts, as explained and expanded below, provide one such bridge. The intention is to present three broad, long-term deterrence problems or scenarios as a way to improve how we think about deterrence activities and capabilities and then cull further ideas for future discussion.

From a strategy perspective, one purpose of this chapter is to provide some long-term context for current thinking on near-term deterrence planning and strategy. The current deterrence framework, outlined in the 2006 *Deterrence Operations Joint Operating Concept*, suggests that we build deterrence strategies in response to our understanding of potential adversary perceptions. These strategies necessarily tend to be dominated by military planning processes, resulting in near-term definitions of the problems and deterrence strategies that emphasize hard-power capabilities and activities. However, as one proceeds across the time horizon of understanding emerging and distant threats, and how potential adversaries might view acquisition or development of nuclear weapons, the role of the military instrument to influence adversary perceptions likely diminishes while soft-power capabilities and activities increase in prominence. Hopefully, this chapter will furnish some conceptual context to better understand how to more effectively address our nation's deterrence challenges.

BACKGROUND

THE DETERRENCE FRAMEWORK

The broad idea that deterrence is about decisive influence is no less germane to long-term deterrence problems than to near-term possibilities. The primary conceptual differences between long-term and near-term deterrence are ones of magnitude and outcomes. A short review of near-term deterrence, stemming from the *Deterrence Operations Joint Operating Concept (DO JOC)*, follows. According to the *DO JOC*,

> Deterrence operations convince adversaries not to take actions that threaten US vital interests by means of decisive influence over their decision-making. Decisive influence is achieved by credibly threatening to deny benefits and/or impose costs while encouraging restraint by convincing the actor that restraint will result in an acceptable outcome.[1]

The goal in near-term deterrence is to influence an adversary to decide to restrain from taking egregious action against us or against our allies (see figure 5.1). We begin by understanding the core decision factors of the adversary; that is, the things that matter most to him from a strategic perspective. Next, we consider those factors in a specific scenario and assess his decision calculus. A calculus is the adversary's perceptions of the consequences of costs and benefits of taking a specific action we seek to

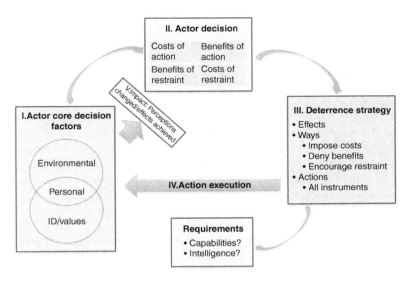

Figure 5.1 Strategic deterrence model

deter as well as the costs and benefits of restraint. This calculus is the focus of near-term deterrence. The calculus informs our strategy development, including desired cognitive effects and potential actions using all instruments of national power. Upon execution, these actions enter and alter the actor's core decision factors. It is the change in core decision factors that influences the actor's decision to act or restrain by changing perceptions throughout his calculus. And so a cycle of assessment, strategy adjustment, and reassessment begins. Importantly, the military means used to accomplish this influence can go beyond nuclear assets and include conventional and even defensive capabilities. Further, nonmilitary capabilities and activities are important to consider precisely because they matter to potential adversary decision making.

Deterrence "Tailoring"

Strategic deterrence is adversary-centric, situation-dependent, and focused on the adversary's decision calculus. Further, this calculus generally comprises perceptions of consequences—that is, what happens if the adversary acts and what happens if he does not act. "Tailored" deterrence is simply the appropriate application of power (both military and nonmilitary) to achieve a deterrence objective, taking into consideration the adversary and his decision calculus. Unpacking an adversary's decision calculus is the essential feature in strategic deterrence strategy development and is the springboard for understanding how to tailor US strategy to effectively deter the adversary's decision to pursue a program intended to develop nuclear weapons.

The features of a tailored deterrence strategy depend in part on whether the strategy is intended to deter near- or long-term threats.[2] For example, if the concern involves a state's acquisition or development of nuclear weapons, one might employ a near-term strategy that includes both denying the adversary access to the various parts of the nuclear fuel cycle and raising, through diplomatic means, the value of cooperation so as to enhance stability through economic interdependencies and treaties. A broad US government strategy might also attempt to incorporate pursuing common interests such as fighting disease, hunger, and famine and promoting education and human capital investment at the societal level, all the while threatening to impose costs for aberrant behavior upon the leadership. In contrast, a long-term strategy might be to lessen the value attributed to nuclear weapons as a means of guaranteeing security by reducing fears of external attack. Considering both long- and near-term aspects of the proliferation problem can help us understand how to sculpt a more consistent long-term US national deterrence strategy. This is accomplished by understanding the actor and how our deterrent actions might need to transition should long-term efforts fail.

On Power

The United States possesses significant national power. This power must be measured, timely, and decisive when applied, even in pursuit of deterrence strategies aimed at nuclear proliferation challenges. The consequences of inappropriate application of US power can include a lasting, tarnished US image in the international community, irrevocable loss of precious resources, strains of over-extension, as well as deterrence failure. Further, failing to plan and organize to marshal and to use US power can frustrate other national security strategies and compound adverse consequences upon us, regardless of the problem at hand.

When we think of power, we often think of an acronym such as DIMEFIL (diplomatic, information, military, economic, financial, intelligence, and law enforcement). In doing so, however, we typically do not associate applying these elements of power in a coordinated or synchronized way toward an end such as deterrence. Economic power, for example, has many aspects and serves many purposes: it undergirds social well-being and trade, taxes and government programs, and so forth, but it can also be used to influence others through, for example, the withholding of economic benefits. Unfortunately, when we think of our nation's "deterrent," or "strategic deterrence" loosely stated, we usually associate such power with long-range nuclear forces.

Strategic deterrence is principally a competition of wills carried out at the most senior levels of political office. In the twenty-first century, our political opponent's decision calculus will include many considerations beyond such weapons. The application of US power to achieve deterrent effects should, therefore, consider all types of power and not be limited to long-range nuclear forces. *How* power is applied is what distinguishes its utility as a deterrent. This is to say, the power to influence others in what matters most is not simply physical destructive power. Rather, "deterrent power," in this way, can be thought of as any power marshaled specifically for deterrent effects. Deterrent power can be either "hard" power or "soft" power or a fusion of the two into what is today termed "smart power."[3] The sum of our nation's varied strategic capabilities is tailorable. A purposeful, disciplined, collaborative, and tailored deterrence campaign development process is needed for deterrent power to achieve its desired cognitive effects. Effectively marshaling deterrent power, however, can be useful in day-to-day conditions, acute deterrent problems, and long-term strategic deterrence scenarios, such as those dealing with nuclear proliferation described below.

Smart power is identified by virtue of the caution and care in which it is applied and the self-limiting objectives guiding its application. Smart power can range from positive policy attraction by others (described by some as soft power) to armed coercion and the decisive use of force (hard power), albeit within a framework of smart power. Smart power can include the power to attract and the power to instill fear; governmental and nongovernmental; military and nonmilitary; kinetic and nonkinetic; as well as less tangible instruments such as US strength of character.

Smart power, as a concept, should be attractive to US policy makers because it offers the potential to deliberately and effectively engage and influence others through positive and negative reinforcement mechanisms in the pursuit of US national security objectives with potentially less risk for adverse consequences for both sides. In particular, smart power can be applied as the capacity to influence in order to more effectively *deter* our potential and immediate adversaries from egregious actions, *assure* our allies and friends of US commitment and resolve, develop improved relations with competitors and indifferent states to *dissuade* them from trends infringing on our interests, *relieve* fears in foreign social groups of US intentions and possibly to foster goodwill among them, and *reassure* our citizens about being free from fear.

LONG-TERM DETERRENCE CONCEPT

Overview

Some long-term deterrence problems and strategies consider actor decisions beyond the alternatives of action or restraint described in the basic deterrence framework above. The long-term deterrence concept suggests that we be prepared to present alternatives to an adversary that are aimed at abandoning an egregious decision altogether for a more favorable policy option that is more attractive to him and potentially of greater long-term significance. Unlike typical near-term deterrence strategies, the long-term deterrence approach provides a pathway to a totally different outcome for all actors involved. The actor is influenced away from egregious action for the indefinite future, not by restraint alone, but by replacing his choice with a mutually acceptable alternative course of action (COA). So while a fundamental distinction exists in that near- and long-term deterrence options presuppose different deterrence pathways (restraint versus alternative COA), the central idea remains the same: decisive influence over an actor's decision making, resulting in enhanced US national security.

Three broad scenarios and strategies germane to the concept of long-term deterrence and nuclear weapons development are summarized below (see figure 5.2):

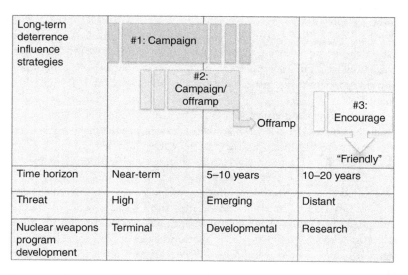

Figure 5.2   Long-term deterrence scenarios and strategies

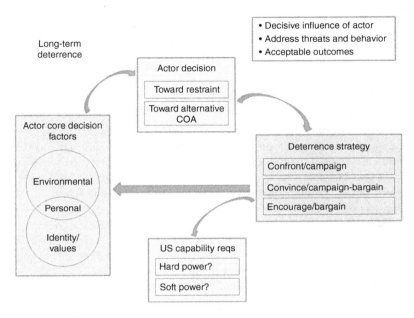

Figure 5.3   Strategy options

1. When we are engaged in a deterrence campaign to influence an actor's decision to act or restrain over an extended period of time;
2. When circumstances arise during an ongoing deterrence campaign in which we can offer an actor an option of an entirely new alternative COA acceptable to both of us; and
3. When we encourage friendly relations early as a preventive measure.

These scenarios also reflect different core decision factors of the actor in question as time and circumstances change, demanding from us appropriate long-term deterrence capabilities, approaches, and strategies (see figure 5.3). Each long-term deterrence scenario, to be explored briefly below, points to three broad approaches to the actor:

1. Deter by *confronting* the actor, given his adversarial identity and values, thus *confounding* the threat and the threatening behavior indefinitely;
2. Deter by *convincing* the otherwise adversarial actor to be friendly, thus *removing* the prospects for threatening behavior by changing the nature of the threat; and

3. Deter by *encouraging* the actor to be friendly before he becomes adversarial, thus *preventing* the threat and threatening behavior from ever emerging.

HISTORICAL INSIGHTS

When considering strategies to influence potential adversaries against pursuing nuclear weapons programs, one could consider past cases where states abandoned them and why they did so. There are several historical cases that one can turn to by way of support or comparison on the subject of an actor's decision to reverse course in its WMD program. South Africa and Libya are two such cases.[4] South Africa, for example, made the decision to abandon its nuclear weapons program,[5] developed principally out of fear of Soviet influence and expansion, if not invasion. However, the collective factors of a decline in Soviet power, internal domestic problems, and a marred international image led South Africa's leadership to see its security position as better off without nuclear weapons. As such, it was not a strategy of external cost-imposition that mattered most, but the drastic alteration of the post–Cold War security environment and how South African leaders came to view it with respect to their security that changed how they valued their nuclear weapons. Certainly, other factors were in play, but security-related conditions fundamentally changed, enabling South Africa's leaders to envision a future that was both secure and free of nuclear weapons.

The most celebrated case of an adversarial state giving up its nuclear weapons program is that of Libya. Libya's nuclear weapons program originated in some of the most trying years of the broader Arab-Israeli conflict and was intended, in part, perhaps a large part, as a deterrent and counter to the Israeli nuclear program. The A. Q. Khan network also aided it. Although Libya never acquired nuclear weapons, its leadership's decision calculus to continue pursuing them changed through a combination of developments that included the loss of a significant program shipment; consideration of the US invasion of Iraq, which heightened fears that Libya could also be attacked; and overtures suggesting that a significant bargain was at hand.

While Libya stood to lose the prestige of eventual nuclear status and the deterrent security afforded by it if it had pursued its program to the end and actually obtained nuclear weapons, Libyan leaders seem to have perceived that their nuclear program might actually make them less secure. The bargain of program abandonment in exchange for lifting economic sanctions, an end to political isolation, removal from the "state sponsors of terrorism" list, and renewal of direct investment in Libya, among others, collectively served Libya's interests, particularly its security position. In the case of both South Africa and Libya, security was understood to be better without nuclear weapons, but in Libya's case in particular, a change in conditions coincided with the opportunity to choose an alternative course of action.

LONG-TERM DETERRENCE SCENARIOS

SCENARIO 1: CONTINUOUS CAMPAIGN

There are two broad possibilities when we consider the sort of long-term deterrence problem in which our response envisions a continuous deterrence campaign. The first is when we are indefinitely deterring an actor presenting a single existing threat. The second is when we are deterring an actor presenting us with a single emerging threat that evolves over a long period of time. The existing *DO JOC* concept applies, but in long-term ways, and can be used to describe the differences between these two in terms of adversary perceptions and appropriate deterrence strategies.

Unlike other deterrence challenges, the pursuit of nuclear weapons entails a series of decisions made by the adversary over a period of several years, beginning with an initial decision to proceed with research and fuel-cycle needs and culminating with final decisions to test a nuclear device and deploy weapons. The issue of an actor pursuing nuclear weapons over several years suggests that we take a broad, long-term view in order to craft and implement an effective deterrence strategy (see table 5.1).

Table 5.1   Long-term deterrence strategy overview

	Continuous campaign	**Campaign-bargain**	**Bargain**
Desired actor choice	Restrain	Offramp to alt. COA	Alternative COA
US strategy approach	Confront	Convince	Encourage
Goal of long-term strategy on threat	Contain	Remove	Prevent
Threat characteristics	Existing threat	Emerging threat	Distant threat
US power emphasis	Hard-soft	Soft-hard	Soft
Strategy's effect on actor's relations with the United States	Adversarial (Unchanged)	Toward friendly	Friendly
Goal of strategy on actor's value of WMD	Confound (Value likely remains high)	Marginalize	Eliminate

In the first scenario, an actor might contemplate taking an action we deem egregious or against our interests and, as a result, might lead us to conduct an active deterrence campaign against this threat over an extended period of time, if not indefinitely. As long as conditions remain basically unchanged, the option available to the actor associated with this situation is simply a decision to act or not act; that is, a decision to proceed with the egregious action or restrain from doing so. Examples of this scenario might include North Korea's contemplation of attacking South Korea over the past several decades or perhaps Soviet decision making relative to a nuclear attack during the Cold War period. Given the actor's historical animosity toward the United States, the US deterrence strategy in this scenario would be to confront the actor and seek to acquire and maintain continuous influence over his decision to restrain from taking hostile action, and doing so indefinitely or until the threat ends. This is done by understanding the actor's decision calculus. The task, then, is to threaten or actually impose costs, deny sought-after benefits, and encourage restraint by reducing the actor's perceived costs of restraint and reinforcing the actor's perceived benefits of restraint. These actions stabilize the threat in conditions of a general deterrence, status quo environment indefinitely, hopefully leading the adversary to eventually abandon the threat to the United States by recognizing its diminishing value.

The key here is that the actor's motivations for considering pursuit of nuclear weapons are value-based. In this case, nuclear weapons are valued to address security concerns, which might for a rogue-type state include its overall relative position of military weakness or significant imbalance, fears of internal political consequences for failing to meet expectations, and vulnerability to being manipulated politically by other states, particularly regional antagonists or competitors. The actor's key question is, what will happen if I *do not* pursue? Years later, when the adversary is at the terminal end of his development program, his decision calculus is likely based more on the benefits of possession, though potential costs would most likely be much higher, and his calculus might be based more on the probabilities. In this case, his key question will be, what will happen if I *continue* to pursue?

Understanding a potential adversary's value perceptions for pursuing nuclear weapons and formulating a deterrence strategy that appropriately applies all elements of national and international power might present several advantages for the United States, its allies, and the international community. First, altering political and regional security conditions that reduce the adversary's fear of attack might be considered a small investment relative to the potential costs and intended consequences of going to war later with a nuclear-armed state. Since changing conditions to be more favorable to the adversary might take a long time to accomplish, the earlier a government assesses this to be a viable strategy to deter the pursuit of nuclear weapons, the higher the likelihood of achieving the outcomes sought. Second, increased use of positive political and economic power, herein described as soft power, might improve the global image of the United States by demonstrating a willingness to explore new non-coercive measures, which may ultimately result in making US threats to use hard power more credible. Further, adversary perceptions of US military overstretch might weaken how those adversaries view US hard-power deterrent threats. Third, an effective deterrence strategy can inform, if not guide, US strategic communication strategy as we seek to promote and strengthen the US position globally. Fourth, employing all instruments of national power, not simply the military instrument, can build trust and confidence in the United States, and possibly increase the viability of nonproliferation inspection regimes. This also might make partnerships on nonproliferation strategies more palatable politically. Fifth, it can assure allies of US regional commitments. Sixth, such a strategy will be more useful in finding coalition members previously unable or unwilling to participate in US nonproliferation initiatives because the military is the sole instrument being used. Seventh, it would make regional security dynamics more stable. And eighth, and most importantly, the specific proliferation problem being considered would be contained, reduced, eliminated, or even prevented because a panoply of instruments and options are in play. Deterrence failure early (or failing to try) makes deterrence success harder at the terminal end, or near-term end, except with higher risks of military force and the potential for second- or third-order effects and unforeseen consequences in the aftermath. But note that, while military threats might be decisive, they probably heighten fears of the adversary and reinforce his belief that he needs nuclear weapons precisely to deter US attack.

Scenario 2: Campaign-Bargain

A second long-term deterrence scenario can occur when an ongoing deterrence campaign is in progress, when in crisis, or when circumstances have changed so much that they might present an opportunity to offer an actor an entirely new course of action. Here, we are concerned with presenting the actor with a choice for a different future, not merely the choice to act or restrain from hostile behavior. That is, we would seek to encourage the actor down the path of an entirely new alternative course of action that presents a different but acceptable outcome for both parties.

The actor must envision an alternative future that is sufficiently secure, without possessing threatening capabilities or behavior. In this scenario, deterrence activities would not be limited simply to near-term incentives, such as financial reward or avoidance of financial loss, but would emphasize a long-term option that sufficiently satisfies the actor's core security concerns and in a way that satisfies our need to reduce or eliminate the hostile threats and capabilities that the adversary poses to us. The actor initially chooses to restrain from egregious behavior, but, more importantly, chooses a value system no longer characterized by the United States as adversarial.

An example of this long-term deterrence scenario would be Libya's decision to reestablish friendly relations with the West and abandon its weapons of mass destruction (WMD) program in 2003–4, not simply to restrain from advancing it along its technological path (see figure 5.4). This long-term deterrence strategy is likely a very difficult challenge when we are in crisis or when the developmental threat has approached completion, especially since our efforts to deter the actor's egregious actions at this point are likely to be increasingly coercive in nature, cost-imposition military capabilities and activities being at the center of our strategy. However, as in the Libyan case, a significant regional security event that

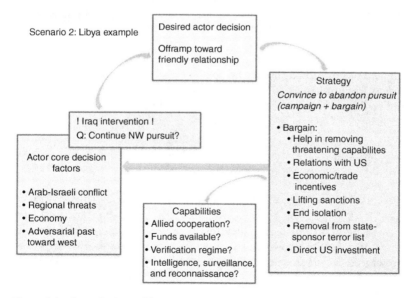

Figure 5.4 Campaigning and bargaining

brought a large number of US combat forces to the region as part of the coalition intervention in Iraq can spur the actor to accept the choice of a long-term alternative course of action marked by a vision of a secure future and friendly relations with the United States.[6]

The 2003 attack on Iraq and the ultimate overthrow of Saddam Hussein altered Muammar Qadhafi's perceptions by increasing the belief in the likelihood that he too faced the possibility of regime change for continuing his nuclear weapons program. Environmental change can and does occur in the international security environment, resulting in change that impacts the decision making of leaders. Such change worked to influence Qadhafi's decision to consider an alternative course of action in the form of a grand bargain to get the result that the United States wanted (a long-term deterrence outcome of good relations with the West and of Libya possessing no threatening or destabilizing capabilities, including nuclear capabilities). US intervention in Iraq triggered the opportunity for the bargain to be offered *and accepted*; that is, Qadhafi would not have accepted the bargain until his perceptions of the probability of cost for continuing to pursue his nuclear weapons program increased.

SCENARIO 3: BARGAIN

The third long-term deterrence scenario considers an actor's option to change strategic course early, while any potential threat to us is but "smoke rising on the horizon." Since this threat is perceptible, yet still on the distant horizon (i.e., as an actor's early decision to pursue a nuclear power capability that could transition later to a nuclear weapons capability), new opportunities present themselves for shaping the actor's perceptions of his security environment and thus his calculus for choosing among broad alternative courses of action. While the tools and ways available to us to influence his decision making remain the same, the actor's choice is not limited to deciding to act or restrain, as described above.

Rather, the concept of long-term deterrence, while the threat is still distant, might involve presenting the actor with multiple alternative choices. However, we are seeking to influence him toward making a choice that takes into account what we deem to be threatening capabilities or intent, even if those capabilities will take years to mature, along with the root security issues driving the actor to value those capabilities (nuclear weapons) in the first place (see figure 5.5). The difference is that we are purposefully and actively packaging a bargain early in the process of an actor's development of a capability that may be a threat to the United States in the future. Properly negotiated, this approach will encourage a potential adversary to choose a value system and behavioral path that are

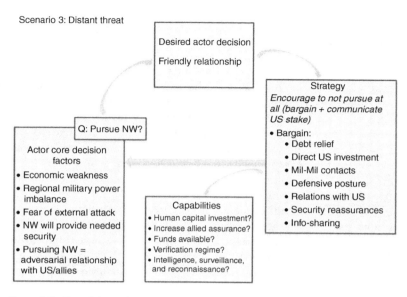

Figure 5.5   Bargaining early

not adversarial to us. As with Scenario 2 above, this requires us to understand and address the root motivations in the actor's decision calculus to pursue a capability that positions him as a potential US adversary. Doing so could include taking political and economic measures that align or even integrate the actor with the United States and its allies. But it would also include removing or reducing the actor's most threatening and destabilizing military capabilities, such as WMD and related means of delivery, however developmental they may be at this point. Thus, his decision goes beyond restraining from pursuit to making a strategic choice that involves a future in which restraint is no longer an option. The US goal is for the actor to choose an alternative bargain that provides enduring, credible, and stabilizing security measures while at the same time reducing or eliminating his perceived costs of restraint. By doing so, the perceived value of WMD and other threatening military capabilities is reduced and ultimately eliminated.

When we consider this third scenario, it is difficult to identify historical cases that match the concept envisioned here as few cases can be cited when the United States acted decisively to influence a distant threat precisely in the manner outlined above. However, there are cases generally representative of the idea. Egypt, for example, explored the possibility of developing a nuclear weapons program during the 1960s and

1970s in response to various perceived threats posed by Israel, including fear of Israel's possible development of its own nuclear weapons. However, an alternative course of action involving peaceful relations with the United States and Israel was presented and eventually accepted, culminating in Egypt's 1979 peace settlement with Israel that the United States brokered at Camp David. Additionally, Egypt's 1980 decision to ratify the Nuclear Non-Proliferation Treaty and an influx of significant US aid and other assurances likely contributed to Cairo backing away from the nuclear option. The goal of influencing Egypt away from continuing its nuclear weapons program was accomplished not merely by influencing its decision to restrain from the pursuit of nuclear weapons, but by crafting a long-term alternative option that amounted to a bargain that addressed its fundamental regional security concerns and other interests. Thus, Scenario 3 illustrates the prevention of a threat when we can only imagine it as potential "smoke rising on the horizon" and when an actor is more amenable to US overtures. Actors like Burma or Venezuela might fit into this category.

ACTOR CORE DECISION FACTORS

GENERAL

The second and third long-term deterrence scenarios emphasize actions and capabilities to not only persuade an actor to restrain from continuing an egregious course, but provide him a credible and durable alternative course that he perceives to enhance his security more than the course he is pursuing currently. Likewise, long-term deterrence emphasizes actions and capabilities that dispel an actor's fears of potential costs of restraint by mitigating long-term motivations pressuring the actor to follow an egregious course of action. Alleviating the actor's perceived costs of restraint intrinsically alters the actor's decision making. More importantly, it strengthens the credibility and the attractiveness of the alternative course of action he is presented.

Long-term deterrence emphasizes consequences of restraint, especially the benefits of changing course, for two important reasons. First, not many costs, especially military ones, can be imposed on an actor presenting a distant threat that will influence him to accept a positive, long-term alternative course of action. This is mainly because threatening significant near-term costs to influence an actor's decision making regarding a threat that might never emerge will not be perceived by that actor as credible. Second, if one waits to threaten heavy cost imposition until the threat posed by an actor is a near-term one, such an approach will likely influence the actor only in terms of his near-term decision to act or restrain. In either case the problem is that threatening heavy costs tends to reinforce an actor's enduring security fears and thus may undergird why he values nuclear weapons (for example) in the first place.

As the Libya case demonstrated, the prospect of near-term and heavy costs upon Libya for development of a nuclear weapons capability in the aftermath of the attack on Iraq only found significant meaning in the regime's decision making when combined with a credible, durable, and beneficial alternative course of action that jettisoned nuclear weapons development and a policy of confrontation with the West. In this case, Libya's security concerns were adequately addressed, allowing Libya to accept a long-term alternative course of action characterized by less confrontational relations with the United States.[7] Libya's strategic "sea change" was, in essence, a decision to change its values made possible by political, economic, and security relational and environmental changes. This is an example of long-term deterrence succeeding under the circumstances of an ongoing deterrence campaign.

It should be noted that emphasizing the cost-imposition or benefit-denial aspects of a decision making might be effective in influencing his decision to act or restrain, but doing so without addressing the consequences of restraint that the actor would face might not be tenable over time. This is because it reinforces his fears and his policy of challenge to us and, therefore, is unlikely to incentivize the actor to a long-term alternative course of action.

In each of these long-term deterrence scenarios, an actor's decision making will include consideration of both external environmental and internal factors. Environmental factors (i.e., political, economic, military) comprise his real world of action and interaction. Internal factors (i.e., his identity, values, and fears) shape how he will interpret his environment and provide motivations for how he might act within and upon his environment, and likewise how environmental change might affect him internally. In long-term deterrence scenarios, however, the internal-external mix of decision factors differs, with salient aspects being how an actor would interpret alternative courses of action and, therefore, differences in the long-term deterrence strategy, actions, and capabilities that we would need to marshal. This also explains why unexpected and radical changes to conditions can be destabilizing and dangerous.

In Scenario 1 (a continuous campaign), environmental factors matter most, since our relationship with an actor is relatively unchanged given the latter's static identity. Given the ongoing threat he poses, our long-term deterrence actions and capabilities, therefore, will emphasize his basic calculus to act or restrain. These will also require coercive measures, including the prospects of defensive and offensive military options. But long-term deterrence strategies, as in the case of deterring conflict on the Korean Peninsula, seek to provide stability to political, economic, and military conditions.

In Scenario 2 (a campaign-bargain), there is time for external factors to change significantly and perhaps affect the actor's basic calculus, possibly presenting us an opportunity for a "grand bargain" with the actor. However, we need insight into his decision calculus, how it might be changing, and a preplanned "bargain" or one that can be cobbled together with little time. Here, internal and environmental factors work together to "motivate" the actor toward a new course of action where he can envision himself securely in a world in which his bilateral and regional relations are significantly altered and the value he places on WMD or other threatening military capabilities is significantly reduced.

In Scenario 3 (a distant threat), the threat is in its earliest stages and the United States might be in a position to decisively influence the actor to move away from further pursuit and toward acceptance of a long-term bargain. The most effective way to achieve this will likely be strategies that reduce the actor's perceptions of external or existential threats. Fostering beneficial conditions or assurances will also be needed. Reducing an actor's fears decreases the perceived benefits for pursuing nuclear weapons, while assurances will persuade the actor to find benefits of restraint attractive. However, the actor must view these perceptions as enduring if we are to expect any long-term alternative option to be of value and accepted.

In Relation to US Deterrence Strategies

When an actor first considers a decision to pursue nuclear weapons, his decision calculus is likely to be dominated by perceptions of various consequences of restraint; that is, what might happen if he chooses not to pursue a nuclear weapons program. Further, they will not likely respond to threats of attack, especially a nuclear threat, as such threats will likely be perceived as premature, hence less than credible. They also might not respond to other potential costs, such as financial or economic sanctions. The thought about deterrence strategy should stretch beyond a capabilities-based approach to "tailor" our deterrence strategies not only to the diverse range of adversaries and diverse deterrence challenges facing the United States today, but also to means beyond the military instrument. This is true for near-term and long-term deterrence problems. However, to do so the United States must be willing to engage adversaries with a view toward making long-term commitments and policy trade-offs.

Providing alternative courses of action, or grand bargains, essentially gives the actor a package of benefits that is irresistible.

An alternative long-term deterrence strategy would shape the conditions that inform decisions to seek nuclear weapons. This is a multifaceted strategy, but one that must, of necessity, have two essential military features to influence the adversary's perceptions favorable to deterrence outcomes. Both must be addressed for a long-term deterrence strategy to be effective. First, discreet or implied threats of military costs if the adversary continues to pursue a nuclear weapons program communicate that the United States will raise the stakes if the adversary jettisons the deal and pursues the full suite of technologies, knowledge, and nuclear weapons capabilities later on. Second, the fears that fuel the adversary's pursuit of nuclear weapons need to be addressed with US allies and partners. Moreover, allies and partners must be reassured about US commitments and enduring stakes in the region. Reassurance would strengthen US relationships with those states.

A US deterrence strategy aimed at influencing adversary decisions to proceed or continue with a nuclear weapons program must guard against adversary perceptions that their security is better off with nuclear weapons and that benefits of restraint are hollow. This would not only raise the specter of renewed interest in WMD in that adversary state, but risk nuclear proliferation among US friends and allies who perceived cracks in the US ability to thwart WMD development and opted to pursue them on their own. For example, it remains to be seen if Libya's commitment to refrain from pursuing nuclear weapons will endure. In recent years, Libya has expressed disappointment that political and economic benefits promised by the United States and others have failed to materialize. Should Arab or Muslim states, such as Iran, continue to be denied a nuclear capability by the United States or Israel? As with Iraq and Syria, it is not difficult to imagine that Libya, coupled with new perceptions of being given a raw deal and feeling less secure for it, might decide to pursue nuclear weapons again.

Considerations

Planning

Long-term deterrence described herein is highly situation-dependent. As history demonstrates, international security circumstances can and do change, impacting relationships among actors. Former adversaries, such as Germany and Japan, became close allies of the United States as well as formidable economic and military powers. Similarly, the aftermath of the Cold War brought about significant changes among several former republics of the Soviet Union that have since become members of the North Atlantic Treaty Organization (NATO). Moreover, as previously mentioned, Libya's relationship with the United States and participation in the international political system shifted shortly after the attack on Iraq. Generally, the point here is not to prescribe a formula for threat reduction, but to acknowledge that conditions, when they change, can afford opportunities to address long-term or long-standing threats by influencing leaders towards alternative outcomes and non-adversarial relationships. Specifically, in relation to nuclear ambitions, whether considering Scenarios 2 or 3, it is important to recognize that other actors have walked away from the pursuit or possession of nuclear weapons, albeit for a variety of reasons. However, some of these reasons included bargains made possible by external actors and changes in external circumstances that are meaningful to the actor in question.[8]

Being prepared for such opportunities requires careful interagency and allied planning. This planning must, first of all, be rooted in an in-depth study and understanding of one's potential adversaries. This planning activity certainly includes an assessment of the actor's existing capabilities, intentions, and willingness of its leadership to act aggressively toward us or our allies. It also means understanding the motivations for adversarial behavior. Further, this study must work diligently, some would argue with greater and more focused investment than in the past, to understand various actors and their values and the cognitive perceptions critical to their decision making. Long-term deterrence strategies would capitalize upon this knowledge and plan for opportunities to present these actors with alternative courses of action to prevent threats from emerging.

The careful planning that is required, but clearly exists today in limited capacity, involves the deliberate coordination of several activities in order for long-term deterrence plans and strategies to be effective. These activities include sharing information, intelligence, and long-term deterrence studies about both state and nonstate threats; policy planning that provides more accurate risk assessments of various policy options in light of existing, emerging, and distant threats; capability assessments germane to long-term deterrence needs, including interagency capabilities that address gaps in nonmilitary instruments of deterrence; and impact assessments of possible alternative courses of action to influence the actor's decision making.

It is a formidable task to organize for long-term deterrence problems, including capabilities to understand and deter various actors to prevent emerging and distant threats. This is particularly true since we are hardly organized to address the myriad of near- and midterm deterrence problems that challenge us with the security complexities inherent in a post–Cold War, twenty-first-century world. Complex deterrence problems, however, are not impossible ones, and consideration for how we can and must organize to address long-term deterrence problems will also provide immediate value as we confront and deter near-term threats.

Recent attention upon deterrence challenges and consistent calls for deterrence-related transformation have come from diverse and authoritative sources. For example, Admiral Michael Mullen, chairman of the Joint Chiefs of Staff, recently argued, "We need a new model of deterrence that helps us bring our own clock up to speed with the pace and the scope of the challenges of this new century. Time hack . . . now."[9] A new capability is needed that authoritatively crafts national deterrence plans to

- provide decision makers comprehensive courses of action for day-to-day, crisis, and long-term deterrence challenges;
- integrate and synchronize national power and activities for deterrence objectives;
- coordinate US government deterrence strategies with those of US allies and partners, as needed;
- expand deterrence-focused adversary analysis in support of deterrence strategies and other national security-related plans and activities; and
- provide national, interagency, and regional leaderships a common deterrence picture and tool for deterrence-oriented decision making.

A national deterrence or "strategic engagement" center, perhaps modeled on the composition and activities of the National Counterterrorism Center (NCTC), especially if combined with other influence-oriented centers (including a NATO Deterrence Center of Excellence), is one way of looking ahead to face these twenty-first-century problems. Doing so could provide a new capability in one location that would develop, integrate, and orchestrate interagency deterrence-focused planning, activities, and effectiveness assessment for our nation's leadership. A national deterrence center would have the capacity for fully integrating national intelligence information into deterrence-specific adversary assessment. This center could also review and update indicators daily for impact assessment of ongoing deterrence actions. Further, if modeled after NCTC, such a center would have the capability to be staffed for planning and cuing of courses of action for coordination, integration, and synchronization with members across the interagency as well as the DOD, the national labs, and expertise from academia and the private sector for research into capabilities, methods, and assessments, as well as allied integration for planning activities, information, and intelligence sharing. This is particularly important in today's security environment where there are threats of mutual interest to our allies, such as NATO, but also with other partners where there are other opportunities to collaborate on combined capabilities, such as integration of missile defenses that could be used to deter or cyber capabilities that could be used to deter, defend, and defeat, as well as other interagency activities such as financial sanctioning.

CONCLUSION

There are three basic values for considering and expanding a concept of long-term deterrence as described in this chapter. First, doing so provides a time-related context for how we currently model the near-term deterrence framework contained in the 2006 *DO JOC*, namely influencing an adversary's decision to act or restrain and doing so usually after the United States is aware of the threat. Continuing to do so, despite recognition that actors consider alternative courses of action[10] in addition to consequences of a single decision, would be to limit future deterrence planning options and fail to recognize how one might effectively develop influence campaigns that span several years or decades.

Second, this concept is intended to illustrate that there might be times and conditions in which preferred deterrence strategies emphasize early proactive measures to head off development of threats emerging "over the horizon." This is because it might be much harder to deter later, when the threatening capabilities are fully developed.

Third, concepts, such as long-term deterrence scenarios, can assist in crafting future experimentation, gaming, and exercises in which deterrence capabilities, activities, and situational conditions can promote better understanding of potential adversaries, threats, and strategies to address them.

NOTES

1. *DO JOC*, page 8. US vital interests might include maintaining the integrity of US territory, preserving basic political sovereignty and societal integrity within the United States, preventing mass casualties among the US population, securing critical US and international infrastructure assets (energy, telecommunications, water, essential services, etc.) that support economic viability, and supporting the defense of US friends and allies.
2. Deterrence can be "tailored" in several ways, including by forming instruments of power appropriate to the need; supporting and complementing, or

at least operating consistent with, all other US national security and foreign policy strategies; addressing one problem at a time; understanding adversaries and their unique motivations, intentions, history, culture, values, goals, and capabilities; and tackling threats as they are understood on the time horizon (above).

3. A thorough report on Smart Power was provided by the CSIS Commission on Smart Power, http://csis.org/publication/smarter-more-secure-america (July 24, 2012).
4. One could consider others, such as Sweden, or Ukraine's decision to return or destroy the nuclear weapons stockpile it inherited by the dissolution of the USSR.
5. While not a clear long-term deterrence case within the concept presented in this chapter, the case of South Africa abandoning its nuclear weapons program does illustrate how changing political, economic, and security conditions impact the value of nuclear weapons and consequently the willingness of leadership to accept an entirely different future and alternative course of action without possessing them.
6. For further background on how the coalition intervention influenced Libya's decision making, see, e.g., Ambassador Robert Joseph's book *Countering WMD: The Libyan Experience* (Fairfax, VA: National Institute Press, 2009).
7. On Libya's relations with the United States, see page 122 of Gawdat Bahgat's article, "Proliferation of Weapons of Mass Destruction: The Case of Libya," *International Relations* 22, no. 1 (March 2008): 105–126. It should be noted that Bahgat's position is that the Libya case was isolated and would not be repeated.
8. In addition to Libya, some of these include South Africa, Kazakhstan, Argentina, and Taiwan[0]. An overview chart of nuclear proliferation since the 1940s, taken from the book *The Nuclear Express*, by Thomas C. Reed and Danny B. Stillman, can be found in the *New York Times* online, http://www.nytimes.com/imagepages/2008/12/09/science/20081209_BOMB_GRAPHIC.html (July 24, 2012).
9. Admiral Michael G. Mullen, "From the Chairman," *Joint Forces Quarterly* Issue 51 (4th Quarter, 2008), p. 3. Col. David H. Gurney, USMC (Ret.), ed., http://digitalndulibrary.ndu.edu/cdm4/document.php?CISOROOT=/ndupress&CISOPTR=20799&REC=10.
10. See the 2006 *Deterrence Operations Joint Operating Concept* (*DO JOC*), 11, 23, 25.

CHAPTER 6

IS A NEW FOCUS ON NUCLEAR WEAPONS RESEARCH AND DEVELOPMENT NECESSARY?

ANNE FITZPATRICK

INTRODUCTION

In the past several years there has been considerable public discussion over the future of the US nuclear weapons program, a topic that raises many large-scope, high-level policy questions ranging from the prospects for nuclear deterrence to the possibility of eliminating nuclear devices altogether. Yet, lying below these 10,000-foot-high debates are important questions about their fundamental epistemological and technical underpinnings. Some of these questions include the following: Is specialized knowledge of nuclear weapons eroding to the point of no return, and does this matter, or is the knowledge instead changing markedly, and does this necessitate a new or reinvigorated focus on nuclear weapons science, research, development, and fielding? Moreover, what is—exactly—a "new" focus on weapons that is markedly different from the pre-1992 design and testing cycles, and do these activities contribute significantly to deterrence in the post–Cold War era?

To various degrees and for divergent reasons, the questions posed above have been raised and analyzed by two main public, nongovernment-affiliated communities: (1) the nongovernmental (NGO) special-interest policy organizations that generally desire to either rid the world of nuclear weapons or at least reduce their numbers, and (2) a small slice of the academic community. Here it is important to note that the published academic literature on the nuclear weapons enterprise as a whole falls all over the place in terms of disciplinary foci. The US nuclear weapons enterprise—its history, science, technology, and culture—has been examined and interpreted by many historians, as well as sociologists, anthropologists, science and technology studies (STS—the branch of academia that studies scientific activity, knowledge, and scientists themselves) experts, and communications studies specialists.[1] Some of this scholarship is very well regarded in academic circles; in addition, a couple of very well researched and written trade histories of nuclear weapons have received international recognition.[2]

Yet within this body of scholarship, only a minority of studies, particularly in the sociological and anthropological fields, delve into nuclear weapons knowledge and expertise. The sociologists Donald MacKenzie and Graham Spinardi's groundbreaking study, "Tacit Knowledge and the Uninvention of Nuclear Weapons,"[3] is the most directly relevant: in this they challenge the long-standing notion that technology will inevitably march forward once it is invented. Specifically, they postulate that if nuclear weapons design ceases and no special, tacit knowledge is passed on to the would-be next generation of designers, the technology may be "uninvented." The value in MacKenzie and Spinardi's piece is the credibility of the research they conducted for it: It was based largely on interviews with technical staff at Los Alamos and Lawrence Livermore National Laboratories, and thus the authors were able to integrate a great deal of firsthand accounts of what it is like to work on nuclear weapons, as opposed to approaching the topic strictly from a sociological theory perspective. Their conclusions are largely speculative about the future and are not a prescription for taking any political course of action.

In 1998 the anthropologist Hugh Gusterson published a full-length book, *Nuclear Rites*, that intriguingly explores Lawrence Livermore National Laboratory as a community and analyzes how activities such as nuclear testing helped form scientists' beliefs, sense of identity, and mission.[4] Also, but to a lesser degree, Gusterson addresses knowledge loss from an outsider's point of view and leaves open the question of what roles the national laboratories should play in the future. His research, like MacKenzie and Spinardi's, relied heavily on numerous interviews with the Livermore Laboratory scientific community.

The most recent among this thread of published studies focusing on knowledge in the US nuclear weapons program is cultural anthropologist Laura McNamara's chapter, "TRUTH is Generated HERE," in a 2007 communications studies edited volume.[5] This is a provocative essay suggesting that the nuclear weapons research and development (R&D) landscape is changing in ways unforeseen by anyone. This piece and all of the above literature will be discussed in more depth later in this chapter. One of the aspects that these studies have in common is that they either explicitly raise or brush up against the subject of deterrence in relation to the process of nuclear weapons R&D and the resulting knowledge and quality of that knowledge, and what the term "new" entails in nuclear weapons R&D.

Why are there so few academic studies of knowledge generation and loss in the nuclear weapons realm that focus on the inside of the national laboratories? Part of this gap in the scholarship, of course, is due to lack of access to classified materials. The few scholars who have gained these privileges, including the author of this chapter, are limited in the depth in which they can discuss the scientific and technical details of their research.[6] Also, there is some evidence that the nuclear deterrent today does not seem to sport the public popularity it once did and that arms control as a public debate does not command the attention of the average US citizen, even if our current national leadership still deems nuclear deterrence as an important national policy.[7] Changes in military requirements after 1992, where nuclear weapons and their delivery systems declined to a lesser priority, have no doubt permanently altered some part of the public view of nuclear weapons and their purpose.[8] Furthermore, partly because of classification barriers, as noted above, but also partly because of the antinuclear lobbyist community's unclear definition of "new" when speaking of nuclear weapons, mostly missing from the public discussion are (1) the nuclear weapons-related knowledge base and its evolution, (2) the nature of the nuclear weapons enterprise's evolution since the end of the Cold War, and (3) the whole spectrum of other critical defensive and offensive national security science and technology that this enterprise directly supports. A review of these subjects is necessary for a better-informed public debate on the role of nuclear weapons and deterrence in general, especially as a serious reconsideration of current US nuclear policy is under way.[9]

Some new government-sponsored and other openly published material has become available in the past several years to complement the small amount of academic literature, which together may begin to address the questions posed in the introduction. Several of the government-sponsored studies address knowledge loss in terms of laboratory staffing and workforce succession planning, topics that are useful to consider.[10] Compared with the analysis of the academic portion, this material raises some intriguing insights into the state of the nuclear weapons enterprise, its value to national security, and its resident expertise and generation of new knowledge. It also helps in understanding how we might better define a new focus on nuclear weapons R&D, and how that may contribute to current thinking on deterrence in a meaningful way.

1992 AND THE STANDUP OF STOCKPILE STEWARDSHIP

When nuclear testing ceased in 1992, no one could predict the future for the nuclear weapons laboratories and their staff, or what exactly the nuclear stockpile's size, configuration, and technology would look like many years down the road. To mitigate this uncertainty and to meet the Comprehensive Nuclear Test-Ban Treaty (CTBT) requirements, the Department of Energy (DOE) and the weapons laboratory managers proposed the Science Based Stockpile Stewardship Program (SBSS)—now called the Stockpile Stewardship Program (SSP).[11] The SSP embodied an ambitious plan to maintain confidence in the nuclear stockpile based on predictive capability through the construction and employment of brand new computational, experimental, and visualization tools—in the absence of full-scale nuclear testing. The program demanded an enormous increase in laboratory capabilities: materials science, computational hardware and software, high energy density physics, and hydrodynamics.[12]

Nothing like this had ever been attempted before, anywhere, and naturally, a great deal of controversy over and criticism of the program emerged throughout the 1990s. In an interview in 1995, the physicist Richard Garwin categorized the program as a payoff that the laboratories received in return for agreeing to stop nuclear testing:

> "What could they get?" Garwin said. "Sandia got the microelectronics research center, which had minimal relevance to the CTBT. Los Alamos got the Dual-Axis Radiographic Hydrodynamic Test [DARHT] facility. Livermore got the National Ignition Facility [NIF]—the white elephant eating us out of house and home. They all maintained these were essential to stockpile stewardship, which they are not."[13]

Indeed, NIF, DARHT, and some of the early SSP high-performance computing projects housed under the Advanced Strategic Computing Initiative (ASCI, now renamed Advanced Strategic Computing, or ASC) were more often than not over budget and behind schedule by several years and faced some serious technical setbacks, at least up until recently.[14] By 2009, NIF and both axes of DARHT were operational (although at the time of this writing, NIF had not yet achieved ignition),[15], the ASC modeling and simulation efforts were maturing, and several lesser-known but equally important additional sets of SSP experimental facilities' results—some examples are noted later in this chapter—had been regularly feeding into improving the collective understanding of how nuclear weapons function and providing data for the annual assessment of the performance, safety, and reliability of the US nuclear stockpile.[16]

Today's means of certifying the US nuclear weapons stockpile is a very different process than that conducted before 1992. Until the underground test moratorium took effect, the nuclear design laboratories engaged in a regular multiphase weapons acquisition cycle: concept studies, scientific feasibility, engineering development, production engineering, initial production, quantity production, and retirement and disassembly.[17] McNamara descriptively analyzed the pre-1992 process, which

> produced confidence in the nuclear deterrent through an iterative cycle of designing, testing, refining, and stockpiling nuclear explosives. That cycle, which structured work practices at the national laboratories for forty-seven years, was abruptly truncated in July of 1992, when Congress approved the Hatfield-Exon-Mitchell Amendment to the Energy and Water Appropriations Act. Within a few months, funding for the DOE's underground nuclear testing program evaporated, and the laboratories' core experimental program was quite literally left hanging, with massive assemblies suspended in mid-completion over the dry desert floor of the Nevada test site (NTS).[18]

This program's successor, the Phase 6.X process, is administered now by the National Nuclear Security Administration (NNSA, the semi-autonomous agency that supports nuclear weapons activities within DOE). In 2001 the Department of Defense (DOD) christened the Phase 6.X process as procedural guidelines to manage the stockpile Life Extension Program (LEP) refurbishment work flow, which mimics the pre-1992 full acquisition process, but only applies to life extension and refurbishment of legacy weapons.[19] Parallel to and supporting this were a whole new series of science and engineering efforts, tools, capabilities, databases, and other components within the overall SSP program. NIF, DARHT, and ASC were among the larger of these—and part of the original proposal for a "troika of computer simulation, experiments, and previous nuclear test data that provides the complete tool box for the assessment process" and as such have perhaps received the most public scrutiny.[20] Yet the SSP's physical, technical, and scientific landscape today looks somewhat different than was described in 1994 by the JASON group, which at that time evaluated the program's viability and prospects for success.[21]

For example, the 1994 JASON report, "Science Based Stockpile Stewardship," stated that the Intel Paragon chip held the world's speed record of approximately 140 Gflops.[22] Since then, commercial computational horsepower has increased exponentially, and partly as a result the nuclear weapons modeling capability—including the required software—has come a long way and is projected to reach the exascale level in the next ten years.[23]

2010 AND AFTER

Today's key SSP scientific and technical tools, facilities, and capabilities are far more numerous than NIF, DARHT, and ASC computers and include, for example, subcritical testing performed at the Nevada Test Site U1A facility, inertial confinement fusion experiments carried out at the Sandia Z-Pinch facility, the high-explosive analysis at Pantex, and many other activities at other sites. The DOE NNSA 2011 Congressional Budget Request states:

> Over the past 15 years, the nation has made significant investment in stockpile stewardship tools and capabilities, which allow the nuclear weapons stockpile to be annually assessed and certified as safe, secure, and effective, without requiring underground nuclear tests. While challenges remain, the growing knowledge and understanding of the stockpile enabled by these tools have reached a level of maturity that not only replaces the need to conduct underground tests, but surpasses the benefits originally realized by previous testing. The data collected from hundreds of previous nuclear tests, along with continued experimental science, remain available to validate predictive simulations of weapons performance. Many of the gaps are closing—or are closed—in understanding the key physics processes, and insights into system and component aging are being realized. These insights will enable better preventative care for the stockpile.[24]

While somewhat generic, the above description is factual. Stated another way, a large portion of the day-to-day nuclear weapons work looks little like it did in the testing era. Here is one way to summarize the difference in the overall approach: Prior to 1992, nuclear weapons experts validated nuclear tests and the loads of data collected from them with computer modeling, but now that has been essentially turned on its head. Today they validate computer simulations of weapon behavior and other phenomenon with a large array of small-scale (small compared to full-scale nuclear tests) experiments. Today computational simulations indeed underpin a significant portion of nearly all nuclear weapons work, and simulation codes play a large part in the nuclear stockpile annual assessment. The result is indeed a significant gain in the knowledge and understanding of how nuclear weapons operate with levels of detail that were not possible in the past.

These evolutions are significant to several debates that range from the need to return to nuclear testing to how this new knowledge's value compares to older Cold War–era knowledge that may be lost as older designers retire.[25] Some government-sponsored analyses even raise concerns that the United States has let the nuclear deterrence knowledge base erode too far to sustain an adequate national nuclear deterrence capability and urge the reinvigorization of these skills.[26] According to the 2008 Office of the Undersecretary of Defense for Acquisition, Technology, and Logistics "Report of the Defense Science Board Task Force on Nuclear Deterrence Skills," the average DOE laboratory worker is old—over age 50—relative to the US workforce, and some personnel perceive the nuclear weapons enterprise as a declining industry.[27] Furthermore, a recent JASON examination of the LEP program went even further, warning that US nuclear expertise was "threatened by a lack of program stability, perceived lack of mission importance, and degradation of the work environment."[28]

The above are valid concerns that require and will continue to demand management and programmatic attention, but from an intellectual point of view they beg the question of how we should interpret "new" when speaking of a new focus on nuclear weapons R&D. The academic anthropologists, sociologists, and communications scholars have not addressed this particular question, while the antinuclear weapons community remains insistent on using the term "new" within the parameters of the nuclear devices: new physics packages in warheads or their specific components. Yet, equally if not more important than the weapons (products) themselves is how the continual generation of new knowledge about the weapons, combined with now established stewardship practices, may force us to rethink to some degree what is meant by "new." In terms of the weapons themselves, Congress has already defined "new" clearly and simply in the fiscal year 2003 National Defense Authorization Act, Section 3143:

> The term "new nuclear weapon" means a nuclear weapon that contains a pit or canned subassembly, either of which is neither—
>
> (A) In the nuclear stockpile on the date of the enactment of the Act: Nor
> (B) In production as of that date.[29]

Furthermore, the 2010 Nuclear Posture Review (NPR) stated that the "United States will not develop new nuclear warheads [and] Life Extension Programs (LEPs) will use only nuclear components based on previously tested designs, and will not support new military missions or provide for new military capabilities."[30]

Congressional verbiage, like that noted in the NPR, is direct and simple, yet various interpretations of this abound, apparently because much of the special-interest NGO community is strictly pinned on the goal of abolishing nuclear weapons based on the argument that nuclear weapons today neither play the Soviet deterrent role they once did nor support any compelling broad set of missions.[31] Furthermore, an even more narrowly focused segment of this community is obsessed with the idea that NNSA and DOD are covertly seeking to design and build new weapons, such as the Reliable Replacement Warhead (RRW).[32] This group does not, curiously, devote much in-depth analysis to the problem of knowledge loss and of what continuing or "new" nuclear weapons work in any form means for workforce replacement and the continuity of nuclear weapons-related skills. Hans Kristensen summarizes this simply:

> The training argument depends on a combination of assumptions: (1) the country will eventually need new nuclear weapons and these will need to be sophisticated weapons requiring high levels of expertise, (2) the expertise needed for continuing stockpile maintenance is not adequate to maintain the expertise needed to design and build new weapons, and (3) the knowledge and skills needed to build new weapons cannot be written down and can only be preserved over the next two or three decades by keeping it alive in people. The truth of all of these assumptions depends in large part on choices we make about the future missions and requirements for nuclear weapons.[33]

Such analyses do not answer the question of whether or not a new focus on nuclear weapons R&D is necessary or why.[34] It goes without saying that the Cold War nuclear mission of deterring a monolithic threat is indeed no longer the same, but it has evolved into a very different set of activities and processes that need to be taken into consideration by all who analyze the current and future role of nuclear weapons and modern-day deterrence. Getting rid of all nuclear weapons and their supporting knowledge and capabilities might indeed be an ideal, peaceful goal, but doing so would also rid us of numerous related essential national security missions for which the nuclear enterprise acts as the technological backbone. LEP activities serve as a good example of the far-reaching effects of this technological backbone, have cumulatively led to some unexpected results, and may help us move beyond the critiques of the nuclear weapons enterprise merely existing to seek new warheads, dream of wild new missions for nuclear weapons, or find work for underemployed weapons scientists, as some critics would have readers believe.[35]

LEPs are not only a means of tinkering with the weapons in a manner void of any intellectual content whatsoever. In *Nuclear Rites*, Gusterson remarked that "university physicists often disparage [nuclear] weapons physics as more high-tech artisanship than science. One physics professor told me that the intellectual challenges in contemporary weapons designs were minimal: 'Weapons design now is just like polishing turds.'"[36] Indeed, some academic physicists may liken the weapons profession to an engineering practice of refining objects and making incremental improvements, but many weapons physicists argue otherwise given the complexity of what they are trying to model, which includes laborious hydrodynamics and rapidly changing densities in materials as a nuclear device operates.

Producing an improved detonator assembly, for example, may be an engineering increment and not scientifically significant, but it is the larger picture that needs to be kept in mind. Not only are LEPs resulting in physical change and evolution in the stockpile over the long term, but in order to certify an LEP as successful, this process needs to match well to recorded underground test data, the current depth of understanding of how the weapons work, and many ongoing nonnuclear and subcritical experiments. Doing this opens a huge array of scientific problems that require solving. Even though nuclear weapons operation has been well studied over the past several decades, it is still not understood completely because of the complexity of the weapons and how their parts and physical phenomena interact, and the extreme physical conditions that occur when they are fired. Getting to a more thorough understanding of these is a key basis for supporting the continuation of a no-testing regime and maintaining confidence in the stockpile.

The issue of stockpile confidence itself and how that relates to current arguments for a need to return to nuclear testing is beyond the scope of this chapter. However, the subject of nuclear testing is worth mentioning here for the purpose of discussing what testing did—and did not—do, since several of the academic scholars cited here spent a significant amount of time analyzing the social, political, and technical role(s) testing played in the Cold War. It is worth comparing a few of their key findings to more recent nuclear weapons enterprise activities.

In *Nuclear Rites*, Gusterson asserts that nuclear tests were "important for their cultural and psychological as well as their technical significance and that they have been vital not only in the production of nuclear weapons but also in the production of weapons scientists and in the social reproduction of the ideology of nuclear deterrence."[37] And toward his conclusion, he argues that the "weapons scientists' sense of mastery over nuclear weapons is reinforced by participation in nuclear tests."[38] But this raises the question: assuming this was true prior to 1992, is this still the case today? Possibly not, because both policy makers' and scientists' own philosophical beliefs about nuclear deterrence are going through a great deal of reinterpretation currently—based on the immense changes in the way nuclear weapons work is rapidly changing.

Since *Nuclear Rites* was published, the process of working on nuclear weapons has evolved drastically. To his credit, in 2004 Gusterson published a collection of articles in the volume titled *People of the Bomb*, where some of the chapters served as an update to *Nuclear Rites*. In one chapter, he deconstructs "virtual weapons science," referring to the increasing use of simulation and computing, as the main activity that weaponeers engaged in as a successor to nuclear testing, but sticks to his earlier argument in *Nuclear Rites* that nuclear tests were traditionally the ultimate means of producing knowledge and power among US nuclear weapons scientists.[39] Gusterson supported his case through several interviews with scientists who expressed doubt about the ability of simulation technologies and the overall viability of weapons work without the testing phase.[40] Although *People of the Bomb* was published in 2004, this particular chapter was written in 2001. In that piece Gusterson reported that older designers—those who have participated in nuclear testing—worried about younger colleagues placing too much confidence in the predictive ability of their computer codes and the basic principles of physics.[41]

Like Gusterson, but for different reasons, MacKenzie and Spinardi concluded in their study that testing was a critical part of nuclear weapons work—in their words, part of the designers' "epistemic culture," a way of making visible their judgment. MacKenzie and Spinardi's interviews with the then current (early 1990s) generation of designers revealed their fear that in the absence of testing, weapons certification would have to rely very heavily on explicit knowledge alone in the form of computer simulation.[42] Yet both Gusterson's and MacKenzie and Spinardi's analyses raise a generational argument. The younger, up-and-coming generation of nuclear weapons experts—those working today, about twenty years after MacKenzie and Spinardi conducted their interviews—has a great deal of faith in computational abilities and with compelling reasons. Also, anecdotal evidence suggests that some older designers are now beginning to place more faith in computation.

MacKenzie and Spinardi's main question, "if there was a sufficiently long hiatus in their [nuclear weapons] design and production (say, two generations) that tacit knowledge might indeed vanish," remains to be proven in the next decades.[43] But just short of twenty years after the cessation of testing—and we can comfortably assume that one generation has passed the torch by now—other new forms of knowledge in the nuclear weapons programs are becoming accepted and institutionalized concurrently as some older tacit knowledge is disappearing.

This is a large and perhaps unexpected paradigm shift for the nuclear weapons RDT&E process. Where MacKenzie concluded that designers circa early 1990s overwhelmingly relied on the empirical testing part—a physical, observable activity—of this process as well as theoretical bases to have confidence in their work, today the high-quality images and results coming from hydrodynamic tests, advanced radiography, subcritical tests, and other small-scale experiments are supplying new empirical scientific bases that may well alter how we should debate and define nuclear deterrence.[44]

Speaking strictly in terms of the information testing provided, and without going into their political and symbolic meanings, McNamara argues that "[n]uclear testing provided an epistemological basis for nuclear confidence but not in a classical statistical sense. Although tests provided a great deal of data about explosive performance, they were far too expensive and difficult to perform multiple trials for any weapon system, much less isolate and repeatedly measure a single feature of a primary or secondary."[45] Furthermore, McNamara correctly argued, "[T]he terrain of weaponeering is simultaneously more stable and more contested than MacKenzie and Spinardi imagined," and "[i]n working to establish new 'ways of knowing' nuclear weapons, which SSP is doing, weapons experts are redefining the very nature of nuclear confidence at a time when the role of nuclear weapons in national security is itself undergoing rapid change."[46]

Even if older, tacit knowledge is lost over time, as MacKenzie and Spinardi predict, the current and future combinations of recorded knowledge—massive amounts of nuclear weapons data are maintained in archives—and the new knowledge being generated and learned by new weaponeers are at least as an important part of the nuclear deterrence calculus as are the presence of the active weapons themselves. This raises the question: in the present day and into the future can we have a scientific-technical-capability-based deterrent? This may be possible; McNamara concluded that "the credibility of the nation's nuclear deterrent was rooted in the expertise of individuals with the most intimate knowledge of nuclear explosives, so that the laboratory's weapons-related judgments were as much the bedrock of nuclear deterrence as were the weapons themselves."[47]

Even during the Cold War the technical basis of the nuclear deterrent was not derived merely from the act of testing or its empirical results. It was also derived in part from the weaponeers' deep knowledge. What scientists know about nuclear weapons and related programs and how well they know these things contributes to credible deterrence in the view of US allies and enemies. If adversaries see the scientific and technical talent as credible, their products—the devices—will be viewed as credible. It is important to emphasize that one cannot simply attend graduate school to learn nuclear weapons design and development. It is a years-long, intensive, hands-on process, akin to apprenticeship, performed only within the design laboratories.

The Defense Science Board summarized these kinds of skills very well in a 2008 study:

> Nuclear deterrence expertise is uniquely demanding. It cannot be acquired overnight or on the fly. It resides in a highly classified environment mandated by law, it crosses a number of disciplines and skills, and it involves implicit as well as requires explicit knowledge. Nuclear weapons expertise is necessary to design and build nuclear weapons, to plan and operate nuclear forces, and to design defense against nuclear attack. It is also necessary to analyze and understand foreign nuclear weapons programs, devise nuclear policies and strategies, deal with allies who depend on the American nuclear umbrella, prevent and counter nuclear proliferation, defeat nuclear terrorism, and—in the event that a nuclear detonation takes place by accident or cold, hostile intent—cope with the catastrophic consequences.[48]

Similarly, the 1994 JASON Stockpile Stewardship study enumerated several nuclear weapons activities spin-off benefits that support arms control and nonproliferation efforts:

> Another major laboratory activity that supports stockpile stewardship both directly and indirectly is the collection of activities involving Non-proliferation, Intelligence, and Arms Control (NIAC).... The groups now doing this work are likely to be the only ones at either laboratory who will continue to study new weapons designs in order to understand both what is happening elsewhere and as part of the study of how to counter such weapons in the hands of others.[49]

Most of this work is, not surprisingly, highly classified and cannot be elaborated on in detail publicly, but its importance is paramount especially given its unique knowledge base that is continually accumulating. Other equally very important—and classified—fields that support nonproliferation, noted generally in the 2008 Department of Defense study, are highly specialized nuclear forensics and nuclear device intelligence analysis and evaluation. These sets of activities rely deeply on those people in the weapons laboratories with experience in US nuclear design to evaluate the technology sophistication, rate of advancement, specific design, materials used, and other factors a foreign country might exhibit. New and fundamental scientific activities in the weapons programs are becoming applicable in these fields, and if our computational models are becoming viable and accepted by the nuclear weapons community, then we, using good intelligence, should be able to model what other nations and nonstate actors are doing.

Older methods of empirical observation of phenomena in weapons work and estimation in the weapons design and development processes are being replaced by new scientific means: for example, the Quantification of Margins and Uncertainty (QMU) methodology, an entirely new—and controversial—nuclear weapons science tool, is currently coming into significant usage. QMU, based on statistical methods and high-level computational capability, calculates uncertainty when it comes to judging the active stockpile's reliability and safety.[50] Exactly how well it does that and the risk one should assign to the uncertainty factor remain to be determined, but the value and utility of computation in general, while still understandably criticized by some skeptics, is providing visual and statistical-like results on stockpile safety and reliability that have not been possible until now. Computational horsepower has improved exponentially over that available in the early 1990s, and simulations are less costly and time-consuming than testing. Computer simulation allows researchers to study anomalies in a weapon over and over, as many times as they want. This cannot be performed using explosive testing, and the ability to do these things directly translates into real benefits to national security endeavors in the areas noted above. This is a genuinely new focus coming out of nuclear weapons R&D that needs to be encouraged and maintained. And not only computing but all of the activities described in the paragraphs above feed into a strong nuclear attribution capability—which itself is a deterrent.

CONCLUSION

Critics argue that we do not need a highly developed scientific and technical capability to support the stockpile because we do not need a sophisticated, advanced stockpile in the post–Cold War world, and that there are no new physics needs to understand nuclear weapons adequately. For example, Ivan Oelrich has argued that "there is little to no technical challenge left for American and other advanced nuclear weapon states in just getting a bomb to explode and we could design bombs that do not require a complex supporting infrastructure." His argument is that the stated need to maintain scientific and technical expertise in the national laboratories rests solely on a blind desire to continue maintaining a Cold War–era mission for our current stockpile.[51]

This kind of reasoning is exactly why we must redefine what we mean by "new" with clarity and careful thought, and move beyond wrangling over the semantic differences between terms such as "life extension" and "modernization," and draw into any discussions about the future of deterrence the significant paradigm shift that is occurring at our laboratories, moving us from testing-based knowledge to simulation-based knowledge dependent on validation methods. Ongoing deepening understanding of these processes does have a significant impact on national security and enriches discussion about what kind of deterrent we may want for the twenty-first century.

While few people would argue that better arms control measures and nuclear weapons-related policies are good things, nuclear deterrence in some form is likely to remain a part of America's national security policy for the foreseeable future. Calls for an end to all nuclear weapons activities and zero nuclear weapons are good goals for an ideal world, but until we live in such a world with no proliferators we still need to maintain as much knowledge as we can while generating new understanding and thinking about scientific and technical means of bolstering national security, and formulating what nuclear deterrence truly means in the twenty-first century.

NOTES

1. For a solid, albeit dated, review of historical studies of nuclear weapons published up through 1990, see Robert W. Seidel, "Books on the Bomb," *ISIS* 81 (September 1990): 519–537. Other, more recent historical studies may be found in the history of science literature. Sociological, anthropological, STS, and communications studies treatments of the nuclear weapons laboratories and their activities and people are discussed later in this chapter.
2. See Richard Rhodes, *The Making of the Atomic Bomb* (New York: Simon and Schuster, 1986); and Richard Rhodes, *Dark Sun: The Making of the Hydrogen Bomb* (New York: Simon and Schuster, 1994).
3. Donald MacKenzie with Graham Spinardi, "Tacit Knowledge and the Uninvention of Nuclear Weapons," in *Knowing Machines: Essays on Technical*

Change, ed. Donald MacKenzie (Cambridge, MA: MIT Press, 1998), 215–260.
4. Hugh Gusterson, *Nuclear Rites: A Weapons Laboratory at the End of the Cold War* (Berkeley: University of California Press, 1998).
5. Laura A. McNamara, "TRUTH is Generated HERE: Knowledge Loss and the Production of Nuclear Confidence in the Post-Cold War Era," in *Nuclear Legacies: Communication, Controversy, and the US Nuclear Weapons Complex*, ed. Bryan C. Taylor, William J. Kinsella, Stephen P. Depoe, and Maribeth S. Metzler (New York: Lexington Books, 2007), 167–198.
6. For some insight on conducting academic research inside the classified environment, see Laura A. McNamara, "Ways of Knowing About Weapons: The Cold War's End at the Los Alamos National Laboratory" (PhD diss., University of New Mexico, May 2001); and Anne Fitzpatrick, "From Behind the Fence: Threading the Labyrinths of Classified Historical Research," in *The Historiography of Contemporary Science, Technology, and Medicine: Writing Recent Science*, ed. Ronald E. Doel and Thomas Soderqvist (New York: Routledge, 2006), 67–80.
7. Henry Kelly, "Arms Control: Where Now?" *FAS Public Interest Report*, Vol. 55, no. 1 (January/February 2002), http://www.fas.org/faspir/2002/v55n1/control.htm.
8. Air Force Nuclear Task Force, *Reinvigorating the Air Force Nuclear Enterprise* (Headquarters United States Air Force, October 24, 2008).
9. David E. Sanger and Thom Shanker, "White House Is Rethinking Nuclear Policy," *The New York Times*, March 1, 2010, 1.
10. For example, see Clark A. Murdock, "The Department of Defense and the Nuclear Mission in the 21st Century: A Beyond—Goldwater-Nichols Phase 4 Report," Center for Strategic and International Studies, March 2008.
11. For more on the SSP's founding, see A. Fitzpatrick and I. Oelrich, "The Stockpile Stewardship Program: Fifteen Years On," Federation of American Scientists Occasional Paper, May 2007.
12. Ibid. "Confidence" in this context means that weapons would perform as required for military operations.
13. Nathan Hodge and Sharon Weinberger, "A Nuclear Family Vacation," *Slate*, July 13, 2005, at http://slate.msn.com/id/2122382/entry/2122493/. Author's note: Garwin was referring to the Sandia Microsystems and Engineering Sciences Application Facility (MESA).
14. D. Post, "Lessons Learned from ASCI," Los Alamos National Laboratory, March 30, 2004, abridged version of LA-UR-04-0388; US Department of Energy, Office of Inspector General Audit Report, "The Los Alamos National Laboratory Hydrodynamic Test Program," Introductory letter, DOE-IG-0699, September 16, 2005; "Interim Report of the National Ignition Facility Laser System Task Force," Secretary of Energy Advisory Board, January 10, 2000; "National Ignition Facility: Management and Oversight Failures Caused Major Cost Overruns and Schedule Delays," GAO-RCED-00-271, August 2009.

15. "DOE NNSA FY 2011 Congressional Budget," Weapons Activities/Inertial Confinement Fusion Ignition and High Yield Campaign, 109–124, http://fire.pppl.gov. For more technical analysis of NIF, see JASON JSR-05-340
16. The annual assessment process is a many-months-long effort in which the nuclear weapons community examines various technical issues affecting the safety, reliability, performance, and military effectiveness of the active stockpile. Their work ultimately results in the Nuclear Weapons Council report on the assessments, accompanied by a joint letter signed by the Secretaries of Energy and Defense and reports from the nuclear weapons laboratory directors and the USSTRATCOM Commander.
17. Gusterson, 132–139. Gusterson provides some lengthy and informative discussion of several of these individual phases. For details on the phases see US Atomic Energy Commission, "An Agreement between the AEC and the DOD for the Development, Production, and Standardization of Atomic Weapons," March 21, 1953.
18. Laura A. McNamara, "TRUTH Is Generated HERE."
19. GAO-02-146R, *Nuclear Weapons: Status of Planning for Stockpile Life Extension*, December 7, 2001, at http://gao.gov/products/GAO-02-146R; and US Department of Defense, Department of Energy, and Nuclear Weapons Council, "Procedural Guidelines for the Phase 6.X Process," April 9, 2000.
20. Statement of Vic Reis at hearing on the Safety and Reliability of the US Nuclear Deterrent, October 27, 1997 - S. Hearing 105–267: Senate Governmental Affairs Subcommittee on International Security, Proliferation and Federal Services.
21. JASON JSR-94-345, "Science Based Stockpile Stewardship," November 1994.
22. Ibid., 92.
23. "DOE NNSA FY 2011 Congressional Budget," Weapons Activities/Advanced Simulation and Computing Campaign, 125–126, http://fire.pppl.gov.
24. "DOE NNSA FY 2011 Congressional Budget Request," 49, http://fire.pppl.gov/.
25. The DOE has made significant investment into preserving documentation of nuclear weapons research and recording individuals' knowledge of all aspects of this. Many DOE sites have participated in this; one example is the Lawrence Livermore Nuclear Weapons Information Project (NWIP). A description of this is available at https://www.llnl.gov/str/Lowns.html.
26. Office of the Undersecretary of Defense for Acquisition, Technology, and Logistics, *Report of the Defense Science Board Task Force on Nuclear Deterrence Skills*, September 2008, 8.
27. Ibid., 61, 25.
28. JASON JSR-09-334E, unclassified "Lifetime Extension Program (LEP Executive Summary)," September 9, 2009, 4.
29. House, *National Defense Authorization Act for Fiscal Year 2003*, 107th Congress, 2nd Session, 2002, H. Rept. 107–772.

30. US Department of Defense, *Nuclear Posture Review Report*, April 2010, xiv.
31. See Ivan Oelrich, "Missions for Nuclear Weapons After the Cold War," Federation of American Scientists Occasional Paper No. 3, January 2005, http://www.fas.org/pubs/_docs/01282005175922.pdf.
32. For a fairly recent analysis of the apparent remaining keen interest in pursuing an RRW, see Hans Kristensen and Ivan Oelrich, "JASON and Replacement Warheads," Federation of American Scientists Strategic Security Blog, November 20, 2009, http://www.fas.org/blog/ssp/2009/11/jason.php#more-2256. In this piece, Kristensen asserts that the "quest for new weapons is not dead yet." For more on the debate over what "new" might mean in terms of weapons, see Hans Kristensen, "Testing the No-New-Nuclear-Weapons Pledge," Federation of American Scientists Strategic Security Blog, March 9, 2010, http://www.fas.org/blog/ssp/2010/03/newnukes.php#more-2784; and Tom Z. Collina, "News Analysis: What Is a 'New' Nuclear Weapon?" *Arms Control Today*, Arms Control Association, April 2010, http://www.armscontrol.org/act/2010_04/NewsAnalysis.
33. Kristensen and Oelrich, "JASON and Replacement Warheads."
34. It is possible that the terminology used in the LEP programs may lead observers to suspect that the door is being left open for brand new warhead development in violation of what Congress has stipulated. LEPs are complex in that they are multi-year, multifaceted, large-scale managed programs intended to extend the "life" or time that a weapon can safely and reliably remain in the stockpile without having to be replaced or removed. The NNSA does provide a public description of how LEPs are intended to function: "Not all weapons and types are the same. NNSA must develop individual life extension programs, sometimes referred to as LEPs, for each weapon type and develop specific solutions to extend the lifetime of each particular warhead or bomb. This includes identifying and correcting potential technical issues with each weapon, and then refurbishing and replacing certain components as necessary. Life extension efforts are intended to extend the lifetime of a warhead or warhead component for an additional 20 to 30 years." See http://nnsa.energy.gov/ourmission/managingthestockpile/lifeextensionprograms. The paths on which LEPs are carried out are specified. NNSA defines the implementation of an LEP as one of three approaches: (1) Refurbishment (current implementation of LEP)—Very generally, individual warhead components are replaced before they degrade with components of (nearly) identical design or that meet the same "form, fit, and function." (2) Warhead Component Reuse—Refers to the use of existing surplus pit and secondary components from other warhead types. Approach may permit limited warhead surety improvements and some increased margins. (3) Warhead Replacement—Some or all of the components of a warhead are replaced with modern design that are more easily manufacturable, provide increased warhead margins, forego no longer available or hazardous materials, improve safety, security, and

use control, and offer that potential for further overall stockpile reductions. JASON JSR-09-334E, "Lifetime Extension Program (LEP) Executive Summary" [unclassified], September 9, 2009, 1. Furthermore, "Modifications (Mod). Normally, changes in components that result in changes to operational characteristics, safety or control features, or technical procedures are designated with a Mod number, which the Nuclear Weapons Council also assigns sequentially. For example, Los Alamos repackaged existing B61 Mod 7 gravity bombs into an earth-penetrating steel case designed by Sandia, resulting in the designation B61 Mod 11. The first component set of a new MK is designated Mod 0, although the Mod 0 designation is usually omitted to avoid confusion if no other modifications exist... and Alterations (ALT). If changes in components do not result in changes to operational characteristics and the differences are transparent to military units and other users, the changes are designated as an ALT. For example, the development of new spin rocket motors for the B61 results in ALTs numbered 356, 358, and 359." Jeffrey Lewis, "After the Reliable Replacement Warhead: What's Next for the US Nuclear Arsenal?" *Arms Control Today*, Arms Control Association, December 2008, http://www.armscontrol.org/print/3463.

35. The Federation of American Scientists (FAS) labeled nuclear weapons activities, particularly in the context of the RRW program, as "nuclear social welfare." See Ivan Oelrich, "A Response to Congresswoman Tauscher's Article on Nonproliferation Review," Federation of American Scientists Strategic Security Blog, October 29, 2007, http://www.fas.org/blog/ssp/2007/10/a_response_to_congresswoman_ta.php.
36. Gusterson, *Nuclear Rites*, 48.
37. Gusterson, *Nuclear Rites*, 132.
38. Ibid., 220.
39. See Hugh Gusterson, *People of the Bomb: Portraits of America's Nuclear Complex* (Minneapolis, MN: University of Minnesota Press, 2004), 147–164, passim, and 178.
40. Ibid., 174–175.
41. Ibid., 156.
42. MacKenzie and Spinardi, 218. Also like Gusterson, MacKenzie and Spinardi published their 1998 piece based on interviews they conducted in the early 1990s. Notably, in this chapter the authors neither prescribe any specific length of time for a design and testing hiatus nor make any moral judgments about doing so. Likewise, although the article's title is provocative, the overall piece is not a call for the elimination of nuclear weapons.
43. MacKenzie and Spinardi, 217.
44. Ibid., 217.
45. McNamara, in Taylor et. al., *Nuclear Legacies*, 176.
46. Ibid., 169.
47. Ibid., 176.
48. Office of the Undersecretary of Defense for Acquisition, Technology, and Logistics, *Report of the Defense Science Board Task Force on Nuclear Deterrence Skills*, September 2008, v.

49. JASON JSR-94-345, "Science Based Stockpile Stewardship," November 1994, 25.
50. For more detail on QMU, see National Research Council, *Evaluation of Quantification of Margins and Uncertainties Methodology for Assessing and Certifying the Reliability of the Nuclear Stockpile* (Washington, DC: National Academies Press, 2008); and Jon C. Helton, "Conceptual and Computational Basis for the Quantification of Margins and Uncertainties," Sandia National Laboratories, SAND2009-3055, June 2009.
51. Ivan Oelrich, "Congressional Commission and Nuclear 'Requirements,'" Federation of American Scientists Strategic Security Blog", May 6, 2009, http://www.fas.org/blog/ssp/2009/05/1280.php#more-1280.

CHAPTER 7

MISSILE DEFENSES AND NUCLEAR ARMS REDUCTIONS: CAN DETERRENCE WITHSTAND THE ATTENTION?

STEPHEN J. CIMBALA

INTRODUCTION

The expectation of improved missile defense technologies and the commitment by the United States and NATO to deploy advanced missile defenses in Europe have raised important issues related to nuclear deterrence. One of the most contentious issues between the United States and Russia in 2011–2012 was the Obama administration's revised version of the US-NATO European-based missile defense plan. Russian political leaders criticized this plan, insisted on a shared Russian-NATO missile defense arrangement going forward, and threatened responsive countermeasures if the United States and NATO proceeded despite Russia's objections.[1] A NATO-Russia summit originally scheduled for May 2012 in Chicago was shelved in favor of other forums for consultations between President Obama and the newly reelected Russian President Vladimir Putin. Regardless of the outcome of dialogue with Russia, NATO planned to announce at its 2012 summit the onset of the first phase of its evolving European Phased Adaptive Approach (EPAA) to European missile defense.

Russian disagreements with the United States and its NATO allies over missile defenses were partly based on high politics, especially during presidential election years in both the United States and Russia. But some of the debate was military-technical in its cast. Russian political leaders, diplomats, and others advanced the claim that the latter phases of EPAA, planned for deployment between 2018 and 2020, might jeopardize the viability of its strategic nuclear deterrent by calling into question Russia's capability for assured retaliation following any nuclear first strike.[2] Although the political absurdity and impossibility of a nuclear first strike by the United States against Russia was recognized by leaders in both states, Russia regarded its strategic nuclear second strike capability as essential for maintaining its great power status and the image of US-Russian strategic nuclear parity. Indeed, satisfying Russia on this matter is a necessary condition for obtaining Russian agreement for post–New START reductions in both states' strategic nuclear forces.

In the following discussion, we first review the political background to the apparent US-Russian impasse over missile defenses in 2012. This includes both domestic and geostrategic aspects of the Russian-American and NATO-Russian disagreements. Second, we apply a methodology to test the "null hypothesis" that the US-NATO missile defense plan as proposed will destabilize mutual deterrence based on of assured second strike retaliation. Third, we draw pertinent conclusions with implications for current and future US-NATO and Russian decision making relative to nuclear-related and other issues.

POLITICAL IMPASSE OR DETOUR?

The United States and Russia have managed to turn the opportunities for post–New START reductions into long-range offensive nuclear forces, and for agreement on a missile defense regime for Europe, into an impasse, within less than two years. There is no military-technical case for this, but politics in Washington and in Moscow have pushed strategic logic and nuclear restraint off the bar stool in favor of draughts of political posturing. From Moscow, the argument is put forward that the EPAA when completed will threaten Russia's strategic nuclear deterrent. In Washington, domestic political opponents of President Barack Obama's "reset" with Russia and of his New START agreement claim that NATO-Russian agreements on European missile defenses could throttle US ballistic missile defense (BMD) technology developments and restrict options for future BMD deployments.

The arrival of 2012 as a presidential election year in the United States and in Russia created additional roadblocks to forward movement in post–New START offensive arms reductions and to resolution of the European missile defense imbroglio. Vladimir Putin, on his way to a second regnum as Russia's president, was in full campaign mode against alleged US interference in Russian politics (particularly with respect to demonstrations in Moscow against electoral fraud in Russia's parliamentary elections). Catching the scent in the prevailing political winds, Russian critics of reset and of NATO European missile defenses sounded tocsins of Cold War retro and possible Russian military reactions to NATO's lack of cooperation on missile defenses. And in the United States, political opponents of President Obama called for a tougher political line against Russia, despite Russia's prior cooperation on Afghanistan, on sanctions against Iran, on civil nuclear energy, and, most pertinent here, on New START.[3] Presumptive Republican presidential candidate Mitt Romney opined in a CNN interview in April 2012 that Russia "is without question our number one geopolitical foe" and that Russia fights every cause for the world's worst actors.[4]

On account of these and other pressures, a NATO-Russia Council meeting originally scheduled to coincide with NATO's summit in Chicago in May 2012 was moved forward to April in Brussels. Some consultations on missile defense doubtless took place at the Brussels meetings between NATO and Russian representatives. Additional discussion of its European missile defense plans was on the menu for NATO's summit in May, but it seemed unlikely from the vantage point of an election year that the gap between NATO and Russian positions on missile defense could be bridged entirely.

Russia sought a legal guarantee from the United States and NATO that the EPAA would not jeopardize the viability of its strategic nuclear deterrent. The United States was unwilling to provide such a legal guarantee, especially in an election year with Congress unwilling to endorse any such document.[5] NATO was reportedly willing to provide an official political statement short of a legal guarantee that EPAA would pose no threat to Russia's nuclear deterrent. Russia was unlikely to be impressed by US or NATO declarations of intent outside a legal framework. The Russian Defense Ministry reportedly planned its own international conference among civilian and military experts for May 2012 at which Russian experts would offer probative analyses of the dangers posed to Russian security by NATO's missile defense shield as now planned.[6]

Although some Russian experts apparently fear the expected proficiency of future US missile defenses, some US experts have expressed concerns over the time table and technology proposed for the European and nationwide US missile defense systems. Lt. Gen. Patrick O'Reilly, head of the Department of Defense's Missile Defense Agency (MDA), has acknowledged that considerable technical challenges are involved in meeting the phased time lines for development and deployment of the EPAA system.[7] Daniel Goure notes that a missile defense capability requires a "system of systems" for effectiveness in design and operation. In addition to developing and deploying interceptors with required velocities, missile defense architectures also require advances in sensors and in battle management-command control systems (BM/C2).[8] Studies by the US Defense Science Board in 2011 and by the nonpartisan Government Accountability Office (GAO) of the US Congress in 2012 have called into question the feasibility of the Obama European missile defense plan. The GAO reportedly noted that the Department of Defense was committed to technologies not sufficiently proved in testing and was risking "performance shortfalls, unexpected cost increases, schedule delays and test problems."[9]

Political criticism in the United States of the Obama missile defense plan for Europe was related to congressional skepticism about the New START strategic nuclear arms agreement signed in 2010 and entered into force in February 2011. Primarily Republican members of Congress and other party notables expressed concerns that that United States had made a tacit or explicit agreement with Russia during New START negotiations to limit US missile defense deployments.[10] In fact, New START contained no such limitations on future US (or Russian) antimissile or antiwar defenses, for at least two reasons.[11] First, the Obama administration was aware that any concessions to Russia on missile defenses would endanger congressional consent to ratification of the treaty. Second, unlike offensive nuclear forces with a long deployment track record whose performance parameters are well known, future missile defense technologies constitute an open-ended menu of technical possibilities. It is difficult to limit something that has not yet been invented or reliably tested. Therefore, New START includes a preamble that acknowledges the generic relationship between offensive nuclear and missile weapons and antimissile and antiwar defenses, provided these are deployed.

GEOSTRATEGY AND ROLE PERCEPTIONS

Of course everyone understood that the New START and any follow-on agreement on offensive nuclear arms reductions, with or without missile defenses, had geostrategic as well as domestic political implications. These geostrategic implications included the self-definitions of the

United States and Russia with respect to their foreign policy objectives. For example, is the United States to regard itself as just another great power in a multipolar power system, or is the United States to attempt to play the role of international sheriff or, even more ambitious, aspiring hegemon? Russia's economic growth under Vladimir Putin's first two terms as president resulted in more assertive foreign and security policies compared with the 1990s, especially regarding NATO enlargement, US missile defenses, and the security of former Soviet territories in Europe and Central Eurasia. Will Putin's victory in the 2012 presidential elections usher in a new period of Russian bare-chested brio or consolidate Medvedev's multilateralism—or split the difference?

Russia's post–Cold War conventional military inferiority relative to NATO made Russia more reliant on its nuclear forces for deterrence and other missions than hitherto. Russia's 2010 Military Doctrine is not necessarily more forward-leaning than previous statements, with respect to any propensity for nuclear first use.[12] But it does acknowledge that Russia reserves the option for nuclear first use in the event of a conventional war that threatens the survival of the Russian state. Some Russian commentators have referred to this as the first use of nuclear weapons as part of Russia's effort to "de-escalate" any conflict by terminating the war in Russia's favor while limiting escalation to the lower rungs of the nuclear ladder. However, given the fact that such threats to remain credible must introduce a large amount of uncertainty into the aggressor's and defender's calculations, it is more likely that Russia's threat in this regard is the existential one created by the forward deployment of sub-strategic nuclear weapons and their inevitable involvement in any large-scale war with NATO or China. Since Russian officials observe a taboo about any discussion of war with China, NATO stands in as the putative adversary in these discussions about Russian doctrine for the possible first use of nuclear weapons in dire straits.[13] On the other hand, Putin has expressed rhetorical support for a Russian modernization program that would reduce Russia's relative dependency on nuclear weapons, as he noted in a February 20, 2012, article:

> In the more distant future, weapons systems based on new principles (beam, geophysical, wave, genetic, psychophysical and other technologies) will be developed. All this will, in addition to nuclear weapons, provide entirely new instruments for achieving political and strategic goals. Such high-tech weapons systems will be comparable to nuclear weapons but will be more "acceptable" in terms of political and military ideology. In this sense, the strategic balance of nuclear forces will play a gradually diminishing role in deterring aggression.[14]

Ironically, regardless of the role perceptions of the United States and Russia, Europe is on the way to growing its security community outward to include additional parts of former Soviet territory, including the Caucasus and Central Asia. This securitization of Eurasian geostrategic space will take place because the prospect of large-scale, interstate war is increasingly becoming politically unthinkable, economically counterproductive, and militarily self-defeating. War is above all a political instrument, and its preferred outcome is victory at an acceptable cost. There are few such wars on offer even for the most imaginative of military planners. Instead, major threats to Eurasia and North America will come from rogue states or regional rivals outside Europe with weapons of mass destruction or a determination to sponsor terrorism against the established order, whatever it is.

In this larger context, nuclear weapons would seem to be political and military liabilities more than assets. Their inability to provide for victory at an acceptable cost would seem to push them into the background of military-strategic thinking, supplanted by the information-based paradigm for high-end conventional war. A more complicated post–Cold War tableau has developed. Nuclear deterrence continues as a required core competency in United States' and other nuclear weapons states' policies even as nuclear first use or first strike becomes more improbable. This apparent paradox exists because, although the threat of nuclear first use or first strike by "responsible" existing nuclear weapons states is judged as slight, the possibility of nuclear attacks by less responsible or irresponsible members of the nuclear club cannot be ruled out. Thus, for example, the Obama administration Nuclear Posture Review creeps toward a "deterrence only" doctrine with respect to nuclear weapons but leaves open the option of a nuclear response to an adversary's use of weapons of mass destruction (WMD) other than nuclear.[15] And NATO continues to deploy several hundreds of nonstrategic nuclear weapons in Europe as part of the alliance's reassurance to Europeans that the American commitment to their defense will be reliable under even the most extreme circumstances.[16]

This geostrategic setting means that theater or shorter-range missile defenses may have a more plausible market and technical performance envelope compared with defenses against weapons of intercontinental and transoceanic range. Ironically, the United States, NATO, and Russia have been discussing cooperative theater missile defenses (TMD) for Europe since the end of the Cold War. These talks have continued among technical specialists without engaging the gears of fear in Washington, Brussels, and Moscow because they are less politically visible, and therefore less contentious, than are the reductions in long-range nuclear force and their implications for antinuclear defenses. Theater missile defenses are also less contentious as between NATO and Russia because the limited ranges of their interceptors and radars are assumed to prevent them from expanding into counters for strategic retaliatory forces of the United States and Russia.

The politics of theater missile defenses prior to 2007, when Putin "went ballistic" over the George W. Bush "third position" proposal for missile defenses in Europe, including interceptors in Poland and a radar in the Czech Republic, shows that missile defenses based in Europe or elsewhere are not necessarily a zero-sum game, as between the United States and Russia or NATO and Russia. It is politically possible, although obviously challenging, to arrive at a modus vivendi that will include NATO's Phased Adaptive Approach or some facsimile of it together with Russia's participation or acquiescence. In the abstract, three possibilities suggest themselves: (1) NATO and Russia establish a merged system with interdependent components for early warning, command-control and battle management, and missile intercept; (2) NATO and Russia establish separate systems with protocols for coordination and sharing of information with respect to launch detection and intercept decisions; or (3) some compromise between (1) and (2), as above, with partly independent and partly shared decision making and operations.

Although in theory it should be possible to reach some sort of compromise, as among the negotiating parties, along one of these trajectories, in practice nontrivial difficulties present themselves. At the political level, NATO members and Russia would have to agree on protocols for defining a genuine threat and for the assignment of any responsibility for a response. The immediate issue is two-sided: at whose territory is the missile headed, and over whose territory should it be intercepted? If these matters can be resolved within the short time available for threat detection and assessment, a third issue is who will, in fact, respond? Will the choice between a NATO and a Russian antimissile response be made on the basis of whose technology is more reliable, closer to the launch site, closer to the flight path of the attacker, or under attack?

The command and control system required for collaboration and prompt response in these exigent circumstances will have to coordinate NATO and Russian launch detection, threat assessment, battle management, and response within decision times perhaps as short as ten minutes or less. And the risks of opposite types of decision failure will have to be resolved consultatively or by preestablished protocols in good time: on the one hand, the risk of false detection of an attack when none is actually taking place, and on the other, the risk of missing the presence of an attack that is actually in progress. Then there is the possibility of divergent political aims and military tactics *after* NATO and Russia have agreed and performed successfully a joint launch detection and intercept. Depending on who the attacker is and prior political relations between NATO or Russia and the offender, the atmosphere of missile defense cooperation may deteriorate into post-intercept conflict. Suppose, for example, that Iran launches a missile toward Western Europe and NATO intercepts the attacker with help from Russian radars in Azerbaijan and Armavir. Further suppose that the regime in Tehran declares that the missile launch was a technical mistake or a usurpation of launch authority by antiregime elements and that no casualties occurred as a result. The United States and NATO might nevertheless demand a more than diplomatic response against Iran that Russia would not automatically support.

Conjecture is open-ended, but we can move to partial closure on one aspect of this great debate over missile defenses: will the Obama Phased Adaptive Approach for Europe pose a substantive threat to Russia's strategic nuclear retaliatory forces if, and when, its four phases are completed in 2020? We cannot know the exact kinds of missile defenses that will be deployed between now and then, nor their performances apart from tests yet to be conducted. Given these imponderables and uncertainties, we can undertake a small thought experiment to evaluate the flexibility and stability of post–New START offensive nuclear arms reductions, with or without defenses.

Research Design and Methodology

Scenarios and Parameters

The Obama administration has reportedly tasked the Department of Defense to interrogate various options for post–New START reductions in deployed long-range US and Russian nuclear weapons, including deployment limits of 1100, 800, and 400 weapons. Taking each of these scenarios as a starting point, we can examine whether stable deterrence based on assured second strike retaliation can be preserved between the United States and Russia. Deterrence stability is not the only mission for strategic nuclear forces, but it provides the essential foundation for the avoidance of nuclear war and for the assignment of other nuclear tasks. Projecting notional but not unreasonable US and Russian strategic nuclear forces forward to 2018–2020, we can subject these forces to a nuclear first strike and calculate the estimated numbers of surviving and retaliating weapons for each state under prewar deployment limits of 1100, 800, and 400 weapons.

If defenses are added to the equation, the scenarios become more conjectural because offensive-defensive interactions compound the uncertainties involved in measuring expected outcomes. The solution here is admittedly improvisational. Assuming that the capabilities of defenses relative to offenses are "known unknowns," we create an artificial or dummy variable by randomizing the penetration probability of retaliating offenses against missile defenses. This randomizing of penetration probability has the same effect as randomizing the "defense leakage" or the proportion of attackers that successfully get through a defense to their intended targets. This randomizing is a stress test for deterrence stability based on second strike retaliation against defenses.

RESULTS AND FINDINGS

Toward these ends, figure 7.1 summarizes the results of a "standard" nuclear exchange model for US and Russian forces with a prewar deployment limit of 1100 long-range nuclear weapons. Figure 7.2 summarizes the numbers of second strike surviving and arriving retaliatory weapons for each state under similar deployment limits, but with the addition of randomized defenses. Figure 7.3 provides the outcomes of the standard (no defenses) nuclear exchange model for a lower prewar deployment limit of 800 weapons, and figure 7.4 summarizes the results of the same model with defenses of uncertain performance added. In the third major

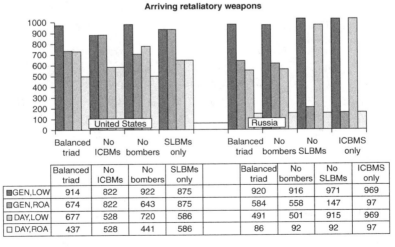

	Balanced triad	No ICBMs	No bombers	SLBMs only	Balanced triad	No bombers	No SLBMs	ICBMS only
■GEN,LOW	914	822	922	875	920	916	971	969
■GEN,ROA	674	822	643	875	584	558	147	97
□ DAY,LOW	677	528	720	586	491	501	915	969
□ DAY,ROA	437	528	441	586	86	92	92	97

Figure 7.1 US-Russia arriving retaliatory weapons, 1100 deployment limit

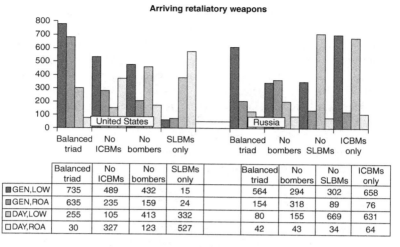

Figure 7.2 US-Russia arriving retaliatory weapons, 1100 deployment limit, random defense penetration

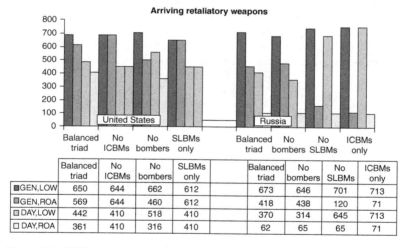

Figure 7.3 US-Russia, arriving retaliatory weapons, 800 deployment limit

step in the analysis, figures 7.5 and 7.6 summarize the outcomes of US-Russian strategic nuclear exchanges for forces limited to 400 prewar deployed weapons. Figure 7.5 provides the standard case without defenses, and in figure 7.6 defenses of uncertain performance relative to offenses are included. All US and Russian forces are contrasted under

MISSILE DEFENSES AND NUCLEAR ARMS REDUCTIONS

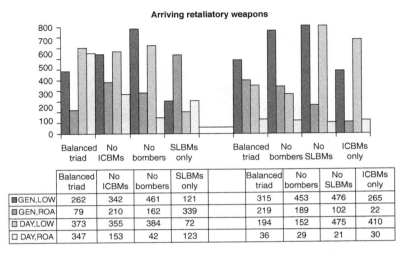

Figure 7.4 US-Russia, surviving and retaliating warheads, 800 deployment limit, random defense penetration

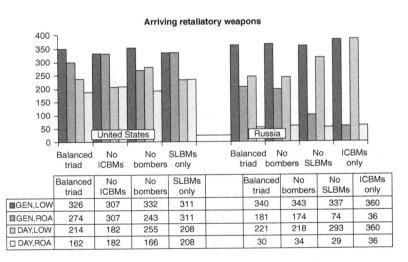

Figure 7.5 US-Russia, arriving retaliatory weapons, 400 deployment limit

four possible states of launch readiness and operational posture: (1) generated alert, launch on warning; (2) generated alert, riding out the attack; (3) day-to-day or normal peacetime alert, launch on warning; and (4) day-to-day alert, riding out the attack.

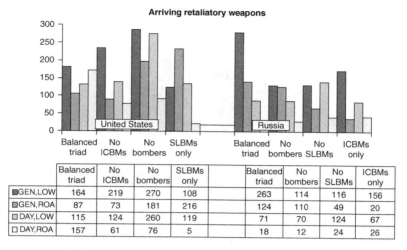

Figure 7.6 US-Russia, arriving retaliatory weapons, 400 deployment limit, random defense penetration

In all cases, the response of four different US and Russian nuclear force structures is modeled for the sake of completeness (and against the possibility that one or the other state might restructure its forces from the nuclear-strategic "triad" of past and current preference to something else). For Russia, a triad of land- and sea-based ballistic missiles and bomber-delivered weapons is contrasted with three alternatives: (1) a dyad of land- and sea-based ballistic missiles without bombers, (2) a dyad of land-based missiles and bombers without sea-based ballistic missiles, and (3) a force composed entirely of land-based missiles. For the United States, in addition to the traditional triad, alternatives include (1) a dyad of sea-based ballistic missiles and bombers without land-based missiles, (2) a dyad of land- and sea-based ballistic missiles without bombers, and (3) a force composed entirely of sea-based ballistic missiles.

The results summarized in figures 7.1 through 7.6 suggest some obvious and some not so obvious conclusions. First, the survivability and flexibility of nuclear retaliatory forces are impressive under even very stressful conditions for them. This finding is apparent in the results for the "standard" cases for prewar deployment limits of 1100, 800, or even 400 weapons (figures 7.1, 7.3, and 7.5). In all cases, US and Russian strategic nuclear forces are able to survive and retaliate with more than sufficient numbers of weapons to inflict unacceptable societal damage by historical standards. In most cases, across force structures and readiness postures, both states are also able to attack additional targets, including opposed forces, command-control systems, and infrastructure.

It gets more complicated when we consider adaptive scenarios with randomized defense leakage or offensive penetrativity. The outcomes for randomized defenses appear in figures 7.2, 7.4, and 7.6 for the prewar deployment limits of 1100, 800, and 400 weapons, respectively. Based on these results, each state would have to assume that, however competent its defenses are thought to be, sufficient numbers of the other state's second strike retaliatory forces would circumvent the defenses and arrive at their intended targets to accomplish unacceptable societal damage and numerous "disasters beyond history."[17] This finding might be disconcerting to those who focus on either the first striker's or the retaliator's dilemma. If both states have deployed missile defenses, then the retaliator's missile defenses complicate the first striker's estimation of expected outcomes. On the other hand, the first striker's defenses increase the uncertainties attendant to the retaliator's ability to accomplish its assured retaliation. Thus studies that attribute defenses to only one side or the other might miss the collision of unknowns that takes place when both do.

What are the implications of the preceding findings for US and Russian nonproliferation objectives? Two perspectives are arguable. The United States and Russia might seek to maintain nuclear forces superior in quality and in quantity to those of all other powers. US-Russian nuclear primacy might be helpful to global nonproliferation and the avoidance of nuclear war, since the United States and Russia together own more than 90 percent of the world's nuclear weapons. Acting in concert, they can overwhelm any system-disrupting nuclear disturber of the peace. An alternative perspective is that the Unites States and Russia must follow through on their nonproliferation obligations under the Nuclear Nonproliferation Treaty (NPT) by reducing their numbers of deployed long-range and other nuclear weapons. If the United States and Russia will not lead in this regard, other nuclear weapons states will not follow and the incentives for currently nonnuclear weapons states to join the ranks of nuclear weapons states will increase. Since the politics of international arms control are complicated, there is probably some truth in both perspectives.

CONCLUSIONS

Analysis shows that the two-sided deterrence relationship between the United States and Russia could be stable at deployment levels of 1100, 800, or 400 weapons, although targeting options would be reduced accordingly.[18] Missile defenses are technological, strategic, and political wild cards. They could stimulate arms races in offsetting offensive countermeasures, but they could also complicate the calculations of prospective nuclear attackers. The thought-experiment here creates a behavior space in which offenses and defenses of unknown effectiveness can interact with random probabilities to help distinguish the relatively plausible from the relatively implausible outcomes.

Projected US and Russian strategic nuclear retaliatory forces should provide for platform survivability and command-control stability even at lower than New START levels. However, reducing their numbers of operationally deployed long-range nuclear weapons below 1,000 will require the United States and Russia to "multilateralize" the reductions talks and engage other nuclear weapons states, especially the larger ones. This multilateral dialogue must be preceded by improving the clarity of the two-way conversation between the United States and Russia. The claim that Russia's nuclear deterrent would be obviated by the EPAA, or by some alternative US or NATO missile defense plan, appears as more of a political pronouncement than a military-technical likelihood. It follows that cooperation among the United States, NATO, and Russia over European missile defenses, notwithstanding technical challenges, is impeded mostly by politics. These politics are apt to be short-sighted and mistaken as they stand in the way of further US-Russian cooperation on security issues, including nuclear nonproliferation and the possibility of nuclear terrorism.

Notes

1. "Russia, NATO Missile Talks Reach 'Dead-End,'" *RIA-Novosti*, May 3, 2012, in *Johnson's Russia List* 2012–#80, May 3, 2012. See also Editorial, "Russia's Last Warnings to Washington," *Moscow Times*, May 5, 2012, in *Johnson's Russia List* 2012–#82, May 7, 2012.
2. BBC Monitoring, "Russia May Have to Launch Pre-emptive Strike on European ABM, Says CGS," *Rossiya 24*, May 3, 2012, in *Johnson's Russia List* 2012–#81, May 4, 2012; and Yelena Chernenko and Ivan Safronov, "Computers vs Ballistic Missile Defense Belts: Computer Model to be Presented in Moscow Will Demonstrate Danger of the United States' and NATO's Ballistic Missile Defense Plans," *Kommersant*, May 3, 2012, in *Johnson's Russia List* 2012–#80, May 3, 2012.
3. Fred Weir, "Why Outlook for US-Russia 'Reset' Looks Bearish," *Christian Science Monitor*, April 11, 2012, in *Johnson's Russia List* 2012–#68, April 12, 2012.
4. Ibid.

5. Yelena Chernenko, "Armed Forces and Means: The Time for Reaching a Compromise on Missile Shields is Running Out," *Kommersant*, April 19, 2012, in *Johnson's Russia List* 2012–#72, April 19, 2012.
6. Ibid.
7. Unclassified statement of Lt Gen Patrick J. O'Reilly, Director, Missile Defense Agency, before the House Armed Services Committee, Subcommittee on Strategic Forces, regarding the *Fiscal Year 2011 Missile Defense Programs* (Washington, DC: House Armed Services Committee, US House of Representatives, April 15, 2010). See also George N. Lewis and Theodore A. Postol, "A Flawed and Dangerous US Missile Defense Plan," *Arms Control Today*, May 2010, http://www.armscontrol.org/act/2010_05/Lewis-Postol.
8. Daniel Goure, "The Obama Administration's Phased-Adaptive Architecture: Technological, Operational and Political Issues," *Defense and Security Analysis*, no. 1 (March, 2012): 17–35, esp. 22–26 on technical challenges.
9. Desmond Butler, "Reports Cast Doubt on European Missile Defense," Associated Press, April 21, 2012, http://www.the-review.com/ap%20washington/2012/04/21/reports-cast-doubt-on-european-missile-defense.html.
10. Jim DeMint, "The Treaty is Mad," *National Review Online*, July 29, 2010, http://www.nationalreview.com/articles/243568/treaty-mad-jim-demint.
The author gratefully acknowledges Mikhail Tsypkin for this reference. See also Mitt Romney, "Obama's Worst Foreign-Policy Mistake," *Washington Post*, July 6, 2010, p. A13, http://www.washingtonpost.com/wp-dyn/content/article02010/07/05/AR2010070502657_pf.
11. *Treaty between the United States of America and the Russian Federation on Measures for the Further Reduction and Limitation of Strategic Offensive Arms* (Washington, D.C.: US Department of State, April 8, 2010), http://www.state.gov/documents/organization/140035.pdf. See also Pavel Podvig, "New START Treaty in Numbers," Russian strategic nuclear forces, blog, April 9, 2010, http://russianforces.org/blog/2010/03/new_start_treaty_in_numbers.shtml.
12. "The Military Doctrine of the Russian Federation," February 5, 2010, http://www.Kremlin.ru, in *Johnson's Russia List* 2010–#35, February 19, 2010. See also Nikolai Sokov, "The New, 2010 Russian Military Doctrine: The Nuclear Angle," Center for Nonproliferation Studies, Monterey Institute of International Studies, February 5, 2010, http://cns.miis.edu/stories/100205_russian_nuclear_doctrine.htm.
13. Jacob W. Kipp, "Russia's Nuclear Posture and the Threat that Dare Not Speak its Name," ch. 10 in Stephen J. Blank, ed., *Russian Nuclear Weapons: Past, Present, and Future* (Carlisle, PA: Strategic Studies Institute, US Army War College, November 2011), 459–503.
14. Vladimir Putin, in *Rossiiskaya Gazeta*, February 20, 2012, cited in Alexander Golts, "The Miracle-Industrial Complex," *Moscow Times*, April 24, 2012, in *Johnson's Russia List* 2012–#75, April 24, 2012.
15. US Department of Defense, *Nuclear Posture Review Report* (Washington, DC: US Department of Defense, April 2010).

16. *NATO 2020: Assured Security; Dynamic Engagement, Analysis and Recommendations of the Group of Experts on a New Strategic Concept for NATO* (Brussels: North Atlantic Treaty Organization, May 17, 2010).
17. The concept of "disaster beyond history" equals ten warheads on ten cities. See McGeorge Bundy, "To Cap the Volcano," *Foreign Affairs*, no. 1 (October 1969), 1–20, citation p. 10, http://www.jstor.org/stable/20039419.
18. Additional support for post–New START reductions, to as few as 900 warheads each for the Untied States and Russia with only half deployed at any one time, has come from a number of former military and political national security officials, including retired Gen James E. Cartwright, formerly commander of US Strategic Command. See Thom Shanker, "Former Commander of US Nuclear Forces Calls for Large Cut in Warheads," *New York Times*, May 15, 2012, http://www.nytimes.com/2012/05/16/world/cartwright-key-retired-general-backs-large-us-nuclear-reduction.html.

Section III

Nontraditional Deterrence

CHAPTER 8

ARE ROGUE REGIMES DETERRABLE?

GARY SCHAUB JR.

INTRODUCTION

How should policy makers approach divining the intentions of revolutionary adversaries who may take actions that the United States wishes to deter? Revolutionary states are those that "consider the international order or the manner of legitimizing it oppressive.... [T]he distinguishing feature of a revolutionary power is not that it feels threatened...but that nothing can reassure it."[1] Such states aim to substantially revise the status quo, challenging those it perceives to threaten or oppress them, perhaps to the point of trying to overthrow the international order and reconstitute it along principles other than that of the sovereign state system.[2] The Soviet Union and Iran have been considered two such states. How have their intentions been gauged? What policies have been proposed to deter them from their messianic missions?

The United States has addressed both states with a policy of deterrence in the service of containment. Although deterrence formed the core mission of the American military throughout the Cold War,[3] a great deal of deterrence theory and planning took place in a strategic and political vacuum, one based on presumptions about the motives of Soviet and other adversaries. Adversary intent was inferred from capabilities analysis married to worst-case scenarios of what they could accomplish. Whether deterrence would succeed in general or in any particular case was likewise considered to be a function of American capabilities and willingness to use them in the event that deterrence failed. Whether something other than a reset of the relationship would happen if deterrence succeeded and the adversary's intent was frustrated was rarely considered.

From a theoretical standpoint, deterrence links a demand that the adversary refrain from undertaking a particular action to a threat to use force if it does not comply. Deterrence places the adversary in a situation in which it has a choice of complying with what has been demanded of it—inaction—or defying those demands and risking the implementation of the deterrer's threatened sanction. How the adversary generate expectations about the consequences of their alternatives—what they consider, the relative importance of these considerations, and how these considerations are combined to yield an estimate of consequences—has been the subject of wide and varied speculation.[4] These expectations are distilled into expected value calculations. Expected value calculations require that the costs and benefits of an outcome be discounted by the probability of its occurrence (i.e., [benefits − costs] * probability) and that the expected value of possible outcomes stemming from a single course of action be summed. In deterrence, the adversary compare the expected value of compliance and defiance. For a deterrence attempt to be successful, the deterrer's threatened sanction must reduce the expected value of defiance to the degree that it is less than the expected value of compliance. The deterrer can do that by threatening to reduce the benefits of defiance or increase its costs. The former would constitute a denial threat, while the latter would be a threat of punishment. And because the adversary will discount these threats by its assessment of the likelihood that the deterrer will implement them, the deterrer must convey these threats credibly.[5]

The *Deterrence Operations Joint Operating Concept (DO JOC)*, a product of Strategic Command (STRATCOM) and Joint Forces Command (JFCOM), adopts this framework and by doing so has improved the official conception of deterrence markedly.[6] It defines "[d]eterrence operations [as those that] convince adversaries not to take actions that threaten US vital interests by means of decisive influence over their decision-making. Decisive influence is achieved by credibly threatening to deny benefits and/or impose costs [if the undesirable action is taken], while encouraging restraint by convincing the actor that restraint will result in an acceptable outcome."[7] The *DO JOC* thus takes an active view of deterrence operations: achieving decisive influence over an adversary's decision making requires deliberate action on the part of a joint force commander or other American policy makers. Such deterrence operations can include force projection, the deployment of active and passive defenses, global strike (nuclear, conventional, and nonkinetic), and strategic communication.[8]

The key to knowing when to practice deterrence is determining an actor's intent. Patrick Morgan notes, "The intentions of opponents are notoriously difficult to fathom."[9] This seems to be especially the case for state actors that have revolutionary orientations. How do joint force commanders, those who populate the staffs of the US government, and the elites upon whom they rely for subject matter expertise, determine adversary intent? Is there doctrinal guidance that military staffs rely upon to perform this key task? Are there certain patterns of thought or interpretive lenses that are commonly employed by officers, civilian policy makers, or scholars? How have these been applied in key episodes in the past? Finally, how can the process of intent determination be improved?

There is little doctrinal guidance for determining adversary intent. What exists is contained in *Joint Publication 2–0 Joint Intelligence*. This doctrine manual contains superficially useful sections, such as "Intelligence and the Levels of War," "Intelligence and the Range of Military Operations," "Prediction—(Accept the Risk of Predicting Adversary Intentions)," and "Intelligence Support During the Deterrence Phase." Unfortunately, most of these sections are unhelpful. Beyond exhorting "intelligence professionals" to "go beyond the identification of capabilities" and take the risk of predicting adversary intent and basing such forecasts on "solid analysis," *JP 2–0* is not particularly helpful in guiding such analysis. Indeed, by indicating that such "an intelligence product... usually reflects enemy capabilities and vulnerabilities," the authors of this doctrine indirectly encourage capability analysis be substituted for intent analysis. While capabilities do suggest some general directions of intent—why invest in a particular capability if you are not going to use it?—it utterly fails to answer questions of the conditions under which such capabilities would be used. These are political issues that the military intelligence process, set as it is at the tactical or operational level of war, does not address.

INTERPRETING INTENT: TWO FRAMEWORKS

If joint military doctrine is not a helpful guide in determining adversary intent, how can operators structure this problem so as to solve it? Intelligence analysts operate in a complex environment and they, like human beings more generally, are unable to process all of the innumerable stimuli that they encounter. In this context, Roberta Wohlstetter usefully distinguished "between signals and noise. By the 'signal' of an action is meant a sign, a clue, a piece of evidence that points to the action or to an adversary's intention to undertake it, and by 'noise' is meant the background of irrelevant or inconsistent signals, signs pointing in the wrong directions, that tend always to obscure the signs pointing in the right way."[10] What Wohlstetter left unsaid was that noise and signals do not come clearly marked for the analysts as they sift through mountains of information. Rather, it is the analyst who determines what is signal and what is noise.

This is a difficult task. Analysts suffer the same cognitive limits as everyone else, and therefore necessarily deal with "a dramatically simplified model of the buzzing, blooming confusion that constitutes the real world."[11] These simplified models of reality focus attention toward certain pieces of information and away from most others, and generally represent the "most significant chains of causes and consequences" as "short and simple."[12] These models allow analysts to discriminate between signals and noise. However, many models may adequately fit the data and it is up to the analyst to determine which best explains the adversary's intent.[13]

American scholars and policy makers have been apt to apply one of two models to comprehend the intentions of other international actors, be they regular states or revolutionary states. The first is the strategic intent model and the second is the internal logic model.

Each model also posits that the actor is purposive: that it seeks to achieve a particular goal with each action. When working retrospectively, this presumption risks making either framework tautological, as "an imaginative analyst can construct an account of value-maximizing choice for any action or set of actions."[14] Tautology can be escaped, however, if it is also presumed that the preferences against which alternatives are considered are relatively stable. This allows an analyst to erect a set of principles that appear to guide the actor's choices over time and across domains. These principles provide generic preferences for particular actors and allow some degree of operationalization of the model. They can be derived from "(1) propensities or personality traits or psychological tendencies of the nation or government, (2) values shared by the nation or government [or organization], or (3) special principles of action [that] change the 'goals' or narrow the 'alternatives' and 'consequences' considered."[15]

The strategic intent and internal logic models differ with regard to the problems that they believe an actor is attempting to solve by taking actions in the interstate arena. The strategic intent model presumes that the actor is solving an external problem, while the internal logic model presumes that it is solving an internal one.

THE STRATEGIC INTENT MODEL

The strategic intent model presumes that state actors direct their behavior toward achieving political goals vis-à-vis external actors. It presumes that they desire to influence the decisions, behavior, or attitudes of these other actors and that they have chosen the most effective means available to them, as delimited by their capabilities and tendencies, to achieve this end. Whether they do so via coercion, inducement, or persuasion,[16] using whatever power resources they have available, matters not. What does matter is that the impact on the external actor is of paramount concern to adversary.

Thus the key variables determining the adversary's intent to act are the costs of undertaking the action, the benefits that would accrue from successful action, and the costs and benefits of not acting. The strategic intent model is vague regarding what factors determine costs and benefits of these two courses of action. Lawrence Freedman has argued that the costs of undertaking the action can be bifurcated into the costs associated with implementing the choice and those associated with enforcing it after the fact.[17] The benefits of undertaking the action have not been given as much attention as the costs, but would be composed of material benefits accrued, intangible benefits—including prestige, reputation, among others—and the new opportunities made possible by successful conclusion of the action. The costs of inaction, or "restraint" in the parlance of the *DO JOC*, can be broken down into the international and domestic costs of foregoing action, including suffering the unwanted reactions of opponents in the near and far term, and the negative reactions of domestic audiences. The benefits of inaction or restraint have not been well-thought out in the literature either, but would include desirable international and domestic reactions—such as praise for being reasonable or a de-escalation of tensions, or tangible benefits provided by those who did not favor action. Despite the obvious utility that considering domestic reactions to the choice made by the adversary's leadership, the strategic intent model generally focuses on externally generated costs and benefits.[18]

THE INTERNAL LOGIC MODEL

The internal logic model, on the other hand, presumes that actors are directing their activities inward, enhancing their support or the cohesion of the group, and that actions directed toward other actors—be they states or otherwise—are judged primarily by their internal effects rather than their external effects. Hence international political behavior is primarily a consequence of domestic (or internal) politics and may be more incidental than intended. "The idea that political elites often embark on adventurous foreign policies or even resort to war in order to distract popular attention away from internal social or economic problems and consolidate their own domestic political support is an old theme in the literature on international politics," argues Jack Levy.[19] Ned Lebow argues that states with weakening political systems, weakening political leaders, or elites engaged in a competition for power may "resort to the time-honored technique of attempting to offset discontent at home by diplomatic success abroad."[20] While success vis-à-vis external actors would certainly be welcomed, the cohesion within the group and support for the leadership generated by conflict abroad is the primary purpose of such actions.

The key variables within this framework are the internal or domestic groups whose support is required to allow the leadership to continue in office. After these have been identified, the relative ability of these groups to influence the leadership by providing benefits such as continued support or imposing costs such as removing leaders from power, the way in which these audiences view the merits of the action to be undertaken (or not), and the relative ability of the leadership to substitute the support of one group for another must be assessed.[21] Thus the internal logic framework requires substantial knowledge of the adversary beyond the leaders and their preferences, especially the leaders' domestic political situation. A great deal of work has addressed the propensities of certain types of regimes to engage in external behavior to ameliorate internal dissension or promote internal cohesion, in democratic states particularly.[22] The manner in which deterrent threats are interpreted and used when external behavior is driven by internal needs has received attention from scholars such as Ned Lebow and Janice Stein, but their insights have not been incorporated into the corpus of deterrence theory—to the detriment of our knowledge.[23]

This has been reflected in how analysts have inferred adversary intent. American policy makers, scholars, and analysts have relied upon these two frameworks of rational action to infer the intent of adversaries. They clearly direct attention toward different aspects of the adversary's makeup, capabilities, and particularly hierarchy of goals. Unsurprisingly, they often provide contradictory prescriptions regarding how to approach adversary and what to do to influence their behavior. Two short examples of each model in action should make the differences clear.

SOURCES OF SOVIET CONDUCT

During the Cold War, there was a grand debate between those who used the strategic intent model to infer Soviet behavior and those who used the internal logic model. Those who utilized the strategic intent model can be divided into those who saw Soviet motivations as an attempt to obtain security in an insecure environment and those who saw the USSR as an opportunistic yet traditional great power.

STRATEGIC INTENT

The first group saw the Soviets operating in an environment in which it had real enemies and "a compulsion to overinsure against potential threats."[24] Soviet leaders inherited traditional Russian insecurities deriving from the lack of geographic barriers to invasions and a history of many such invasions married to "a politically xenophobic Communist ideology that interpreted the external world as implacable to the Socialist state."[25] In this conception, the Soviets were seen as sensitive to the influences of their environment and the behavior of external actors. George Kennan put it thusly: "What is called 'Soviet behavior' is, in far higher degree than seems to be realized in Washington, a reaction by the leaders of that country to the manner in which we ourselves treat them."[26] These analysts, therefore, argued that American actions should bear in mind Soviet sensitivities and that Washington should pursue policies that avoided unnecessary provocation. Indeed, they saw in this room for cooperation between the superpowers on the basis of overcoming common threats to their security, particularly those caused by the existence of nuclear weapons. Hence, they advocated arms control to enhance strategic stability, nonproliferation efforts to halt the further spread of nuclear weapons, and greater transparency in the form of cooperative security arrangements—all designed to reassure the Soviets that their environment was less dangerous than they perceived and therefore influence its behavior.[27]

A related strategic view accepted that the Soviet Union received an inheritance from Tsarist Russia, particularly its self-image as a great power. According to Kissinger, "Soviet policy is also, of course, the inheritor of an ancient tradition of Russian nationalism. Over centuries the strange Russian empire has seeped outward...across endless plains where no geographical obstacle except distance set a limit to human ambition, inundating what resisted, absorbing what yielded."[28] Its continued outward drive manifested itself in the Cold War-era in traditional great power fashion as continued consolidation of the empire, the control over the buffer states of Eastern Europe, prevention of encirclement by hostile states, and the reshaping of the rules of the international system to its liking.[29] In essence, those who held this view saw the mellowing of Bolshevik ideological fervor and decreasingly reluctant acceptance of the Soviet Union's role in the established international system. But they did not infer that Soviet intentions were benign.

This conception emphasized the opportunistic nature of Soviet forays abroad. In his famous article, "The Sources of Soviet Conduct," George Kennan argued that Soviet "political action is a fluid stream which moves constantly, wherever it is permitted to move, toward a given goal. Its main concern is to make sure that it has filled every nook and cranny available to it in the basin of world power."[30] Kissinger agreed that "Soviet strategy [is] essentially one of ruthless opportunism."[31]

In both variants of the strategic intent conception of Soviet intent, the Soviet leadership was composed of clearheaded and rational statesmen operating in an environment where their behavior was determined by the expected value of available courses of action. They were therefore viewed as amenable to influence from external actors—amenable in the sense that they were not implacable or insensitive to the consequences of their actions deriving from the reactions of others. For this reason Kennan prescribed "that the main element of any United States policy toward the Soviet Union must be that of a long-term, patient but firm and vigilant containment of Russian expansive tendencies."[32] Kissinger likewise counseled, "To foreclose Soviet opportunities is thus the essence of the West's responsibility. It is up to us to define the limits of Soviet aims."[33]

This view became the basis for deterrence theory as it developed in the Cold War. The Soviet leadership might desire to take advantage of every opportunity to increase its security, material power, or political influence, but American strategists believed that it would not risk war with the United States to obtain these goals. It held this belief for two reasons. First, it knew that Soviet leaders—Stalin in particular—could count and America's military and economic preponderance was obvious to all. Therefore, the Soviets would ultimately content themselves with consolidating that which they already had to avoid overt conflict with the United States. Second, Communist ideology would reinforce this tendency. "[T]he Kremlin is under no ideological compulsion to accomplish its purposes in a hurry," argued Kennan. "[I]t can be patient. It has no right to risk the existing achievements of the revolution for the sake of vain baubles of the future."[34] The Soviets believed that time was on their side and that tactical withdrawals were not indicative of a strategic retreat. Indeed, Kennan continued, "[T]he Kremlin has no compunction about retreating in the face of superior force.... [I]f it finds unassailable barriers in its path, it accepts these philosophically and accommodates itself to them."[35] Successful deterrence would depend on this peculiar Soviet trait. As Bernard Brodie put it, "[T]he saving grace of the Soviet philosophy so far as international relations are concerned is that, unlike the Nazi ideology, it incorporates within itself no time schedule.... The Soviet attitude appears to be much more opportunistic. The Soviets may be unshakably convinced that ultimately there must be war.... What we can do, however, is to persuade them each time the question arises that 'The time is not yet!'"[36]

INTERNAL LOGIC

Those who saw Soviet behavior through the prism of the internal logic model also began their analyses with George Kennan, but discounted the ability of external influences to affect Soviet calculations. In this view, dealing with internal solidarity was

> one of the most basic of the compulsions which came to act upon the Soviet regime: since capitalism no longer existed in Russia and since it could not be admitted that there could be serious or widespread opposition to the Kremlin springing spontaneously from the liberated masses under its authority, it became necessary to justify the retention of the dictatorship by stressing the menace of capitalism abroad.... [T]he stress laid in Moscow on the menace confronting Soviet society from the world outside its borders is founded not in the realities of foreign antagonism but in the necessity of explaining away the maintenance of dictatorial authority at home.[37]

Analysts such as Richard Pipes, Colin Gray, and William Odom continued this line of argument in the late 1970s and early 1980s.[38] Their analyses suggested that the Soviet system of governance was characterized by "endemic militarism" and that it was "as central to Soviet communism as the pursuit of profit is to societies with market-oriented economies."[39] Thus the use of force abroad was seen as a good in itself, one that enhanced the identity of the Soviet state. "According to this view," wrote Seay, "the Soviet iteration of an implacable foreign threat results not from paranoia or from fear of invasion but rather from the regime's self-interest, a foreign threat being an indispensible element in the regimentation of Soviet society."[40] Indeed, this posture had "the additional benefit of helping to legitimize an otherwise illegitimate regime."[41]

The internal logic view of Soviet conduct implied that there was a fundamental impediment to changing their behavior. They could not be influenced on a case-by-case basis through coercive strategies, such as deterrence, or induced through acts of goodwill, or persuaded through diplomacy. Given that the sources of Soviet conduct were internal and endemic, only physical barriers to Soviet action would affect them. Only if they were physically denied the ability to achieve their goals would they refrain from acting. Analysts who held this view argued strenuously for national missile defense as an alternative to an inherently unreliable deterrent,[42] against strategic nuclear arms control, and opposed détente.

These analysts did believe that it was possible for the United States to achieve its objectives vis-à-vis the Soviet Union—once it collapsed. Kennan had argued that the internal contradictions of the Soviet system and the unbearable strain that it would place on its population could result in a collapse of the Soviet system. "Soviet Russia might be changed overnight from one of the strongest to one of the most pitiable of national societies," he argued.[43] But those who emphasized the internal logic of the Soviet system as the motivator behind its policies saw such a collapse as perhaps the only way to ultimately affect Soviet behavior. Pipes, for instance, argued, "The Soviet Union will be a partner in peace only when it makes peace with its own people. Only then will the danger of nuclear war recede."[44]

Clearly, there were substantial differences in the views and prescriptions of analysts who utilized the strategic intent model to infer Soviet intentions and those who used the internal logic model. These views helped shape the debates of American foreign policy, particularly after the Vietnam War, and continue to have echoes today. Some of these are evident in the way in which the intentions of Iran's leaders are debated.

THE ISLAMIC REPUBLIC OF IRAN

There has been a similar debate regarding Iran between those who use the strategic intent model to infer Iranian behavior and those who use the internal logic model. Most analysts who use the strategic intent model locate the drivers of Iran's foreign policy in a sense of insecurity among its leaders, a sense of national and cultural pride, and a sense of mission. In this view Iran is an opportunistic heir to the ancient Persian Empire, surrounded by unfriendly neighbors and motivated by an ideological zeal to achieve regional hegemony, if not export its revolution.

STRATEGIC INTENT

Many analysts who use the strategic intent model recognize that Iran is located in a region in which it is in many ways an outsider. "A Persian, Shiite nation struggling in an Arab, Sunni Middle East, Iran has always lived with the fear of being surrounded by foes."[45] Its recent history has been characterized by the intervention of external powers in its internal affairs, from the British and American support of the coup that overthrew Mosaddeq in 1953 and installed Reza Pahlavi as Shah to the diplomatic and economic sanctions leveled against it in the aftermath of the 1979 revolution. Iran has been further isolated and contained by the United States military presence in the region, from its continuous naval presence in the Persian Gulf to its forces in the Arab monarchies after Operation Desert Storm and in Afghanistan and Iraq after the invasions of 2001 and 2003. And, of course, Saddam Hussein's Iraq attacked Iran in 1980.

Analysts with this view see Iran's foreign policy as primarily driven by the insecurities of its situation but do not see their policies as benign; rather they have the flavor of a revolutionary power that desires to make its environs more congenial. Early in its history, at least through the tenure of Ayatollah Khomeini, "[t]he Islamic Republic of Iran [was] a self-professed revolutionary state...[that] rejected the status quo and deliberately incited regional instability.... Its revisionism was related to status, not land."[46] It combined a pride in its cultural heritage with a sense of aggrievement to form a positive international "manifest destiny" for itself.[47] "To this sense of nationalism and historical grievances, the mullahs added an Islamist dimension. Ayatollah Khomeini bequeathed his country an ideology that divided the world between the oppressed and the oppressors. The Islamic Republic was to be a vanguard state leading the subjugated masses toward freedom and justice.... The old balance between ideology and pragmatism has yielded to one defined by power politics and religious fervor."[48]

Along these lines Posen argued that "it is reasonable to expect that revolutionary Iran, like Iran under the Shah, has pretensions to regional hegemony."[49] Eisenstadt contended that "Iran is not pursuing nuclear weapons just to enhance its ability to deal with perceived threats. There are other powerful motives at work here, including the regime's drive for self-reliance and its desire to transform Iran into a regional power."[50] Others see this balance a bit differently, with Timmerman arguing that a "nuclear-ready Iran will not stop at violently suppressing domestic dissent, but will actively seek ways of lashing out at what it sees as the sources of that dissent: the United States and Israel."[51] Ledeen goes further, arguing that "the mullahs do not share our dreams; they dream of our destruction.... Western civilization will be consigned to the garbage heap of history by the twelfth Imam.... These are dreams of global conquest and domination."[52] Thus these analysts see a wide prism of possible Iranian behavior that can be pragmatic, opportunistic, or aggressive—but all expect it to be expansionist and motivated by the value of the stakes sought.

In this strategic narrative, Iranian leaders are seen as rational statesmen acting upon their estimates of the costs and benefits of various courses of action, be they strategic or tactical. These leaders can therefore be influenced by the actions of external actors such as the United States. As Pollack puts it,

> Our goal should be to present the Iranians with two different paths. If they choose to go down the path of confrontation—stubbornly clinging to their nuclear program, their support for terrorism, and their violent opposition to a Middle East Peace—then at each step they will be hit with progressively more painful consequences. If they choose the path of cooperation—by giving up those same patterns of behavior—then at each step they will be rewarded with progressively more advantageous benefits.[53]

Where analysts using the strategic intent model differ is their assessment of the risk attitudes among Iranian leaders. Some see Iranian leaders as risk-neutral or even risk-averse. Pollack argues that "Iran's behavior over the past fifteen years suggests that it can probably be deterred from taking the most harmful offensive actions even after it has acquired nuclear weapons.... In fact, all of the reporting... indicates that they want nuclear weapons to deter an American—or, to a lesser extent, Israeli or Iraqi—attack. Nor does the current Iranian leadership have a history of reckless behavior.... None of this makes it certain that Iran could be deterred once it acquired nuclear weapons, but all of it indicates that there is a strong basis for believing it could be."[54] Posen agrees, arguing that "the strategy of deterrence and containment has worked for the United States before; there is no reason why it cannot work again.... In a confrontation with the United States, Iran could run risks of complete destruction, and it cannot threaten the United States with comparable damage."[55] And Eisenstadt emphasizes,

> Because Shi'i religious doctrine exalts the suffering and martyrdom of the faithful, and because religion plays a central role in the official ideology of the Islamic Republic, Iran is sometimes portrayed as an "undeterrable" state driven by the absolute imperatives of religion, rather than by the pragmatic concerns of statecraft.... However, the perception of Iran as an irrational, undeterrable state with a high pain threshold is wrong. Iranian decision-makers are generally not inclined to rash action. Within the context of a relatively activist foreign and defence policy, they have generally sought to minimize risk.[56]

On the other hand, some see Iran's leaders as risk acceptant or even reckless. Rubin argues that "Tehran may not be suicidal, but it is prone to risk taking, and as a highly ideological regime that profoundly misunderstands the West, it is likely to miscalculate in ways that could lead to war.... Iran's regime is the farthest thing from a rational state that the United States has confronted since Nazi Germany."[57] A group of analysts from the Heritage Foundation concur:

> The United States' unrivalled military power would be a powerful deterrent against an Iranian direct nuclear attack, but relying on the threat of massive retaliation could be risky. The Iranian hard-liners could miscalculate and misperceive; they are profoundly ignorant about the outside world and have shown a tendency to gamble recklessly. They frequently proclaim their conviction that the United States would not or could not attack them. In addition, there are legitimate questions about whether Ahmadinejad, who reportedly harbors apocalyptic religious beliefs regarding the return of the Mahdi, or others in the Iranian regime like him would have the same cost-benefit calculus about a nuclear war that other leaders would have.[58]

INTERNAL LOGIC

Although the complex and factional nature of Iranian decision making is widely noted, those who offer an internal logic analysis of Iranian motives are few. In general, those of this view hold that the Iranian government uses foreign conflict to enhance domestic unity and support for the regime and their policies. "[T]he empirical record seems to suggest that public dissatisfaction has led to the regime exacerbating tensions with the US to distract the population's attentions from domestic political problems and demonstrate [Ahmadinejad's] revolutionary credentials," argues Graeme Davies.[59] "For self-proclaimed revolutionary regimes like Iran," writes Shahram Chubin, "foreign policy is an expression of its values and a validation of its struggle. Hence, there is an intimate connection between domestic legitimization and foreign policy conduct. Foreign policy and foreign threats are routinely invoked to control domestic politics.... Foreign policy, therefore, is at once an extension of domestic politics, an expression of the regime's identity, and a barometer of its intentions.... Regime survival, equated with [the hard-liner's] primacy, depends upon embattlement."[60] The authors of a recent RAND study agree, albeit within an elite-centric frame of reference, arguing that "leadership factions frequently wield foreign policy issues as tools to outmaneuver their rivals and form tactical alliances that will aid their domestic standing.... The actual issues debated are secondary to the larger prizes of patronage, power, and privilege."[61]

The internal logic view of Iranian conduct leads to the conclusion that its leaders are not particularly amenable to external influence. They are difficult to coerce, induce, or persuade to change their behavior—be it with regard to their nuclear program, their sponsorship of terrorist organizations throughout the region, or their conflict with Israel. The legitimacy of the regime, founded on the basis of "a transnational mission of redeeming the Middle East for the forces of righteousness" and being "a vanguard state leasing the subjugated masses toward freedom and justice," deprives their leaders of the political space necessary to comply with Western, especially American, demands.[62] "[T]he influence of powerful hard-line minorities in each country [Iran and the United States] and a number of outstanding disputes that push domestic political buttons have held back efforts at conciliation."[63] Indeed, as Pollack put it, "[t]he backing of the United States has generally proven to be the kiss of death for Iranian leaders. Khatami himself is the best proof of this: his effort to reach out to the United States early on in his presidency was a serious mistake that convinced the hard-liners that he opposed the fundamental principles of the revolution upon which their legitimacy was based."[64]

Surprisingly, however, few of these analysts offer prescriptions that derive from the internal logic framework. Pollack, for instance, treats Iran as a unitary actor when proposing a three-tiered approach of offering a grand bargain, then using carrots and sticks if that fails, and finally preparing to contain Iran indefinitely.[65] So does Takaeyh in offering his strategy of engagement.[66] Eisenstadt, on the other hand, argues for a deterrence by denial strategy that "depriv[es] Iran of the resources it could have otherwise used for a military build-up" because "regime factionalism ... could make it difficult to establish a stable deterrent relationship with a nuclear Iran."[67] And the RAND team of Wehrey et al. proposes "essentially reversing the traditional good cop/bad cop roles" of the United States and its allies, and letting the Russians and Chinese lead multilateral coercive efforts, so as to deprive Iranian factions the unifying force of a continuous American or European threat. Unlike prescriptions based on the domestic needs of Soviet leaders, this literature eschews regime change, externally assisted or not, as the best way of dealing with leaders preoccupied by their own domestic travails.[68]

PRESCRIPTIVE PROBLEMS

The strategic intent model and the internal logic model of adversary intent produce very different pictures of what motivates adversary. Do they desire to influence external actors so as to achieve a political outcome vis-à-vis that actor? Or do they desire to bolster their domestic solidarity in the face of centrifugal forces? Is the outcome of the action that we wish to deter of primary or secondary importance to adversary? Making this determination is important when deciding whether to attempt to deter the adversary's actions or to take another approach, such as preemptive brute force or actions to increase or decrease the adversary's feelings of insecurity.

Deterrence is a strategy to pursue when one judges that the adversary's intended action is motivated primarily by strategic goals. Given that this strategy is directed toward external actors in such situations, identification of the adversary's goal is a matter of routine. Focusing deterrent demands toward that objective—"don't do *that*"—places the adversary in a decision situation in which it can either comply with what has been demanded of it, or defy those demands and risk the implementation of the deterrer's threatened sanction. As the *DO JOC* rightly suggests, denying the adversary's leadership the potential benefits of the actions that it intends to take and imposing costs that reduce the net utility of the action are the two ideal ways of reducing the likelihood that the adversary will choose to act.[69] The objective of this deterrent threat is to reduce the expected value of "doing that" to a point that the consequences of compliance are of greater value. As the *DO JOC* explains, "[A]dversaries weigh the perceived benefits and costs of a given course of action in the context of their perceived consequences of restraint or inaction. Thus deterrence can fail even when the adversary perceives the costs of acting as outweighing the benefits of acting if he believes the costs of inaction are even higher still."[70] When the adversary is basing his choice upon these considerations, deterrence is correctly targeted and has a chance of success.

Deterrence may not be the strategy to pursue if the adversary's external behavior is directed toward enhancing internal cohesion or the power of the leadership. Providing overt signs of an external threat is precisely the outcome desired by the adversary's leadership. A threat from an external actor allows them to take actions to increase their support, silence moderates or critics, mobilize resources that might otherwise be unavailable, and provides the opportunity for common in-group identities to be forged or reinforced. These goals can be achieved only if the deterrer provides the missing ingredient: its hostile reaction. If the deterrer falls into the trap, then the adversary has the means its needs to achieve its goal of increased cohesion. If the deterrer refrains from reacting, then the adversary may still capitalize on the lack of a reaction to motivate support for strong leadership. Yet this is less likely than action provoking hostility, as people are less motivated to act to seize opportunities than they are to avoid potential losses.[71]

DETERRING ADVERSARIES MOTIVATED BY INTERNAL LOGIC

If the adversary is motivated by internal logic, is it really a no-win situation for the deterrer? Is deterrence a nonstarter? Are there alternatives to issuing an immediate deterrent threat directed against their intended external action or doing nothing and letting the adversaries' provocation pass unanswered? There are a number of options.

First, one can still attempt to deter the adversary directly through passive measures that deny them the opportunity to carry out their intended action and also deny them the visible indicators of hostility that they seek to engender. There are a number of means that can be used to do this. One denial measure is to harden soft targets, for example police stations, through passive point defenses. This makes it less likely that spectacular successes can be had against these targets, and given their passivity—barriers, reinforced concrete, or even ballistic missile defenses (provided that they are well beyond the ability of the adversary to observe)—they deprive the deterrer of the ability to overreact and justify the adversary's actions.[72] Passive area defenses can also be used to deny the adversary the interaction that they need with the deterrer to achieve its internal goals. Possibilities in this realm include measures such as the fence that Israel has erected around Palestinian areas, which have decreased suicide attacks substantially since its completion,[73] or diplomatic isolation such as that imposed on the People's Republic of China, Cuba, or Iran after their revolutions. A potential drawback to passive area defenses is that they themselves might become symbols of implacable and unyielding hostility that the adversary can use repeatedly to rally their domestic constituents.[74]

Second, one can attempt to deter adversary indirectly—by directing the deterrent threat toward the members of the group that the leadership is attempting to bolster or recruit from. The adversary's external challenge is designed to attract these followers, and a deterrent threat that is directed toward the group's members and potential members may cleave them away by highlighting personal over group interests.[75] All groups engaged in conflict that are attempting to recruit or retain members ask these people to put aside their personal interests for the benefit of the group's cause, even though their individual contributions will be marginal (in most cases, suicide terrorism is designed to overcome this recruitment challenge). "Thus rebels confront the possibility of disastrous private costs and uncertain public benefits.... Unless the collective action problem is somehow overcome, rational people will never rebel—rebellions, that is, require irrationality."[76] Israel has pursued a policy of deterring group members by threatening to destroy the family homes of young Palestinians who were involved in attacks.[77] Aerial surveillance capabilities, such as that of the Predator unmanned aerial vehicle, have been key to operationalizing this strategy. Such an option would be an attempt to deny adversary leaders the domestic benefits of intended action by threatening to punish individual members of the group.

Third, one can pursue a similar goal but through inducements to members of the adversary's constituency rather than through coercion. COIN strategies, such as those discussed in FM 3–24 *Counterinsurgency*, work on this principle. "The real battle is for civilian support for, or acquiescence to, the counterinsurgents and host nation government. The population waits to be convinced. Who will help them more, hurt them less, stay the longest, earn their trust?"[78] Indeed, the "Anbar Awakening" in Iraq is quite a vivid example of using inducements to cleave potential supporters away from an adversary—in this case al Qaeda in Iraq.[79]

Fourth, one can attempt to "encourage adversary restraint," as the *DO JOC* puts it, by "try[ing] to communicate...benign intentions...to reduce the fear, misunderstanding, and insecurity that are often responsible for unintended escalation to war."[80] Engaging in such persuasion is an alternative to influence through coercion or inducement. It involves altering the considerations by which compliance and defiance are evaluated. The persuader does not promise or threaten action, but convinces the adversary to see the situation in such a way that they realize that it is in their own interests to act in a certain way. This can be done by highlighting—without altering—costs or benefits related to complying with or defying the persuader's demands or by offering new alternatives that allow the adversary to achieve their goals in ways that do not harm the persuader's interests. These persuasion strategies treat the definition of the problem facing the adversary—in this case increasing cohesion, recruitment, or retention of members—as given or settled. Another avenue of persuasion requires understanding the basis upon which the target frames the issue and shifting it.[81] Persuasion is generally seen as a fruitless option, particularly when dealing with an adversary whose primary concerns are internally generated or have revolutionary orientations.

Fifth, one can forego influence altogether and use brute force against adversary to prevent them from undertaking action.[82] This can take the form of disarming the adversary to deny them the capability to pursue the action that they intend or decapitating them so as to disrupt their ability to act. Either action risks increasing the cohesion of the adversary by justifying their hostility toward the deterrer or creating a martyr of the leadership. Decapitation of the leadership could also disrupt the internal cohesion of the adversary to some degree.[83]

Overall, if it is determined that an adversary decision maker is motivated by the internal logic of his group's situation, deterrence may work–but not in the manner prescribed in the *DO JOC*. Rather, deterrent demands and other influence attempts should be directed at the primary objectives of the adversary in these situations: the internal constituencies whose support the leadership hopes to rally by its external actions. Clearly, actions should also be taken to mitigate the impact of those actions as well, since nothing fails like failure, but it should be borne in mind that mere signals of hostility directed toward the group (or nation) as a whole in an attempt to deter the unwanted action could provide the adversary leader precisely what he or she wants: an external enemy that his or her people can oppose in unity.

CONCLUSION

How should policy makers approach divining the intentions of revolutionary rogues who may take actions that the United States wishes to deter? Although deterrence formed the core mission of the American military throughout the Cold War, adversary intent was based on capabilities analysis married to worst-case scenarios of what they could accomplish. Whether deterrence would succeed in general or in any particular case was likewise inferred to be a function of American capabilities and willingness to use them in the event that deterrence failed. The consequences that would befall adversary if deterrence succeeded in frustrating their objectives were rarely considered.

The *DO JOC* rectified a basic problem in previous deterrence thinking by recognizing that an adversary has a choice between complying with a demand to refrain from action and defying that demand—and that the adversary will consider the expected value of each of these options. No longer is "restraint" considered to be an option that is outside the deterrence calculus for the adversary or the deterrer. This has opened significant doors to making the deterrence planning and assessment processes used by the US military, from Strategic Command to the regional combatant commands, much more sophisticated and, hopefully, effective.

Getting the basic framework correct has led to the next issue: determining how much the adversary desire to undertake particular actions, those that the United States would prefer that they not undertake, and others that might provide less offensive alternatives. This requires assessing adversary intent. Regrettably, there is no set process or framework for undertaking this necessary analysis. US joint military doctrine merely exhorts intelligence analysts to "take risks" to "predict" adversary intent. Intelligence officers, uniformed and civilian, have indicated that producing such analyses is considered more of an art than a science and that no processes have been established; rather, intelligence analysts are left to develop their own methods to produce their analytic products.[84] Hoping that particular analysts in key positions are da Vincis or Michelangelos is simply unacceptable. Military staffs excel at planning and use set processes to yield acceptable and improvable products. Such a process needs to be established to infer adversary intent on a continuous basis so that a usable product is available to assist in routine planning or in the event of a crisis.

Such a process should begin with a skeleton framework that focuses on producing at least two narratives of adversary behavior: a strategic intent model and an internal logic model. The strategic intent narrative would build a case that the adversary was intending to act to achieve external goals. It should begin with an overview of the grand strategy of the adversary: the goals that their leadership has traditionally sought, the goals sought by their current leadership, the environment in which they find themselves and how it facilitates or hinders pursuit of those goals, and the capabilities in their possession to overcome these obstacles and take advantage of situations as they arise. The narrative should also locate the adversary's potential actions in their strategic culture and operational procedures so that indicators and warnings can be identified to provide information about intent as events unfold.

The internal logic narrative would build a similar case to explain what adversary might intend to do, but its focus would be on the internal or domestic imperatives and constraints facing adversary leaders. Such a narrative would begin by identifying the structure of the leadership, those who hold those positions, and their relations to one another. It would also identify various internal constituencies upon whom the leadership is dependent or responsible, in particular those who are in a position to sanction or reward those leaders given their behavior. Finally, it would attempt to identify the internal problem that the adversary leaders would attempt to solve by acting externally. As with the strategic intent model, indicators and warnings keyed to the reactions of these domestic constituencies should be constructed to provide information that can confirm or invalidate hypotheses about the adversary's intent as events unfold.

As I have discussed in the preceding sections, these two frameworks have provided the basis for rival interpretations of adversary behavior from that of the Soviet Union during the Cold War to Iran today. They have also provided alternative prescriptions for American behavior. Their explicit use would allow debate and discussion in the intent assessment process that could inform a commander or political leader about the issues, foreign and domestic, that are pressing on adversary's leaders, provide the commander's planning staff the basis for recommending whether deterrence or some other strategy is wise in the present circumstances, and also provide a basis upon which to assess the likelihood of success. Prescribing that at least two frameworks be used, rather than a single consolidated one, will assist in highlighting the biases inherent in each framework as well as those introduced by the analysts themselves and mitigate the dangers of groupthink.[85] This would greatly enhance the ability of commanders to determine when deterrence was wise, and necessary, and how to best implement it.

NOTES

1. Henry A. Kissinger, *A World Restored: The Politics of Conservatism in a Revolutionary Age* (New York: Grossett and Dunlap, 1964), 2.
2. See Henry A. Kissinger, *Nuclear Weapons And Foreign Policy* (New York: Harper & Brothers, 1957), 316–324; Hans J. Morgenthau, *Politics Among Nations: the Struggle for Power and Peace*, 5th rev. ed. (New York: Alfred A. Knopf, 1978), 57–67; Robert Gilpin, *War and Change in World Politics* (Cambridge: Cambridge University Press, 1981); Randall L. Schweller, "Bandwagoning for Profit: Bringing the Revisionist State Back In," *International Security* 19, no. 1 (Summer 1994); Randall L. Schweller, "Neorealism's Status Quo Bias: What Security Dilemma?" in *Realism: Restatements and Renewal*, ed. Benjamin Frankel (London: Frank Cass, 1996); and Robert S. Snyder, "The US and Third World Revolutionary States: Understanding the Breakdown in Relations," *International Studies Quarterly* 43, no. 2 (June 1999).
3. Indeed, as Bernard Brodie famously put it, "Thus far the chief purpose of our military establishment has been to win wars. From now on its chief purpose must be to avert them. It can have almost no other useful purpose." Bernard Brodie, "Implications for Military Policy," in *The Absolute Weapon: Atomic Power and World Order*, ed. Bernard Brodie (New York: Harcourt, Brace and Company, 1946), 76.
4. See, for example, William W. Kaufmann, "The Requirements of Deterrence," in *Military Policy and National Security*, ed. William W. Kaufmann (Port Washington: Kennikat Press, 1956); Alexander George and Richard Smoke, *Deterrence in American Foreign Policy: Theory and Practice* (New York: Columbia University Press, 1974); and Paul Huth and Bruce Russett, "What Makes Deterrence Work? Cases From 1900 to 1980," *World Politics* 36, no. 4 (July 1984).
5. For a discussion of the constituents of credibility, see Daryl G. Press, *Calculating Credibility: How Leaders Assess Military Threats* (Ithaca, NY: Cornell University Press, 2005).
6. Previous official conceptions of deterrence have been underdeveloped. *Joint Publication 1–02, Department of Defense Dictionary of Military and Associated*

Terms, as well as its predecessor, *JCS Publication 1, Dictionary of United States Military Terms for Joint Usage*, defines deterrence as "the prevention from action by fear of the consequences. Deterrence is a state of mind brought about by the existence of a credible threat of unacceptable counter action." This definition does not specify the relationship between "fear" and reasoned consideration of consequences, the nature of the "credible threat of unacceptable counter action," or its origin. It also reflects and encourages considering deterrence only in the nuclear context. As late as January 2007, the US Air Force, for example, subsumed deterrence under nuclear operations. Air Force Doctrine Document 1–2, Air Force Glossary, only mentions deterrence in its definition of "mutual assured destruction," Air Force Doctrine Document 1–2, Air Force Glossary (Maxwell AFB, AL: USAF Doctrine Center, January 11, 2007), 58.

7. *Deterrence Operations Joint Operating Concept, Version 2.0* (December 2006), 3. Hereafter *DO JOC*.
8. *DO JOC*, 6.
9. Patrick Morgan, *Deterrence*, Second Edition (Beverly Hills: Sage Publications, 1983), 39.
10. Roberta Wohlstetter, "Cuba and Pearl Harbor: Hindsight and Foresight," *Foreign Affairs* 43, no. 4 (July 1965): 691.
11. Herbert A. Simon, *Administrative Behavior: A Study of Decision-Making Process in Administrative Organization*, 3rd ed. (New York: The Free Press. 1945/1976), xxix.
12. Ibid., xxx.
13. Any framework that simplifies reality will not be neutral. It will bias the decision maker's observations and inferences. It will therefore result in at least some misperceptions. See Robert Jervis, *Perception and Misperception in International Politics* (Princeton, NJ: Princeton University Press, 1976). Although Jervis and others make the case that misperceptions inherently undermine the quality of decision making, this is not necessarily the case, as argued by Jack S. Levy, "Misperception and the Causes of War: Theoretical Linkages and Analytical Problems," *World Politics* 36, no. 1 (October 1983); Gerd Grigerenzer and Daniel G. Goldstein, "Reasoning the Fast and Frugal Way: Models of Bounded Rationality," *Psychological Review* 103, no. 4 (1996); and J. M. Goldgeier and P. E. Tetlock, "Psychology and International Relations Theory," *Annual Review of Political Science*, ed. Nelson W. Polsby, 4 (2001).
14. Graham T. Allison, *Essence of Decision: Explaining the Cuban Missile Crisis* (Boston: Little, Brown and Company, 1971), 35.
15. Ibid., 36–37.
16. For the relations between these forms of influence, see the *Strategic Communication Joint Integrating Concept, v 0.5* (April 25, 2008), 101–103.
17. Lawrence Freedman, "Strategic Coercion," in *Strategic Coercion: Concepts and Cases*, ed. Lawrence Freedman (New York: Oxford University Press, 1998), xx.

18. The lack of domestic level independent variables is considered in Gary Schaub Jr., "Deterrence, Compellence, and Rational Decision Making" (PhD diss., University of Pittsburgh, 2003).
19. Jack S. Levy, "The Diversionary Theory of War: A Critique," in *The Handbook Of War Studies*, ed. Manus I. Midlarsky (Boston: Unwin Hyman, 1989), 259.
20. Richard Ned Lebow, *Between Peace and War: The Nature of International Crisis* (Baltimore: The John Hopkins University Press, 1981), 66–69.
21. For an overly abstract discussion of these variables, see Bruce Bueno de Mesquita, Alastair Smith, Randolph M. Siverson, and James D. Morrow, *The Logic of Political Survival* (Cambridge, MA: MIT Press, 2003).
22. For a recent study, see David J. Bulé, "Congress, Presidential Approval, and US Dispute Initiation," *Foreign Policy Analysis* 4, no. 4 (October 2008).
23. Rather their work is seen as providing an alternative to deterrence theory. See Richard Ned Lebow and Janice Gross Stein, "Beyond Deterrence," *Journal of Social Issues* 43, no. 4 (1987); Richard Ned Lebow and Janice Gross Stein, "Rational Deterrence Theory: I Think, Therefore I Deter," *World Politics* 41, no. 2 (January 1989); Paul Huth and Bruce M. Russett, "Testing Deterrence Theory: Rigor Makes A Difference," *World Politics* 42, no. 4 (July 1990); and Richard Ned Lebow and Janice Gross Stein, "Deterrence: The Elusive Dependent Variable," *World Politics* 42, no. 3 (April 1990).
24. Douglas Seay, "What Are the Soviets' Objectives in Their Foreign, Military, and Arms Control Policies?" in *Nuclear Arguments: Understanding the Strategic Nuclear Arms and Arms Control Debates*, ed. Lynn Eden and Steven E. Miller (Ithaca, NY: Cornell University Press, 1989), 71.
25. Ibid., 72.
26. George F. Kennan, "Toward Peace on Two Fronts," *Christianity and Crisis* (December 13, 1982), 378.
27. Paul C. Warnke, "Apes on a Treadmilll," *Foreign Policy* 18 (Spring 1975); and Seay, "What are the Soviets' Objectives?" 76–87.
28. Henry A. Kissinger, *White House Years* (Boston: Little, Brown, and Company, 1979), 118. "The result is a foreign policy free to fill every vacuum, to exploit every opportunity, to act out the implications of its doctrine. Policy is constrained principally by calculations of objective conditions," 117.
29. Dmitri K. Simes, "Assessing Soviet National Security Strategy," in *Understanding US Strategy: A Reader*, ed. Terry L. Heynes (Washington, DC: National Defense University Press, 1983), 210–212.
30. George F. Kennan, "The Sources of Soviet Conduct," *Foreign Affairs* 65, no. 4 (Spring 1987): 861.
31. Kissinger, *White House Years*, 119.
32. Kennan, "Sources of Soviet Conduct," 861.
33. Kissinger, *White House Years*, 119.
34. Kennan, "Sources of Soviet Conduct," 860–861.

35. Ibid., 861. Here Kennan was elaborating on Lenin's dictum: if one encounters steel, withdraw; but if one finds mush, push on.
36. Bernard Brodie, "The Atom Bomb as Policy Maker," *Foreign Affairs* 27, no. 1 (October 1948): 23. Also see Raymond L. Garthoff, *Soviet Military Doctrine* (New York: The Free Press, 1953), 11; and William W. Kaufmann, "Limited Warfare," in *Military Policy and National Security*, ed. William W. Kaufmann (Port Washington: Kennikat Press, 1956), 103.
37. Kennan, "Sources of Soviet Conduct," 856–857.
38. See Richard Pipes, "Militarism and the Soviet State," *Daedalus* 109 (Fall 1980); Richard Pipes, *Survival Is Not Enough: Soviet Realities and America's Future* (New York: Simon and Schuster, 1984); Colin S. Gray, "SALT II: The Real Debate," *Policy Review*, 10 (Fall 1979); Colin S. Gray, *Missiles Against War: The ICBM Debate Today* (Fairfax, VA: National Institute for Public Policy, 1985); and William E. Odom, "Whither the Soviet Union?" *The Washington Quarterly*, 4 (Spring 1981).
39. Seay, "What are the Soviets' Objectives?" 54; and Richard Pipes, "Militarism and the Soviet State," 1.
40. Seay, "What are the Soviets' Objectives?" 55.
41. Ibid.
42. "Both Nitze and Gray have in mind using the perceived advantages of SDI to push the Soviet Union toward a reformulation of deterrence, from an offense-based MAD to a deterrence based upon defensive systems." Seay, "What Are the Soviets' Objectives?" 69–70.
43. Kennan, "Sources of Soviet Conduct," 868, 866.
44. Pipes, *Survival Is Not Enough*, 278.
45. Ray Takeyh, *Guardians of the Revolution: Iran and the World in the Age of the Ayatollahs* (New York: Oxford University Press, 2009), 1–2. Also see Barry R. Posen, *A Nuclear-Armed Iran: A Difficult but not Impossible Policy Problem. A Century Foundation Report* (New York: The Century Foundation, 2006), 9; and Gregory F. Giles, "The Crucible of Radical Islam: Iran's Leaders and Strategic Culture," in *Know thy Enemy: Profiles of Adversary Leaders and Their Strategic Cultures*, 2nd ed., ed. Barry R. Schneider and Jerrold M. Post (Maxwell AFB, AL: USAF Counterproliferation Center, July 2003), 146.
46. Daniel Byman, Shahram Chubin, Anoushiravan Ehteshami, and Jerrold Green, *Iran's Security Policy in the Post Revolutionary Era* (Santa Monica, CA: RAND, 2001), 8. Also see Michael Eisenstadt, "Living with a Nuclear Iran?" *Survival* 41, no. 3 (Autumn 1999): 125.
47. Giles, "The Crucible of Radical Islam," 146.
48. Takeyh, *Guardians of the Revolution*, 2, 6. Also see Frederick Wehrey, David E. Thaler, Nora Bensahel, Kim Cragin, Jerrold D. Green, Dalia Dassa Kaye, Nadia Oweidat, and Jennifer Li, *Dangerous But Not Omnipotent: Exploring the Reach and Limitations of Iranian Power in the Middle East* (Santa Monica: RAND Corporation, 2009), 9.
49. Posen, *A Nuclear-Armed Iran*, 8.

50. Eisenstadt, "Living with a Nuclear Iran?" 129.
51. Kenneth R. Timmerman, "The Day After Iran Gets the Bomb," in *Getting Ready for a Nuclear-Ready Iran*, ed. Henry Sokolski and Patrick Lawson (Carlisle, PA: Strategic Studies Institute, US Army War College, October 2005), 121.
52. Michael A. Ledeen, *The Iranian Time Bomb: The Mullah Zealots' Quest for Destruction* (New York: Truman Talley Books of St. Martin's Press, 2007), 24–25.
53. Kenneth M. Pollack, *The Persian Puzzle: The Conflict between Iran and America* (New York: Random House, 2004), 406.
54. Ibid., 384–385.
55. Posen, *A Nuclear-Armed Iran*, 24.
56. Eisenstadt, "Living with a Nuclear Iran?" 134–135. Also see Michael Eisenstadt, "Deter and Contain: Dealing with a Nuclear Iran," in *Getting Ready for a Nuclear-Ready Iran*, ed. Henry Sokolski and Patrick Lawson (Carlisle, PA: Strategic Studies Institute, US Army War College, October 2005).
57. Barry Rubin, "The Containment Conundrum: How Dangerous is a Nuclear Iran? The Right Kind of Containment," *Foreign Affairs* 89, no. 4 (July-August 2010): 164.
58. Ilan I. Berman, Peter Brooks, Patrick Clawson, Mackenzie M. Eaglen, James Phillips, Baker Spring, Owen Graham, and Eric Sayers, "Iran's Nuclear Threat: The Day After," Heritage Foundation Special Report No. 53, June 4, 2009, 2.
59. Graeme A. M. Davies, "Inside Out or Outside In: Domestic and International Factors Affecting Iranian Foreign Policy Towards The United States 1990–2004," *Foreign Policy Analysis* 4, no. 3 (July 2008): 213. It should be noted that Davies's analysis of dyadic event data from 1990–2004 "suggests that the Iranians tend not to engage in diversionary hostility; rather they encapsulate their problems and avoid confrontation with the United States. The model indicates that the greater the level of domestic conflict within Iran the more cooperative the Iranians become toward the United States," 220, 221–222).
60. Shahram Chubin, "The Iranian Nuclear Riddle after June 12," *The Washington Quarterly* 33, no. 1 (January 2010): 165.
61. Frederick Wehrey, David E. Thaler, Nora Bensahel, Kim Cragin, Jerrold D. Green, Dalia Dassa Kaye, Nadia Oweidat, and Jennifer Li, *Dangerous But Not Omnipotent: Exploring the Reach and Limitations of Iranian Power in the Middle East* (Santa Monica, CA: RAND Corporation, 2009), 22. Also see Eisenstadt, "Living with a Nuclear Iran?" 131.
62. Takeyh, *Guardians of the Revolution*, 2.
63. Jahangir Amuzegar, "Iran's Crumbling Revolution," *Foreign Affairs* 82, no. 1 (January/February 2003): 45.
64. Pollack, *The Persian Puzzle*, 388.

65. Ibid., 400–416. "If the Iranians can ever get over their psychological and political hurdles regarding the United States, the Grand Bargain would be the best way to handle our mutual problems," he begins.
66. Takeyh, *Guardians of the Revolution*, 261–265.
67. Eisenstadt, "Living with a Nuclear Iran?" 142, 136.
68. Those who do advocate regime change, such as Timmerman and Ledeen, base their analyses upon the strategic intent model and posit extreme goals for Iran.
69. *DO JOC*, 26–27.
70. *DO JOC*, 21, emphasis in original.
71. On the differential weighting of gains and losses generally, see Daniel Kahneman, Jack L. Knetsch, and Richard H. Thaler, "Anomalies: The Endowment Effect, Loss Aversion, and Status Quo Bias," *Journal of Economic Perspectives* 5, no. 1 (Winter 1991). For an application to the domestic costs of conflict, see Miroslav Nincic, "Loss Aversion and the Domestic Context of Military Intervention," *Political Research Quarterly* 50, no. 1 (March 1997).
72. This is an application of Schelling's art of the commitment. See Thomas C. Schelling, *The Strategy of Conflict* (New Haven, CT: Harvard University Press, 1960).
73. Daniel Byman, "Do Targeted Killings Work?" *Foreign Affairs* 85, no. 2 (March/April 2006): 96, 105–106.
74. Matthew Kalman, "Israeli Fence Puts 'Cage' on Villagers: More Palestinians Scrambling to Keep Barrier from Going Up," *San Francisco Chronicle*, March 9, 2004, http://www.sfgate.com/cgi-bin/article.cgi?file=/chronicle/archive/2004/03/09/MNGIP5H0IL1.DTL.
75. See Julian Tolbert, *Crony Attack: Strategic Attack's Silver Bullet?* (Maxwell AFB, AL: School of Advanced Air and Space Studies, 2003); and Mark Irving Lichbach, *The Rebel's Dilemma* (Ann Arbor, MI: University of Michigan Press, 1998). On the other hand, Jerrold Post argues, "Once in the group, though, the power of group dynamics is immense, continually confirming the power of the group's organizing ideology and reinforcing the member's dedication to the cause." Jerrold M. Post, "Deterrence in an Age of Asymmetric Rivals," in *Understanding the Bush Doctrine: Psychology and Strategy in an Age of Terrorism*, ed. Stanley A. Renshon and Peter Suedfeld (New York: Routledge, 2007), 171.
76. Lichbach, *The Rebel's Dilemma*, 7.
77. "Israeli officials said that the destruction of an Arab home with dynamite or bulldozers was a rare, deliberate, and highly publicized event, designed to serve as an effective deterrent to adults who might permit or encourage illegal acts by younger members of their families." Jimmy Carter, *Palestine: Peace, Not Apartheid* (New York: Simon and Schuster, 2006), 123. Israel stopped this policy in February 2005 after it was challenged domestically by human rights groups. BBC News, "Israel to Destroy Attacker's Home," July 4, 2008, http://news.bbc.co.uk/go/pr/fr/-/2/hi/middle_east/7490212.stm.

78. Sarah Sewall, "Introduction to the University of Chicago Press Edition: A Radical Field Manual," in *The US Army/Marine Corps Counterinsurgency Field Manual* (Chicago: University of Chicago Press, 2007), XXV.
79. A nice account can be found in Thomas Ricks, *The Gamble: General David Petraeus and the American Military Adventure in Iraq, 2006–2008* (New York: Penguin Press, 2009), 61–72. For an analysis see Andrew W. Koloski and John S. Kolasheski, "Thickening the Lines: Sons of Iraq, A Combat Multiplier," *Military Review* 89 (January-February 2009).
80. Richard Ned Lebow and Janice Gross Stein, "Beyond Deterrence," *Journal of Social Issues* 43, no. 4 (1987): 40.
81. There are generally three such bases: consequentialism, authority, or principles. Consequentialism is the easiest basis within which to operate as the adversary is considering outcomes, and these bases are all potential as opposed to actual. They can therefore be altered by shifting the type of problem to be solved, and hence the solution set from which it is appropriate to consider options. Authority-based frames are more difficult to affect because they are given to the adversary by another party, one to which the adversary have previously ceded decision authority. Thus a better target for the influence attempt is that entity. But another approach here is to provide the adversary with another authority to which they have previously ceded the decision, one that conflicts with the current authority frame, and make the case that they should switch. Finally, frames based on principle are likewise difficult to affect, although the mechanism is similar: find a principle to which the adversary adhere and make the case that they apply more than the principle that provided the basis for defiance.
82. Jones and Libicki find that only 7 percent of terrorist groups that "ended" in their sample of 268 such groups were defeated by military force. "Militaries tended to be most effective when used against terrorist groups engaged in an insurgency in which the groups were large, well armed, and well organized. Insurgent groups have been among the most capable and lethal terrorist groups, and military force has usually been a necessary component in such cases. Against most terrorist groups, however, military force is usually too blunt an instrument." Seth G. Jones and Martin C. Libicki, *How Terrorist Groups End: Lessons for Countering al Qa'ida* (Santa Monica, CA: RAND Corporation, 2008), xiii–xiv.
83. Lisa Langdon, Alexander J. Sarapu, and Matthew Wells, "Targeting the Leadership of Terrorist and Insurgent Movements: Historical Lessons for Contemporary Policy Makers," *Journal of Public and International Affairs*, 15 (Spring 2004), found that killing the leader of a nonstate movement led to the disbanding or moderation of the movement in 61 percent of the cases that they examined.
84. Personal interviews with the author.
85. For more on motivated and unmotivated biases see Jervis, *Perception and Misperception in International Politics*. On groupthink see Irving L. Janis, *Groupthink: Psychological Studies of Policy Decisions and Fiascoes* (Boston:

Houghton Mifflin, 1982); and Marlene E. Turner and Anthony R. Pratkanis, "Theoretical Perspectives on Groupthink: A Twenty-Fifth Anniversary Appraisal," *Organizational Behavior and Human Decision Processes* 73, no. 2/3 (February/March 1998). Alexander L. George prescribes multiple assessments and other process fixes to this dilemma in "The Case for Multiple Advocacy in Making Foreign Policy," *American Political Science Review* 66, no. 3 (September 1972), as does Paul Hart, in "Preventing Groupthink Revisited: Evaluating and Reforming Groups in Government," *Organizational Behavior and Human Decision Processes* 73, no. 2/3 (February/March 1998).

CHAPTER 9

How Can the United States Deter Nonstate Actors?

Adam B. Lowther

In the aftermath of World War II, the United States took center stage in an international system dramatically different from the one that existed a decade earlier. As the Cold War took shape in the late 1940s, the United States played the protagonist to a Soviet Union seeking to export communism around the world. One school of thought regarding US foreign policy holds that Americans traditionally prefer to remain aloof from international politics.[1] In the twentieth century, US policy makers repeatedly departed from this perspective—by participating in both world wars and the Korean War and by taking the lead to form the United Nations and the North Atlantic Treaty Organization—to pursue and protect the country's interests. As the expansionist ideology of the Soviet Union, armed with the atom bomb, threatened to overwhelm the free world during the Cold War, American policy makers developed a grand strategy for containing the Soviet Union that ultimately succeeded.[2]

Among the most important of these early strategies was deterrence. In the early years of the Cold War, the Eisenhower administration's New Look Policy focused on deterring the Soviet Union by threatening to launch a massive nuclear strike in response to conventional or nuclear aggression.[3] Although deterrence and nuclear weapons need not be coupled, they became inextricably linked for more than half a century.

As the Cold War came to an end after nearly half a century, deterrence fell by the wayside as the United States sought to take advantage of the peace dividend that was the fruit of victory.[4] In the 1990s, deterrence was supplemented by a strategy of globalization and a policy of engagement with the world. No longer did the United States simply seek to prevent the spread of communism. It also sought to assist former Eastern Bloc countries as they attempted to develop market economies and democratic institutions. This approach to the world saw the United States take on the role of world policeman, as it made the world safe for democracy by addressing threats to international order.[5]

Lasting less than a decade, the relative tranquility of America's "hegemonic moment" was shattered by the attacks of September 11, 2001. Although the United States was well aware of al Qaeda's desire to strike a painful blow, as the amorphous organization attempted on at least five previous occasions, the use of commercial aircraft as missiles to strike the US homeland caught the nation off guard.[6] Where America's previous responses to al Qaeda attacks were largely ineffective, a new president and an enraged public would bring the full might of the American military to bear in Afghanistan and anywhere else al Qaeda and its affiliates might seek refuge. The "global war on terror" had begun.[7]

Within the United States, this new approach to terrorism signaled a dramatic shift in the balance of power within the international relations liberalism school of thought. Throughout the 1990s, a war of words filled the pages of Beltway publications as the two factions—economic globalists and neoconservatives—fought for supremacy.[8] Advocates of economic globalization came to dominate public policy and succeeded in keeping their ideological competitors from ascending to power in the federal bureaucracy. This changed with the 2000 election and the victory of neoconservatism. Where economic globalists sought to remake world order through the largely peaceful development of social-market democracy and international institutions, neoconservatives believed in the utility of force to achieve similar objectives.[9] Preemption and a concerted effort to impose democracy in strategic regions became the underlying initiatives of the post-9/11 Bush administration.[10] Conspicuously absent from any position of prominence in the debate were the realists, who had dominated foreign policy decision making throughout the Cold War, but this, too, would eventually change.

On October 7, 2001, the United States invaded Afghanistan. Early success had been followed by a persistent and growing Taliban insurgency. Thus, few were surprised when former NATO commander in Afghanistan, Gen. Stanley McChrystal, wrote of the urgent need for more troops to secure victory. US operations in Iraq turned out very differently and appeared to indicate the emergence of a stable government. Some analysts are concerned, however, that opponents of the regime are biding their time as the Americans withdraw forces from the country.[11] Only time will tell if Iraq was a victory.

Whatever the final outcome of these two conflicts may eventually be, they had a profound effect on the 2008 US presidential election. After eight years of conflict, war fatigue was apparent during the campaign—Americans wanted change. That change came in the form of Senator Barack Obama (D-IL) and a Democrat majority in both houses of Congress. With his election as president, it became clear that US foreign policy would take a new approach. It was from this milieu that an emphasis on deterrence reemerged. It did so, however, in a world much different from the one in which it once held sway. Rather than facing a peer competitor in a bipolar international system, the primary security challenges that the United States appears to confront in a post-9/11 security environment come in the form of nonstate actors.

Although post–World War II deterrence strategy was designed to deter a Soviet nuclear attack, today's scholars and policy makers are asking if deterrence can be applied against the nation's current adversaries.[12] This chapter seeks to examine that possibility by addressing five central questions:

1. What is deterrence?
2. What is a nonstate actor?
3. Do nonstate actors pose a threat to the United States?
4. Is it possible to deter a nonstate actor?
5. How do you deter nonstate actors?

WHAT IS DETERRENCE?

According to Joint Publication 1–02, *Department of Defense Dictionary of Military and Associated Terms*, deterrence is the "prevention from action by fear of the consequences. Deterrence is a state of mind brought about by the existence of a credible threat of unacceptable counteraction." By design, deterrence aims to achieve a specific psychological effect that causes an adversary to alter potential behavior. Since deterrence comprises two components—capability and credibility—its success or failure is based on the ability of A to convince B that altering the status quo presents risks that outweigh potential benefits.

Although deterrence and nuclear weapons have been closely linked for half a century, the concept of deterrence is far older than its modern understanding. The history of mankind is replete with examples of individuals, tribes, empires, and states using deterrence to dissuade adversaries from taking an undesired action.[13] One familiar example is worth noting.

After the Congress of Vienna (1814–1815), Great Britain served as the balancer in Europe by ensuring that neither a Franco-Russian alliance nor the German states and Austria-Hungary were able to dominate the Continent. By siding with the weaker alliance, Britain sought to deter the stronger.[14] This is only one of many examples of deterrence at work. As historians will certainly note, the Concert of Europe ultimately failed with the outbreak of World War I—after nearly a century of relative stability on the Continent. Like all approaches to foreign policy, deterrence does not guarantee permanent peace. The relevant point is that deterrence may be applied against actors at any level of analysis (individual, domestic, or international).

One recent effort to revitalize deterrence is the US Strategic Command's (STRATCOM) *Deterrence Operations Joint Operating Concept* (*DO JOC*), which clearly illustrates that the US military is not "stuck in a Cold War mindset."[15] The *DO JOC* is a clear sign that STRATCOM and the DOD understand the changing nature of the strategic environment and the need to evolve deterrence strategy. The document exemplifies the collaboration taking place between academia and the military as the two work together to develop a broader approach to nuclear and conventional deterrence in a world that is no longer dominated by the bipolar competition of the United States and the Soviet Union. In attempting to develop an approach to deterrence that incorporates the range of conventional and nuclear threats, the authors of the *DO JOC* have undertaken a very difficult task.

While somewhat different than the approach used in the *DO JOC*, one way of conceptualizing deterrence is to think of it as a continuous spectrum with three components. At one end is deterrence by dissuasion.[16] At the other end is deterrence by threat.[17] In the middle is deterrence by denial.[18] Moving from left to right increases the level of action by the state seeking to deter an ally or adversary. The specific design of a deterrence strategy will depend on the value of the interest at stake and the capabilities of both A and B. Because the target of deterrence may be either an ally or adversary, a hostile relationship is not required.

Deterrence by dissuasion, the most passive component of deterrence, can take a number of forms, such as efforts to influence target-nation public opinion, public diplomacy, or propaganda, or the offer of a benefit for maintaining the status quo. Dissuasive efforts are notably different from deterrence by threat because they do incorporate the threat of violence or punitive action.[19]

Deterrence by denial seeks to deny the target a desired objective through largely defensive measures. By increasing the risks a target must accept to achieve an objective while also reducing the probability of success, it may be possible to effectively deter a target. Denial can take a number of forms as well. Effective policing, passenger and cargo screening, intelligence gathering, and "no fly" and watch lists are all among the ways deterrence by denial can be carried out.[20]

Deterrence by threat relies on the overt use of a specific threat. It can range from the low (targeted strike) to the high (invasion) end of conflict.[21] Threats can also incorporate punitive measures, including diplomatic and economic sanctions. For the threat to be effective, it must pose greater costs on the target than the reward for altering the status quo. Credibility is the key if deterrence by threat is to work.[22] Empty threats only serve to undermine deterrence. Once a threat is issued, its issuer must be prepared to carry it out.

Any or all three components of deterrence can be combined at any time. There is no requirement that a deterrence strategy begin with dissuasion and progress to a threat. The interests at stake, the actor's objectives—seeking to deter—and the available means for deterrence play a vital role in determining the design of a strategy. The greater the interest at stake, the more likely deterrence by threat will play a role in a deterrence strategy.

In the event that deterrence fails, reversing the new status quo may require applying punitive measures against the target. Compellence, as this strategy is called, attempts to force a return to the previous status quo. If effective, the credibility of future deterrence may increase. Thus, deterrence and compellence can work as a feedback loop where the effectiveness of one increases or decreases the need and effectiveness of the other.

WHAT IS A NONSTATE ACTOR?

When major European powers agreed to the Peace of Westphalia (1648) ending the Thirty Years' War, the modern nation-state was born.[23] In the 361 years since the nation-state came to dominate the international system, states have never been its only actors. Super-empowered individuals, private organizations, religious movements, transnational ethnic groups, and economic interests have long exerted influence in international relations. While the term "nonstate actor" is generally associated with the likes of al Qaeda and other terrorist groups, the term is not limited to these groups. The International Committee of the Red Cross, established in 1863, is one example of a nonstate actor founded to provide medical aid to wounded soldiers—very different from the negative stereotype. Modern violent Islamic fundamentalists are not even unique in their role as a negative example of a nonstate actor. In the half-century between

1881 and 1914, left-wing revolutionary anarchists assassinated a number of world leaders and prominent citizens in their efforts to spark social revolution.[24] They, too, were nonstate actors.

Modern nonstate actors fall into two categories—peaceful and violent.[25] Peaceful nonstate actors are the most numerous. They include international nongovernmental organizations, international religious organizations, multinational corporations, super-empowered individuals, and transnational diaspora groups. Violent nonstate actors include international criminal organizations, terrorist networks, and insurgent groups.[26] Because the former operate within the bounds of national and international law, they need not be deterred. The latter, however, flaunt national and international laws and are the focus of deterrence. Violent nonstate actors are divided into the three groups mentioned above because the composition, objectives, and tactics of each often differ.

INTERNATIONAL CRIMINAL ORGANIZATIONS

International criminal organizations include a variety of groups.[27] The Mexican and Colombian drug cartels, for example, grow, process, and export illegal drugs. The majority of cartel members are young men who view the drug trade as their best opportunity for material success. When governments interfere with their enterprise, violence frequently results. Currently, Mexican cartels present a legitimate challenge to Mexico's government in its border states.[28]

The Italian, Japanese, and Russian mafias engage in the distribution of drugs, arms trafficking, prostitution, human trafficking, and other illegal activities. They, too, are composed largely of young men who desire greater economic success through criminal enterprise. With few exceptions, the various criminal organizations have shown a reluctance to challenge national governments directly. However, their methods and their products weaken societies at both the production and distribution ends of the supply chain.

TERRORIST GROUPS

In *How Terrorist Groups End*, Seth Jones and Martin Libicki suggest that terrorist groups can be divided into four types: left-wing (Marxist-Leninist, animal rights, environmental, anarchical, and antiglobalization), right-wing (neo-Nazi and neofascist), nationalist (Hamas, Hezbollah, Irish Republican Army, Kurdistan Workers Party, and Tamil Tigers, etc.), and religious (al Qaeda and Jemaah Islamiyah, etc.).[29] While each focuses on violence against civilians to achieve political objectives, each group's motivation and desired end state varies. As Jones and Libicki note, the end state sought by a group largely determines its probability of success. The more limited the objectives, the higher the likelihood of achieving them. For example, the Irish Republican Army (IRA), a nationalist group, was able to negotiate a political settlement with the British government through *Sin Fein* because IRA objectives were finite and both parties were willing to negotiate. On the other hand, al Qaeda seeks to topple the governments of the Middle East to restore the Caliphate.[30] Neither al Qaeda nor the governments of the region are willing to negotiate. Thus, reaching some sort of accommodation is unlikely.

Modern history suggests that types of terrorism often wax and wane.[31] As mentioned earlier, the first episode of terrorism in the modern era began late in the nineteenth century with assassinations by left-wing anarchists. By espousing an ideology in opposition to ordered society, anarchists proved difficult to organize. Thus, their efforts to destroy society ultimately ended with the onset of World War I.

The dramatic change in the international system brought about by World War II led to a second episode of terrorism. As European colonialism collapsed in the postwar years, nationalist groups turned to terrorism to garner independence for their nation or ethnic group. Some achieved their objectives in a few years; others did not and continue to exist. By the 1960s, left-wing terrorism was on the rise again as Marxist-Leninist groups used terrorist tactics to spur revolution around the globe, often with the support of the Soviet Union. The Red Brigade (Italy), Red Army Faction (Germany), and Weather Underground (USA) all struck domestic targets between 1960 and 1990. Like their left-wing predecessors, they too failed.[32] Today, religious terrorism directly challenges international order. Led by imams preaching a violent interpretation of Salafism, al Qaeda and its affiliates are responsible for the deadliest period of terrorism in history.[33] While they are unlikely to achieve victory, these groups are proving to be resilient.

INSURGENT GROUPS

Separating insurgents and terrorists into distinct categories is a common practice, but it is a somewhat arbitrary distinction.[34] Both terrorists and insurgents seek to alter the status quo, but terrorists, by virtue of their weakness, are defined by the tactic they employ. Insurgents, on the other hand, are defined by their objectives. As David Galula wrote, insurgents are driven by perceived grievances into "challenging a *local* ruling power controlling the existing administration, police, and armed forces." Galula adds, "an insurgency is a *protracted struggle* conducted methodically, step by step, in order to attain specific intermediate objectives leading finally to the overthrow of the existing order."[35] Insurgents engage in revolutionary warfare, but their violence focuses primarily on the military, police, and government supporters. While insurgents may use terrorism on specific occasions, as Mao Zedong recognized, the people are the center of gravity for insurgents and counterinsurgents alike, and their support is the key to victory.[36]

Perhaps because insurgents actively engage in attempts to seize and hold territory and to replace an existing regime, they are accorded a status above terrorists, but they often vary only in their capabilities. Both terrorists and insurgents are fundamentally dissatisfied with the existing order and are willing to use violence to alter it.[37]

Do Nonstate Actors Pose a Threat to the United States?

To understand the threat that nonstate actors pose to the United States, it is helpful to first have a firm grasp of the United States' national interest.[38]

Vital interests are most important to the nation and are of sufficient importance that the United States will go to war to protect them.[39] Major interests will not precipitate the large-scale use of military force, but a threat to them can lead to limited use of military force. Diplomatic coercion and economic sanctions are, however, much more common. Peripheral interests do not directly affect state sovereignty (survival) or economic interests. In many instances, they are associated with the cultural and moral preferences and norms of the nation and its citizenry but are not of significant importance to the United States to solicit more than a negligible response to their violation.

Historically, violent nonstate actors have not presented existential threats to the United States. This is to say they are limited in the risk they can pose to the vital interests of the nation and have yet to threaten its survival.[40] As the Conflict Pyramid illustrates, nonstate actors are likely the most numerous threat, but also the least dangerous of any potential adversaries.

Violent nonstate actors are capable of posing threats to the major and peripheral interests of the United States and may one day prove much more formidable, but the current state of technology (even with cyberterrorism) and the structure of the international system does not provide nonstate actors with the means to challenge the United States' sovereignty or vital interests directly.[41]

As the attacks of 9/11 illustrate, the United States is susceptible to terrorist attack. On that day, almost 3,000 civilians were killed and over $1 trillion worth of damage was inflicted.[42] Since the invasion of Afghanistan, more than 900 Americans have given their lives in Operation Enduring Freedom. In Iraq, more than 4,000 Americans have died fighting an insurgency that, until 2011, proved difficult to defeat.[43] The fiscal cost of both wars exceeds $1 trillion and continues to rise.[44] While the ultimate outcome in Afghanistan and Iraq is yet to be determined, it is clear that the cost of defeating nonstate actors in both countries is significant. Thus, nonstate actors clearly pose a risk to the United States, but fortunately, this risk is limited.

CAN VIOLENT NONSTATE ACTORS BE DETERRED?

Providing an answer to this question is as complex and varied as the actors that the United States seeks to deter. According to terrorism experts Paul Davis and Brian Michael Jenkins,

> Although causing a member of al Qaeda to change his stripes may be out of the question, deterring individuals from attacking individual targets is not. To the contrary, the empirical record shows that even hardened terrorists dislike operational risks and may be deterred by uncertainty and risk. A foot soldier may willingly give his life in a suicide mission, and organizations may be quite willing to sacrifice such pawns, but mission success is very important and leaders are in some ways risk-averse.[45]

With three distinct types of violent nonstate actors (international criminal organizations, terrorist groups, and insurgents), the motivations, objectives, and grievances of each make it difficult to develop a standard approach to deterrence. Thinking about deterrence in terms that were appropriate during the Cold War offers limited utility for today. Three examples illustrate the differences in deterring a nonstate actor and a Cold War–era nation-state. First, unlike states, nonstate actors do not exercise sovereignty over a given territory—in fact, they often seek to undermine state credibility by attacking the state's ability to exercise sovereign control over territory.[46] Because the sovereign territory of a nation-state is more easily held at risk, it is possible to threaten that control and deter a nation. This is a key difficulty in the relationship between states and nonstate actors; often nonstate actors can deter states more effectively than states can deter their nonstate adversaries. Second, nonstate actors lack a clearly identifiable center of gravity that can be readily targeted.[47] For a nation-state, the capital, military forces, or political leadership usually function as the center of gravity. Third, nonstate actors exist to change the status quo, unlike nation-states.[48] States have an inherent desire to protect that which they already possess, making them susceptible to coercion should they desire a change in the status quo. These and other differences between nonstate actors and nation-states make deterrence of violent nonstate actors a far more complex and difficult task today.

If deterrence is understood as operating along the spectrum proposed—with deterrence by dissuasion, denial, and threat available for application—it may be possible to devise a deterrence strategy that is effective in deterring some, if not all, violent nonstate actors. As in economics, there is a diminishing marginal utility for deterrence efforts.[49] Although it may be possible to deter every threat by putting a Border Patrol agent along every inch of the US border, turning every American home into a fortress, or conducting a complete background investigation of every person entering the United States, such efforts would be cost prohibitive. Absolute certainty is not possible when attempting to deter nonstate actors. Thus, it is imperative that any deterrence strategy provide the greatest level of deterrence at the lowest possible cost.

Some nonstate actors, such as al Qaeda, are less likely to be deterred permanently.[50] With objectives that offer little room for negotiation or addressing specific grievances, there are virtually no options but destruction of the group.

Developing a detailed understanding of each nonstate actor's motivations, objectives, and desired end state is necessary to determine the efficacy of a deterrence strategy.[51] Simply dismissing a terrorist group as a gang of bloodthirsty killers—and therefore not susceptible to deterrence—may play well with an angry public, but it ignores what may be legitimate grievances that can be redressed with varying degrees of effort. Nonstate actors should not be dismissed because of the tactics (terrorism, assassination, ambush) they use. This is helpful neither in determining the most effective ways of deterring them nor in designing a strategy for their defeat.

How Do You Deter Violent Nonstate Actors?

Developing an effective deterrence strategy presents no easy task or readily apparent solution. The simple application of force is insufficient to coerce deterrence targets into maintaining the status quo. Success requires far more than in decades past, but it is possible in some if not every instance.

KNOW YOUR ENEMY

As previously mentioned, before an effective deterrence strategy can be developed, it is necessary to understand the conditions that gave rise to the criminal organization, terrorist group, or insurgency. Understanding the cultural, economic, historical, and political conditions of the nation in which a nonstate actor develops provides a clear sense of the potential appeal, strength, and longevity of the group or organization. It also enables the strategist to design a set of policies that effectively apply dissuasion, denial, and threat at each of the three levels of analysis (individual, domestic, and international). As the following illustration shows, a multipronged approach to deterrence may be most appropriate. But, in order to develop such an approach, a thorough knowledge of an adversary and his environment is an essential criterion for success.

While suggesting "know thy enemy" may appear so fundamental to any deterrence effort that it need not be said, the United States does not have a history of developing an in-depth understanding of its adversaries—Iraq and Afghanistan are cases in point. Instead, American leaders have long relied on the nation's economic and military power to overwhelm any potential adversary. When engaging with nonstate actors, this approach is less successful because it is this very strength that they are actively seeking to challenge.

Violent nonstate actors, particularly those that pose a threat over an extended period of time, are most often found in states with nondemocratic regimes, low levels of economic development, constrained upward mobility, and restrictions on human rights.[52] Rarely do they arise in states with the most oppressive regimes—North Korea, for instance. Instead, they develop and thrive in countries where the citizenry often have legitimate grievances against the government and where bright and well-educated young people experience what Ted Robert Gurr calls "relative deprivation."[53] According to Gurr, citizens rebel because they perceive that their absolute condition should be better than it is, not because it is unacceptable. This state of affairs can give rise to all three types of violent nonstate actors.

For a deterrence strategy to work, specific policies must be developed that target the individual group member, the nation, society giving rise to a group, and the international system in which nonstate actors operate. A multilayered approach to deterrence offers the greatest chance for success.

Recommendations at the Individual Level

The design of a deterrence by dissuasion approach can take a number of forms. First, the United States could wage an active propaganda campaign targeting those most likely to join criminal organizations, insurgencies, or terrorist groups.[54] In most instances the United States is not directly responsible for the deprivation facing many around the globe, but it does a poor job of selling American ideals and efforts to improve lives around the world, leaving millions with an incorrect impression of the United States. Second, the United States could actively support and assist those individuals and groups actively challenging the ideologies espoused by many nonstate actors.[55] The imams, for example, who do not support a violent global jihad, are, in many cases, an effective tool in preventing potential members from joining a terrorist group. Third, the United States could sponsor alternative organizations that provide an outlet for disaffected individuals to express their concerns, turn to for support, and find alternatives to violence. As Marc Sageman notes, those who join the jihad tend to be new to a foreign country, lonely, unhappy in their current circumstances, and susceptible to influence.[56] Providing alternative organizations to radical mosques can prevent the conversion of many to the terrorists' cause.

Deterrence by denial can also take a number of forms. First, effective security measures at airports, border crossings, and seaports act as an active defense that may deter some seeking to carry out terrorist attacks.[57] As the probability of a successful attack decreases, the probability of successful deterrence increases. In the case of terrorism, a failed attack is worse than no attack at all. Second, potential targets should be hardened. A passive defense may be sufficient to convince an attacker that success is unlikely. Third, effective intelligence gathering, policing, and forensic investigation may be successful in convincing individual group members that they will be denied the anonymity they seek.

Deterrence by threat is undoubtedly what Americans are most familiar with, but current efforts have not proven as effective as desired. As Audrey Kurth Cronin notes, targeted assassination and related approaches to addressing terrorism may have some deterrent value, but they are difficult for democratic leaders and societies to accept as a legitimate means of deterring violent nonstate actors.[58] However, the threat of violence can have a positive effect, but only if backed by a credible ability to target that which a violent nonstate actor values most and seeks to prevent its harm. While violent nonstate actors use what Moises Naim calls "the five wars of globalization"—illegal trade in drugs, arms, intellectual property, people, and money—to further their causes, current government efforts to control these adversaries is having only limited effect.[59] Although a number of cases exist where governments used massive repression and violence in an attempt to eradicate terrorist organizations—some successfully—the indiscriminate use of violence often leads to a Pyrrhic victory.[60]

Instead, the threatened use of violence should be precisely targeted at that which individual violent nonstate actors hold dear. Developing the ability to devise such an approach is built on an intimate knowledge of the individuals that comprise a network or organization. Again, the threat of violence and its ultimate use is not a singular approach to deterring and defeating violent nonstate actors. It is part of an integrated strategy that layers a variety of policies designed to prevent terrorism and other acts of violence.

While the threat of massive retaliation must always remain an option to underscore deterrence credibility and eradicate criminals, insurgents, and terrorists, states will stand a better chance in the competition against violent nonstate actors if they have a robust tool kit that applies an array of options to the deterrence calculus.

RECOMMENDATIONS AT THE DOMESTIC LEVEL

Because nonstate actors are dissatisfied with the status quo in a world dominated by nation-states, focusing deterrence at the state or society levels is as important, if not more so, as directing it at the individual. In much counterinsurgency literature, "the people" are described as the center of gravity.[61] Win the support of the people and the insurgency can be defeated. While accomplishing this feat is no easy task, it plays an important role in defeating criminal organizations and terrorist groups as well.

Deterrence by dissuasion offers the opportunity to apply a number of policies directed at political leaders and societies. First, the United States should work with foreign leaders to address the possible legitimate grievances of some nonstate actors.[62] While political leaders in the nondemocratic nations from which most terrorist and insurgent groups develop will not accede to free and fair elections, it is possible for American policy makers to use the considerable leverage of the United States to promote economic and human rights reforms. This is a desirable option because it has the potential to reduce or eliminate the grievances that give rise to violent nonstate actors and the opportunity to show the United States in a positive light. As the civil war in Libya illustrates, American leaders are apt to interpret the United States' interests very broadly, which can lead to intervention when a nation experiences internal instability. Thus, encouraging national leaders to address grievances well before terrorist groups and insurgencies develop stands to limit more invasive American involvement around the world.

Second, and related, a more effective societal-wide use of pro-American propaganda could dramatically improve the United States' image around the world.[63] Such efforts were highly successful during the Cold War and may be successful in the present security context. Since the end of the Cold War, organizations such as the Voice of America have been largely ineffectual in promoting a generally positive view of the United States. It is time to mobilize national capabilities to combat poisonous ideologies as was done against communism during the Cold War. This can be done with relatively limited fiscal resources while repeating significant gains.

Third, the president and the secretary of state could take a more active role in discouraging allies—those with large populations of discontented citizens—from using state-controlled media to blame domestic ills on the United States, which is rarely responsible.[64] This is a practice in the Middle East that is more than half a century old. Authoritarian regimes employ this tactic as a method of obfuscation in order to turn the ire of their people away from the regime's failures. In many instances, the regimes that are guilty of this practice are allies or friends of the United States.

Deterrence by denial can also play an important role at the domestic level. Illiberal regimes are susceptible to a denial of economic benefits that can be tied to reform.[65] Again, eliminating the grievances that give rise to nonstate violence and lead segments of society to support them is necessary. The United States can also provide many states the training and support necessary to create honest and effective police forces—a common problem in many countries.[66] Denying nonstate actors anonymity through successful local policing may be sufficient to defeat them. Additionally, the United States can deny allies the military aid they often receive. American troops play a key role in assisting, funding, and training local military forces as part of ongoing foreign internal defense (FID) programs. Absent US assistance, these regimes may be forced to address the grievances of nonstate actors or face a serious challenge to the regime.[67]

Deterrence by threat may be the most effective way to apply domestic pressure. American forces can assist local forces in presenting a clear military threat to insurgent or terrorist groups.[68] The United States can also encourage political leaders—in susceptible countries—to place significant resources and time into addressing their internal problems by clearly communicating that the United States will not respect territorial sovereignty when hunting down those who have attacked the American people. The

United States can also make it clear that it will hold governments accountable for the acts of their citizens.[69] For example, Saudi Arabia turned a blind eye to Wahhabi jihadists as long as terrorism was directed externally. Only when the kingdom became a target did the king act. Other "allies" are undertaking similar, and unacceptable, approaches. Thus, a change in approach by the United States could go a long way in deterring violent nonstate actors.

RECOMMENDATIONS AT THE INTERNATIONAL LEVEL

Because nonstate actors are not recognized participants in the international system, it is more difficult to design deterrence policies at this level. There are, however, three specific policies that can assist in deterring these groups. First, the international community, led by the United States, can bring significant weight to bear in creating a broad cultural rejection of the tactics used by violent nonstate actors.[70] If the international community could, for example, reach consensus on a definition of terrorism, it may be possible to create a broader dissuasive effect that filters down to the societal and individual levels. As examples such as the Irish Republican Army (IRA) and al Qaeda illustrate, significant funding and support for local activities comes from international sources.[71] Thus, developing a consensus on what is and is not acceptable behavior has the potential to assist in eliminating these sources of support.

Second, improved intelligence gathering and greater cooperation across national intelligence agencies can significantly contribute to denying potential criminals and terrorists the ability to travel internationally, launder illicit funds, and communicate with other members and supporters around the globe.[72] Interagency and multinational cooperation does occur, but there is certainly room for improvement. However, the case of PVT Bradley Manning and Wikileaks has undermined efforts to promote openness among the federal government's information and intelligence-gathering organizations, making this recommendation more difficult than before.[73]

Third, the United States could shift to a policy of offshore balancing in much of the world. As Robert Pape notes in his work on suicide terrorism, the presence of American troops in the Middle East and elsewhere is perceived as a threat to the "homeland" by groups within countries where American forces are present. Pape suggests that moving US forces offshore will likely reduce the perceived threat. Thus, a reduction in terrorism and insurgent activity may occur as a result.[74]

CONCLUSION

Developing an effective deterrence strategy for today's adversaries is more complex and difficult than at any time in American history. The range of adversaries confronting the United States is staggering. Developing tailored approaches to deterring its adversaries may provide the United States with a more effective solution to the challenges facing the nation. Addressing common misconceptions in a variety of areas will enable the United States to develop a clearer picture of the threats facing the American people and assist in developing workable approaches to protecting the nation's interests.

In some instances, deterrence will prove effective. In others, it will not. Neither political leaders nor the American people should expect deterrence to work in every case in which it is applied. Deterrence can never be the sole strategy of the United States. It must work in conjunction with other strategies designed to accomplish national objectives through alternative means. Through the layered approach suggested, the United States may have a greater probability of succeeding in ongoing efforts to defend itself and its interests.

NOTES

1. Justus Doenecke, "American Isolationism, 1939–1941," *Journal of Libertarian Studies* 6, no. 3–4 (Summer/Fall, 1982), 201–217; William Astore, "The New American Isolationism," *The Nation* (November 1, 2010), http://www.thenation.com/article/155725/new-american-isolationism; and Thomas Patterson et al., *American Foreign Relations* (Boston: Wadsworth, 2009), 133–135.
2. John Lewis Gaddis, *Strategies of Containment* (Oxford: Oxford University Press, 2005), 53–96.
3. Ibid., 162–196.
4. Thomas Nichols, *Eve of Destruction: The Coming Age of Preventive War* (Philadelphia: University of Pennsylvania Press, 2008), 46–52.
5. Joseph Stiglitz, *Globalization and Its Discontents* (New York: W. W. Norton, 2002), 3–22.
6. Ophir Falk and Henry Morgenstern, *Suicide Terror: Understanding and Confronting the Threat* (New York: Wiley, 2009), 275.
7. Amy Belasco, *The Cost of Afghanistan, Iraq and Other Global War on Terror Operations Since 9/11* (Washington, DC: Congressional Research Service, 2009).
8. The debate between these two perspectives was, and is, regularly debated in publications such as *The Weekly Standard, The Nation, The New York Times, The National Interest, The New Republic, Blueprint Magazine, Foreign Affairs,* and *The Atlantic Monthly.* Perhaps the most well-known neoliberal is Joseph Nye, Harvard University professor and former Clinton administration

Assistant Secretary of Defense for International Security Affairs. During the George W. Bush administration, neoconservatives such as William Kristol, Robert Kagan, Paul Wolfowitz, and Douglas Feith rose to prominence. See John Ehrman, *The Rise of Neoconservatism* (New Haven, CT: Yale University Press, 1995).
9. Irving Kristol, "The Neoconservative Persuasion," *On the Issues*, September 2003, 1–3; and Justin Vaisse, *Neoconservatism: The Biography of a Movement* (Cambridge, MA: Harvard University Press, 2010), 110–147.
10. Benjamin Miller, "Explaining Changes in US Grand Strategy: 9/11, the Rise of Offensive Liberalism, and the War in Iraq," *Security Studies* 19, no. 1 (2010): 26–65.
11. "Al Maliki Defiant in Face of Regime's Opponents," *Arizona Daily Star*, March 13, 2011, http://azstarnet.com/news/world/article_2c6247ac-573d-54d7-8fbb-aa5567a88841.html.
12. See James Lebovic, *Deterring International Terrorism and Rogue States* (New York: Routledge, 2007).
13. Raoul Naroll, Vern L. Bullough, and Frada Naroll, *Military Deterrence in History: A Pilot Cross-historical Survey* (Albany, NY: State University of New York Press, 1974).
14. Michael Sheehan, *The Balance of Power: History & Theory* (New York: Routledge, 1996), 122–145.
15. United States Strategic Command, *Deterrence Operations Joint Operating Concept* (Washington, DC: Department of Defense, 2006).
16. Brad Roberts, "Deterrence and WMD Terrorism: Calibrating Its Potential Contributions to Risk Reduction," in *Jihadists and Weapons of Mass Destruction*, ed. Gary Ackerman and Jeremy Tamsett (Boca Raton, FL: CRC Press, 2009), 275.
17. Keith Payne, *Deterrence in the Second Nuclear Age* (Lexington, KY: University Press of Kentucky, 1996), 129–132.
18. Brian Jackson et al., *Evaluating Novel Threats to the Homeland* (Santa Monica, CA: RAND Publishing, 2008), 95.
19. Edward Luttwak, *Strategy: The Logic of War and Peace* (Cambridge, MA: Belknap Press, 2003), 225–232; and Richard Kugler, "Dissuasion as a Strategic Concept," *Strategic Forum* 196 (December 2002).
20. Robert Pape, "Coercion and Military Strategy: Why Denial Works and Punishment Doesn't," *Journal of Strategic Studies* 15, no. 4 (Winter): 423–475; and Daniel Byman and Matthew Waxman, *The Dynamics of Coercion: American Foreign Policy and the Limits of Military Might* (Cambridge, UK: Cambridge University Press, 2002), 50–56, 80–91.
21. Bernard Brodie, *Strategy in the Missile Age* (Princeton, NJ: Princeton University Press, 1959), 264–304.
22. Herman Kahn, *On Thermonuclear War* (New Brunswick, NJ: Transaction Press, 2007), 26–35.
23. George White, *Nation, State, and Territory* (Lanham, MD: Rowman and Littlefield, 2007), ch. 4.
24. Colin Ward, *Anarchism* (Oxford: Oxford University Press, 2004).

25. Klejda Mulaj, *Violent Non-state Actors* (New York: Columbia University Press, 2009), 1–27; and Anne Peters et al., *Non-State Actors as Standard Setters* (Cambridge: Cambridge University Press, 2009).
26. Moises Naim, "The Five Wars of Globalization," *Foreign Policy* (January/February, 2003): 29–36.
27. James Richards, *Transnational Criminal Organizations, Cybercrime, and Money Laundering: A Handbook for Law Enforcement Officers, Auditors, and Financial Investigators* (Boca Raton, FL: CRC Press, 1999), 2–20.
28. Max Mainwaring, *A Contemporary Challenge to State Sovereignty: Gangs and Other Illicit Transnational Criminal Organizations in Central America, El Salvador, Mexico, Jamaica, and Brazil* (Carlisle, PA: Strategic Studies Institute, 2007), 23–33.
29. Seth G. Jones and Martin C. Libicki, *How Terrorist Groups End* (Santa Monica, CA: RAND Publishing, 2008), 15.
30. Christopher Blanchard, *Al Qaeda: Statements and Evolving Ideology* (Washington, DC: Congressional Research Service, 2007).
31. Caleb Carr, *The Lessons of Terror* (New York: Random House, 2003), 161–165.
32. Jones and Libicki, *How Terrorist Groups End*, 25–29, 35–43.
33. Malcolm Nance, *An End to Al Qaeda: Destroying bin Laden's Jihad and Restoring America's Honor* (New York: St. Martin's Press, 2010), 134–136; and Angel Rabasa et al., *Beyond al Qaeda* (Santa Monica, CA: RAND Publishing, 2006), 35–36.
34. Richard Shultz and Andrea Dew, *Insurgents, Terrorists, and Militias: The Warriors of Contemporary Combat* (New York: Columbia University Press, 2006), 17–37.
35. David Galula, *Counterinsurgency Warfare* (Westport, CT: Praeger Security International, 2006), 1–2.
36. Mao Tse-tung, *On Guerilla Warfare*, trans. Samuel Griffith II (Urbana, IL: University of Illinois Press, 1961), 41.
37. See Donald Snow, *Uncivil Wars: International Security and the New Internal Conflicts* (Boulder, CO: Lynne Reiner Publishers, 1996), 3–24; and Brian Michael Jenkins, *Unconquerable Nation: Knowing Our Enemy, Strengthening Ourselves* (Santa Monica, CA: RAND Publishing, 2006), 74–76.
38. While the *National Security Strategy* (NSS) describes the nation's "enduring national interests" as "[t]he security of the United States, its citizens, and US allies and partners; A strong innovative and growing US economy in an open international economic system that promotes opportunity and prosperity; respect for universal values at home and around the world; and an international order advanced by US leadership that promotes peace, security, and opportunity through stronger cooperation to meet global challenges," the NSS is overly generic in its description of national interests and fails to provide a set of interests that are readily translated into policy.

39. For a detailed explanation of the vital, major, and peripheral categorization used above, see Donald Snow and Dennis Drew, *Making 21st Century Strategy* (Maxwell AFB, AL: Air University Press, 2006), ch. 3.
40. Rik Coolsaet, *Jihadi Terrorism and the Radicalization Challenge in Europe* (Burlington, VT: Ashgate, 2008), 19; and Ian Lesser et al., *Countering the New Terrorism* (Santa Monica, CA: RAND Publishing, 1999), 3.
41. Bruce Hoffman, *Inside Terrorism* (New York: Columbia University Press, 2006), 229–256.
42. Stephen Biddle, *American Grand Strategy After 9/11: An Assessment* (Carlisle, PA: Army War College, 2005), 20.
43. Hannah Fischer, *US Military Casualty Statistics: Operation New Dawn, Operation Iraqi Freedom, and Operation Enduring Freedom* (Washington, DC: Congressional Research Service, 2010), 5.
44. Amy Belasco, *The Cost of Iraq, Afghanistan, and Other Global War on Terror Operations Since 9/11* (Washington, DC: Congressional Research Service, 2010).
45. Paul Davis and Brian Michael Jenkins, *Deterrence and Influence in Counterterrorism* (Santa Monica, CA: RAND Publishing, 2002), xii.
46. Hoffman, *Inside Terrorism*, 229–256.
47. Brian Steed, *Piercing the Fog of War* (Minneapolis, MN: Zenith Press, 2009), 251.
48. Frederick Gareau, *State Terrorism and the United States* (Atlanta, GA: Clarity Press, 2004), 14–15.
49. The law of diminishing marginal utility holds that as a person increases consumption of a product, while keeping consumption of other products constant, there is a decline in the marginal utility of consuming each additional unit of that product.
50. Joshua Alexander Geltzer, *US Counterterrorism Strategy and al Qaeda* (New York: Routledge, 2010), 43–65.
51. Davis and Jenkins, *Deterrence and Influence in Counter-terrorism*, ch. 3.
52. Jones and Libicki, *How Terrorist Groups End*, 3–4.
53. Ted Robert Gurr, *Why Men Rebel* (Princeton, NJ: Princeton University Press, 1970).
54. Max Mainwaring, *Deterrence in the 21st Century* (New York: Frank Cass, 2001), 87–88.
55. See Salwa Ismail, *Rethinking Islamist Politics: Culture, the State and Islamism* (London: I. B. Taurus, 2006).
56. Marc Sageman, *Understanding Terror Networks* (Philadelphia: University of Pennsylvania Press, 2004), ch. 4.
57. James Lebovic, *Deterring International Terrorism and Rogue States* (New York: Routledge, 2007), ch. 6.
58. Audrey Kurth Cronin, *How Terrorism Ends* (Princeton: Princeton University Press, 2011), 25.
59. Naim, "The Five Wars of Globalization," 35–36.
60. Audrey Kurth Cronin, *How Terrorism Ends*, 141–144.

61. See James Forest, ed., *Countering Terrorism and Insurgency in the 21st Century* (Westport, CT: Praeger, 2007), 38.
62. Assaf Moghadam, *The Roots of Terrorism* (New York: Chelsea House, 2006), 45–65.
63. Forest, *Countering Terrorism and Insurgency in the 21st Century*, 394; and David Altheide, *Terrorism and the Politics of Fear* (Lanham, MD: AltaMira Press, 2006), ch. 8.
64. Nancy Snow, *Information War* (Toronto: Hushion House, 2003), 130–132.
65. Paul Wilkinson, *Terrorism Versus Democracy* (New York: Routledge, 2006), 49–58.
66. Sharon Pickering et al., *Counter-terrorism Policing* (New York: Springer, 2008), ch. 4.
67. David Ucko, *The New Counter-Insurgency Era* (Washington, DC: Georgetown University Press, 2009), 88–90.
68. Boaz Ganor, *The Counter-Terrorism Puzzle* (Piscataway, NJ: Transaction Publishers, 2005), ch. 4.
69. Lebovic, *Deterring International Terrorism and Rogue States*, chs. 5–6.
70. Mariya Omilecheva, *Counter-Terrorism Policies in Central Asia* (New York: Routledge, 2011), 8–10.
71. Laura Johannes and Marc Champion, "Irish Nationalists May Feel US's Funding Squeeze," *Wall Street Journal*, September 27, 2001; and Eric Lichtblau, "Threats and Responses: The Money Trail; US Indicts Head of Islamic Charity in al Qaeda Financing," *The New York Times*, October 10, 2002.
72. Yehuda Schaffer, "Detecting Terrorist Financing Through Financial Intelligence: The Role of FIUs," in *Countering Terrorist Financing*, ed. Mark Pieth, Daniel Thelesklaf, and Radha Ivory (Bern: Peter Lang, 2009).
73. Joe Gould, "Pfc. Faces 22 New Charges in Wikileaks Case," *Army Times*
74. Robert Pape, "Suicide Terrorism and Democracy: What We've Learned since 9/11," *Policy Analysis*, no. 582 (November 1, 2006).

CHAPTER 10

Is Space Deterrence Science Fiction?

Dale Hayden

America's Vulnerability in Space

Today, America's preeminence in space is being challenged. The United States relies more heavily on space than any other nation. However, that reliance has also created a vulnerability—thus presenting an attractive target for potential adversaries. The nation's vulnerabilities in space are most apparent in the area of assured access to space—a national priority. At present, the United States has limited ability to protect its space assets or to deny the actions of others in space, which has made "space superiority" only a term and not an operational reality. Without a direct strike against a launch site, the United States lacks any true capability to deny another nation's access to space.

Before going further into the discussion of strategic space deterrence, it might be helpful to understand more about the medium and how the United States arrived at its current reliance upon space assets. Operational space exists principally of near-, low-, and high-earth orbit. Space is identified by international treaty as beginning at 65,000 feet. It extends upward in all directions from the earth's surface and is thus a global common. Near-earth orbit begins at 65,000 feet—a little over 12 miles up, low-earth orbit ranges from approximately 100 to 1240 miles, and high-earth orbit generally means geostationary orbit, approximately 22,240 miles up. Near earth has eddies and wind currents and is capable of sustaining high-altitude balloons. Low-earth orbit is where most satellites and the International Space Station (ISS) operate, and high orbit, or geostationary orbit, is where the capability exists to position a satellite over a specific area on earth and keep it geographically stationary.

WHY IS SPACE IMPORTANT?

Today, no one questions the importance of space operations as an integral part of American national strategy. During the Cold War, the space race represented not only national pride, but national security as well. In the 1960s Vice President Lyndon B. Johnson stated, "One can predict with confidence that failure to master space means being second best in every aspect, in the crucial arena of our Cold War world. In the eyes of the world first in space means first, period; second in space is second in everything."[1] In the past fifteen years, reliance on space has grown geometrically. Global Positioning Systems (GPS) receivers are commonplace in many of today's vehicles, commercial banking is dependent on satellite communications, and both land-based and satellite cable television receivers rely on space-based assets. Military reliance is no less dramatic. From intelligence, surveillance, and reconnaissance (ISR) to targeting, satellites provide a technological infrastructure that enables today's precision strike and superiority of the battlespace. However, our increased reliance on space capabilities has turned our advantage into a vulnerability and us into a likely target for potential adversaries. Thus, deterrence becomes paramount in the defense of a critical national asset.

Directly related to the missions of deterrence and denial, in 1984 and 1985 the United States tested anti-satellite (ASAT) technology, going as far on four separate occasions as to launch an interceptor missile from an F-15 at a point in space. Finally, in September 1985 the missile was launched against an actual target, destroying a gamma-ray spectroscopy satellite, Solwind P78-1, that had been launched in February of 1979. Congress refused to fund further testing of this technology in 1988, in part due to technical difficulties, in part due to cost growth. In February 2008, the Missile Defense Agency successfully destroyed a failing ISR satellite by firing an interceptor from the Navy's ballistic missile defense cruiser USS *Lake Erie*, in cooperation with targeting data from the US Air Force. This, however, was not an ASAT demonstration, as the demonstrated capability is designed for suborbital warheads, objects below the lower limits of low-earth orbit. Further complicating the issue is the question of how the US distinguishes an anti-satellite weapons launch from any other launch.

During the past forty years, space has moved from exploration under direct governmental control to public and private exploitation; in other words, a medium not that different than the land, sea, or air. Gordon

Adams, director of Security Policy Studies at George Washington University, puts it this way: "Space is no longer a frontier, used and occupied solely by governments. From an environment in which only governments operated, largely for exploration and military purposes, space has rapidly filled with assets used for intelligence and military operations to civilian communications, to observation and commerce. Today, more launches are dedicated to commercial purposes than to military ones."[2] The numbers support his views. In the year 2010, the commercial space industry generated over $189 billion in worldwide revenue.[3] The largest share of this commercial market was in space products and services such as satellite services, or the use of satellites to deliver telephone, television, radio, data communications, remote sensing data, and government services, accounting for 44.5 percent of total commercial space revenues in 2000.[4]

Today, space exploration has even wider connotations. The European Union (EU) asserts, "Space systems are strategic assets demonstrating Europe's independence and readiness to assume global responsibilities. The strategic mission of the European Space Policy, jointly developed by the European Commission and the European Space Agency (ESA), is based on the peaceful exploitation of outer space.[5]

As with Europeans, over the past fifty years space asset usage has become a commonplace occurrence for the average American, no different to our blind acceptance of the technology of television. When we turn on the TV, we simply expect the picture and sound to be there; no one speaks with awe about how the video and audio waves appear. Many Americans will start their day by driving to work in an automobile with a graphic display that depicts their present location, directs them across town following instructions to a predetermined destination, stop to gas up by using a credit card at the pump, and remove money from an automated bank teller machine from their account that could be from a different bank in another part of the country. They will think nothing about the technological wizardry, but this set of transactions—location, directions, and link to credit card and banking accounts—are all made possible by instantaneous access to multiple satellite constellations, something we all take for granted.

These and other satellite systems can provide navigation for civilian airliners, identify underground water in Sub-Saharan Africa, and mark the destruction of the Amazon rainforests, in addition to numerous other everyday services we have all come to expect from a modern society. The failure of a single satellite in May 1998 disabled 80 percent of the pagers in the United States, as well as video feeds for cable and broadcast transmission, credit card authorization networks, and corporate communication systems. If the GPS, a multisatellite constellation originally designed for military navigational assistance, were to experience a major failure, it would disrupt fire, ambulance, and police operations around the world; cripple the global financial and banking system; and could in the future threaten air traffic control.[6] Space, therefore, whether we realize it or not, plays an increasingly important role in everyday life.

The evolution of space from a frontier to an operating environment serving numerous customers raised a new set of issues for American policy makers. Recognizing the importance of space to US national interests, Congress chartered a review of national security space activities. Released in May 2001, "The Report of the Commission to Assess United States National Security, Space Management and Organization," better known as the Space Commission Report, concluded that the security and economic well-being of the United States and its allies and friends depend on the nation's ability to operate successfully in space. To be able to contribute to peace and stability in a distinctly different but still dangerous and complex global environment, the United States needs to remain at the forefront in space, technologically and operationally, as it has in the air, on land, and at sea. Further, it must deter others from taking hostile actions against US space assets. Specifically, the United States must have the capability to use space as an integral part of its ability to manage crises, deter conflicts, and, if deterrence fails, prevail in conflict.[7]

Not surprisingly, military reliance on space is no less dramatic than that of today's American public. Satellites provide the technological infrastructure that enables today's precision strike and superiority of the battlespace. The military has long understood the significance of space, which is recognized as the ultimate "high ground" for military operations. Space provides the opportunity for surveillance without the issues of over flight, and instantaneous communications capability that enables command and control of forces across the globe. Secretary of the Air Force Dr. James G. Roche stated, "Space capabilities in today's world are no longer nice-to-have, they've become indispensable at the strategic, operational and tactical levels of war."[8] A decade ago, Peter B. Teets, undersecretary of the Air Force and director of the National Reconnaissance Office and the senior Department of Defense (DOD) space official, emphasized the critical nature space plays today when he remarked, "I think the recent military conflict [Afghanistan] has shown us, without a doubt, how important the use of space is to national security and military operations."[9]

General Ralph E. Eberhart, as commander in chief of United States Space Command, noted, "Most anyone involved in military operations, whether military or civilian, would tell you space is becoming increasingly important. Looking back to how we leveraged our space assets in Desert Storm, compare that to Kosovo—or how we can leverage them even today as we have made advancements since Kosovo—and I think it is obvious how important and how much we rely on capabilities that are resident in our information that moves through space."[10]

General Norman Schwartz, Air Force Chief of Staff, stated as recently as 2012 that "even with extraordinary budget pressures, we are protecting—and in some cases, even increasing—investments in our top acquisition priorities, including space systems that we deem critical to Joint warfighting requirements. In fact, space acquisitions represent 21 percent of all Air Force investment spending, and include four of our ten largest procurement programs: Space-Based Infrared, Global Positioning System–III, Advanced Extremely-High Frequency systems, and the Evolved Expendable Launch Vehicle."[11]

How Did We Get to Where We Are Now? The Evolution of US National Space Policy

While it is too simple to state that it all began with a single launch—it all began with the Soviet Union's Sputnik launch in 1957, which made the USSR the first space-faring nation. That launch shook the United States like nothing since the opening days of the Korean War. How could anyone but US scientists have the necessary background with which to accomplish such a feat? The Eisenhower administration moved rapidly to determine a direction for America's space effort and created the National Aeronautics and Space Administration (NASA) on October 1, 1958, which dictated the civilian route of the US entry into space. During this same period, the US Air Force moved quickly to stake its claim to military operational interests. General Thomas D. White issued the first Air Force space doctrine on November 29, 1957, which included the ideas that spacepower would someday prove as dominant in combat as the Air Force believed that airpower already was, and that the Air Force should have operational control over all forces within this medium.[12]

Today, civilian-operated NASA controls manned space flight and space exploration, while the DOD directs the nation's military space efforts, with the Army, Navy, and Air Force operating separate organizations within their services responsible for space application. Following the Space Commission Report in May 2001, the DOD identified the Air Force as the military's executive agent of space, reporting to the undersecretary of the Air Force.[13] Within the Air Force, Air Force Space Command serves as the "space corps" discussed in the commission's report, with cradle-to-grave responsibility for space systems acquisition and operations.[14] Further streamlining the administrative function of space within DOD, effective October 1, 2002, United States Strategic Command assumed control of military space as the nation's unified command.

One significant change since the earliest days of the US space program is the current state of cooperation between NASA and the military. Through much of US space history, NASA and the military competed for resources, which is understandable with space being an extension of Cold War expectations. During the post–Cold War era, the paradigm changed, culminating in May 2002, when Congress directed the secretary of the Air Force to continue the growing cooperative relationship with NASA and explore the possibility of a joint development project for future spacelift that could meet each organization's requirements.[15] One outgrowth of this new direction was the Air Force's XB-37B orbital test vehicle, an unmanned vehicle capable of multiple launch and recovery while sustaining low-earth orbit for months at a time.

Just as the US national security strategy evolved and adapted to a changing international environment, so did space policy. During the Cold War, it reflected the struggle between East and West. According to Matthew J. Mowthorpe, author of *US Military Approach to Space During the Cold War*, during the early period of the Cold War, American administrations generally viewed space from a sanctuary point of view; that is, the realm of space should not be used for military purposes and should remain free from weapons. Space could then provide strategic stability by providing surveillance of missile launches, which increased the survivability of retaliatory strategic forces.[16] During the 1980s, the Reagan administration shifted US policy from viewing space as a surveillance medium to exploring the feasibility of using space for strategic defense.[17] Announcement of the Strategic Defense Initiative in March 1983, coupled with the *Challenger* disaster in January 1986, led to a revised US space policy in January 1988 that set out four new pillars for space: deterring or defending against enemy attack, accessing assured US space, negating hostile space systems, and enhancing operations of US and allied forces.[18]

The Reagan administration's shift in policy implied for the first time space was not a pristine environment, but, like land, sea, and air, was another arena for military operations. As the first post–Cold War statement of national space policy, the 1996 US National Space Policy continued this trend and announced, "Access to and use of space is central for preserving peace and protecting US national security as well as civil and commercial interests."[19] Completing the transition in national space policy, President Clinton's secretary of defense, William Cohen, wrote in a letter to his service secretaries and senior military personnel, "Space is a medium like the land, sea, and air within which military activities will be conducted to achieve US national security objectives."[20]

Recognizing the increasing importance of space, the National Security Strategy (NSS) of December 1999 declared for the first time that the "unimpeded access to and use of space is a vital national interest."[21] The congressionally chartered "Space Commission" completed the current evolution of US space policy when it reached five unanimous conclusions in its report:

> 1. The present extent of US dependence on space, the rapid pace at which this dependence is increasing, and the vulnerability it creates all demand that US national security space interests be recognized as a top national security priority.
> 2. The US government—in particular, the Department of Defense and the Intelligence Community—is not yet arranged or focused to meet the national security space needs of the twenty-first century.
> 3. US national security space programs are vital to peace and stability.
> 4. We know from history that every medium—air, land, and sea—has seen conflict; reality indicates that space will be no different. Given this virtual certainty, the US must develop the means both to deter and to defend against hostile acts in and from space.
> 5. Investment in science and technology resources—not just facilities, but people—is essential if the US is to remain the world's leading space-faring nation.[22]

The Bush administration's National Security Strategy of September 2002 remained consistent with the policy transition began during the Reagan administration. The 2002 Bush NSS addressed space in the post-9/11 environment:

> Before the war in Afghanistan, that area [space] was low on the list of major planning contingencies. Yet, in a very short time, we had to operate across the length and breadth of that remote nation, using every branch of the armed forces. We must prepare for more such deployments by developing assets such as advanced remote sensing, long-range precision strike capabilities, and transformed maneuver and expeditionary forces. This broad portfolio of military capabilities must also include the ability to defend the homeland, conduct information operations, ensure US access to distant theaters, and protect critical US infrastructure and assets in outer space.[23]

Recognizing a need to update the 1996 US space policy to reflect both the post–Cold War and post-9/11 situations, on June 28, 2002, President Bush directed the National Security Council to chair a review of US space policy and report back during 2003.[24] The destruction of the shuttle *Columbia* during reentry on February 1, 2003, caused an almost three-year delay in the report. On August 31, 2006, President Bush signed off on the new space policy—a document that superseded the September 1996 version of the directive. The new policy not only supported a Moon, Mars, and beyond exploration agenda, but also responded to a post-9/11 world of terrorist actions, such as the need for intelligence gathering internal and external to the United States. The directive recognized that "[s]pace has become a place that is increasingly used by a host of nations, consortia, businesses, and entrepreneurs.... In this new century, those who effectively utilize space will enjoy added prosperity and security and will hold a substantial advantage over those who do not."[25]

In 2010, President Barack Obama's administration announced that it would shift spending from government projects, for example, the decision to cancel NASA's Constellation manned spaceflight program and rely more heavily on commercial endeavors like those of SpaceX. Marking a potentially dramatic change in American space policy, the United States, in the second decade of the twenty-first century, appears poised to place a greater emphasis on private companies rather than relying heavily upon government developed programs.[26]

Who Are the Players?

Throughout most of the Cold War, the United States and the Soviet Union were the only nations with the industrial infrastructure and political will to break the bounds of earth. Today, in addition to the European Space Agency consortium, no less than seven countries have space launch capability.[27]

Furthermore, space activities are moving away from government operation and are becoming increasingly commercially oriented. The proliferation of space activities broadens the threat. The US industrial base finds new invigorated competition, potentially driving the few remaining American companies abroad to remain competitive, while directly challenging the decades-old US space preeminence. The US dependence on space further highlights its vulnerability. Today, any nation with adequate funding can purchase capability for almost any purpose. This dramatically changes the dynamic from the Cold War–era.

A decade ago, Charles V. Pena of the Cato Institute suggested that space, as it relates to national security, may be shaped and influenced more by the future of commercial space activities rather than international military competition.[28] During the 1990s, the United States, Europe, China, and Russia developed proven commercial launch capabilities.

Orbital Sciences Corporation of Dulles, Virginia, launched a Department of Defense satellite aboard an air-launched Pegasus rocket in 1990, becoming the first privately developed space launch vehicle and launch to be sold to the government on a commercial basis.[29] The European Space Agency's family of Ariane vehicles has been the chief US competitor in the international launch market and has dominated the market by launching 55 percent of all commercial payloads between 1990 and 1995; China's Long-March vehicle captured 9 percent of commercial payloads in the first half of the decade, compared to the United States' 36 percent share.[30] Russia entered the commercial launch market through a consortium with Lockheed Martin called International Launch Services, while offering other independent commercial launch services at the same time. India, Israel, Japan, and Australia round out the list of countries with proven space launch capabilities, and with the exception of Japan, have yet to offer international commercial services. This reality has provided a significant opening for such privately owned companies as SpaceX and Orbital to enter the marketplace.[31]

As is proving evident, the future space exploitation may not be restricted primarily to governments and multinational corporations, but may follow the proliferation pattern exhibited by aviation. One such example is an attempt to emulate the aviation industry of the early 1920s, when private organizations offered monetary rewards in an attempt to spur technological development. In the spirit of Charles Lindbergh and his winning the race for the first solo flight across the Atlantic, a group of St. Louis, Missouri-based business leaders started the X-Prize in 1996 to promote private space travel. In all, twenty-one teams from six countries—Argentina, Canada, Romania, Russia, Great Britain, and the United States—joined the competition for the $10 million prize to be the first amateur team that builds and flies a manned craft into space.[32] On September 29 and October 4, 2004, *SpaceShipOne* broke the 100-kilometer mark (62.5 miles), the internationally recognized boundary of space. A public company, Virgin Galactic, is now poised to ferry paying customers into suborbital flight out of a New Mexico spaceport.

Amateur unmanned programs have proliferated as capabilities increase and cost decreases. The California-based Reaction Research Society sent a rocket payload up 53 miles in 1996, while the Civilian Space eXploration Team (CSXT), a Minnesota-based group, has twice attempted to reach the edge of space, most recently in September 2002.[33] By 2010, Elon Musk's company, SpaceX, successfully launched light and medium lift vehicles in Falcon 1 and Falcon 9. Attempting to shape space launch through the public sector, both the Falcons 1 and 9 significantly reduce cost against their Boeing and Lockheed Martin rivals, designed to undercut their rivals by a factor of 10.³⁴ In December 2008, NASA selected SpaceX to resupply the International Space Station during the hiatus of US manned flight following the last Space Shuttle mission in July 2011.³⁵

Nevertheless, despite great commercial and private involvement, for the immediate future, space principally remains the purview of nation-states. Space exploration reflects national pride, as well as represents strategic national interests. Henry Kissinger, President Nixon's secretary of state, noted that the "international system of the twenty-first century will contain at least six major powers—the United States, Europe, China, Japan, Russia, and probably India."³⁶ These also happen to be the nations most capable of independently projecting national aspirations into space in both the present and near term. Each has highly capable industrial infrastructure and possesses the will to expend scarce resources to support its space-faring goals. None of these powers yet has the ability to directly threaten US dominance in space; however, to obtain an accurate picture one must look not only at capabilities, but future intent as well. But, before determining what impact each might have on future US policy, and ultimately deterrence, it is first necessary to review the state of play in each nation. A logical place to begin is with Russia, the inheritor of much of the Soviet Union's Cold War space heritage.

RUSSIA

The Russian government inherited both vast capabilities and significant challenges from its Soviet predecessor. The Russian Space Agency and the Russian Militant Space Forces, both founded in 1992, were given the responsibility for maintaining a diverse constellation of approximately 170 operational spacecraft and the industry behind them.³⁷

Today, the Russian space program faces many daunting challenges with shortfalls in financing being blamed for a series of rocket explosions in the 1990s.³⁸

Yuri Koptev, Russian Aerospace Agency director, concluded that the steady decline of Moscow's space program meant that it was only capable of providing services to others and could no longer independently launch any major missions. The Russian space budget has shrunk to one-nineteenth of what it was in 1989. Mr. Koptev remarked at a conference on space research in December 2002, "Our NASA colleagues are terrified by the fact that their budget amounts to $15 billion a year, but Russia's space budget totals $309 million." He added that India spends nearly $530 million annually on space research.³⁹

Underfunding affects not only the Russian space effort, but its infrastructure as well. A May 2001 fire at Serpukhov, 150 miles from Moscow, severely damaged Russian command and control capabilities, while in May 2002, a roof collapsed at the Baikonur Cosmodrome, killing six workers and damaging the Buran shuttle spacecraft, the only one of three built to have flown in space. The Soviets initiated the Buran project in 1976 in response to the US shuttle program, but abandoned it after the fall of the Soviet Union.[40]

Further hampering the Russian space effort is the location of its main launch site at the Baikonur Cosmodrome in the now independent Republic of Kazakhstan, in the former Soviet Central Asia. Moscow leases the facility from its neighbor, but has been trying to shift launches to its own Plesetsk Cosmodrome, which represents yet another funding challenge.[41]

The increased revenue generated by Russian oil fields is, for now, providing the financial wherewithal for a resurgent Russia. Russia retains a robust launch capability able to place objects in both near-earth and deep-space orbits. Its Soyuz rocket, the backbone of Russia's space operations, traces its origins to the rocket that sent the first man, Yuri Gagarin of the Soviet Union, into space in 1961. It remains highly reliable and has experienced only one failure within the past eleven years. Following the space shuttle *Columbia* accident of February 2003, Russia's launch capability represents the only viable lifeline to the International Space Station (ISS), of which Russia is a full partner. While the past presents a proud heritage for the Russian space program, and the present displays hope, the future may not be as bright.

CHINA

Another Cold War adversary and potential competitor is the Peoples' Republic of China, which has made significant advances in reaching its goals as a space-faring nation. It launched its first satellite on April 24, 1970, and possesses a robust family of boosters called Long-March. Launching from three sites—Jiuquan, Xichang, and Taiyuan—it has established an integrated command and control network capable of directing satellites in both near-earth and geostationary orbit, the largest models being three tons.[42]

On November 20, 1999, China launched and then recovered the next day an unmanned experimental spacecraft, taking its first steps toward reaching manned space flight.[43] The *China Business Times*, a Chinese government-run publication, noted the military implications for the space flight, as well. It quoted a Chinese military expert as stating the same low-power propulsion technology used to adjust a spacecraft's orbit could also be used to alter the path of offensive missiles, helping them evade proposed US antimissile defense systems.[44]

Luan Enjie, administrator of the China National Space Agency, proclaimed at the Third United Nations Conference on the Exploration and Peaceful Uses of Outer Space on October 4, 2000, "The development and application level of the space technology has become an important indicator of a nation's comprehensive strength. Sustained development and application of the space technology has been the important topic of every country dedicated to its own development." He went on to state that "China will actively and pragmatically implement a comprehensive multilayer and multi-form strategy of international cooperation and exchange in space technology according to the market demands of space science, space technology and space application. The new century is a century for Chinese space industry to develop continuously."[45]

China's tenth Five Year Plan, published in December 2001, gave more details of its space goals and articulated a new generation of boosters with greater thrust, higher reliability, and lower cost. It also described aspirations for a manned space program that could potentially lead to lunar and deep-space exploration.[46] China became the third country with a successful manned space program by sending an astronaut into space aboard Shenzhou 5 on October 15, 2003, for more than 21 hours. Since then, China has turned its focus to extraterrestrial exploration beginning with the Moon. The first Chinese Lunar Exploration Program unmanned lunar orbiter—Chang'e 1—was successfully launched on October 24, 2007, making China the fifth nation in the world to master this technology. Further demonstrating advanced capabilities, the Chinese government has placed a space station in low-earth orbit, successfully docking and undocking.[47] Again, something only two other nations have successfully accomplished. Attempting to avoid public missteps of both the US and Russian space programs, China's manned space program goals remain simultaneously guarded and deliberate.

China, however, faces many challenges in the near future as it strives to fulfill its promise. To date, it appears to be effectively transforming itself from a command economy to more of a capitalist model. A new moneyed elite is emerging, and entrepreneurs were welcomed for the first time at a Chinese Communist Party Congress in November 2002, yet vast areas within China remain unaffected by the economic boom of the first part of the twenty-first century. Furthermore, officials are struggling with the question of how to reform the Party while retaining control of the government, something that few one-party systems have ever accomplished effectively. While there is no guarantee China will reach its potential, underestimating it would be foolhardy. China sees itself as a future world player and must be taken seriously.

JAPAN

Long in the shadow of shared US space technology, Japan is beginning to strike an independent path. The National Space Development Agency (NASDA), established in 1969 to oversee most of Japan's space effort, witnessed its first satellite launch in 1970. Over the next two decades, Japan based its booster program on shared US technology, but during the 1980s, it began developing a domestically designed booster to take advantage of the growing commercial market and to increase its flexibility.[48]

While Japan was poised to enter the competitive commercial market with its domestically produced H-2 booster, Japan experienced failure after failure, and eventually canceled the H-2 program in 1999.[49] In August 2001, Japan successfully launched its H-2A booster, which ended six major setbacks in seven years, restoring much of Japan's sapped morale.[50] Today, the Japanese vision for space development is based on the following NASDA doctrine: (1) Establishing a strong foundation for the future of Japanese space development programs; (2) Involvement in developing new and innovative space technologies and systems; and (3) Promoting international cooperation programs by sharing philosophical ideas behind the future of space development.[51] As a result of this direction, Japan has placed higher priority on four areas: construction of a global earth observation system, promotion of advanced space science and unmanned lunar exploration, operation of an in-orbit laboratory, and development and operation of new space program infrastructures.[52]

The Japanese space program continues to evolve and since 2003 has been guided by the Japanese Aerospace Exploration Agency (JAXA). Formed from three previously existing organizations, the Institute of Space and Astronautical Science (ISAS), the National Aerospace Laboratory of Japan (NAL), and the National Space Development Agency of Japan (NASDA), JAXA is responsible for research, technological development, and satellite launch. Under JAXA, the new Japanese space goals are articulated in JAXA 2025, but even there the challenges Japan faces are clearly evident.[53] Terms such as "establish space transportation system," "revive aircraft manufacturing," and "establish indigenous technologies for human space activities," foreshadow the difficult path ahead.[54]

Looking toward space exploration and exploitation Japan is moving further into the marketplace on an almost two-decade quest to compete in the world's commercial satellite-launch business.[55] While built on the success of the Japanese economy at the close of the twentieth century, the interviewing decades have not been a kind. Presently, Japanese space expenditures hover around $4 billion annually.[56] Nevertheless, despite lofty goals and aspirations, the Japanese space program faces significant challenges.

In addition to financial issues, a significant limiting factor for Japan will probably be human capital, as the Japanese cadre of scientists and engineers that constitute the space workforce diminish further in the face of demographic challenges. The estimated space workforce for Japan today is roughly 6,500 workers, in comparison to China's 50,000. One virtue of the small satellite development efforts in Japan is that disseminating this work to universities and other institutes helps to cultivate younger engineering and scientific talents.[57] Further complicating finances, Hughes satellite manufacturing pulled out of a contract with Japan to launch ten of its satellites on the H-2A, and other clients seem reluctant to risk their satellites on this still unproven rocket, when other, more established launch vehicles are available.[58]

In addition, the commercial launch business is becoming more competitive with the introduction in 2002 of Boeing's Delta IV and Lockheed Martin's Atlas V new generation of boosters. An editorial in the *Yomiuri Shinbun* newspaper expressed public concerns about the Japanese space program in light of Japanese involvement in the International Space Station and the economic stagnation of the Japanese economy over the past decade. Labeling the national goal for space as "unclear mission creep," the editorial concluded with the questions: "How much money is needed for space development? What can be done when? Or, what cannot be done? Is the final goal a practical space manned flight? Or is it just a fundamental technological experiment?"[59] These are questions that both the government of Japan and its people must answer.

EUROPEAN SPACE AGENCY

The most immediate commercial competitor to the United States space effort is the European Space Agency (ESA). The ESA is a consortium of European nations founded in 1973 and today represents fifteen member states.[60] The ten founding members of ESA included the largest Western European countries: France, Germany, Italy, Spain, and the United Kingdom, together with Belgium, Denmark, the Netherlands, Sweden, and Switzerland. Five others joined later: Ireland, Austria, Norway, Finland,

and Portugal. Canada is a cooperating state. Most member states also belong to the European Union, but some do not. Conversely, some members of the EU do not yet belong to the ESA. The two bodies are independent of each other, but they interact in evolving European space programs and policy.

The ESA's charter is to "provide for and to promote for exclusively peaceful purposes, cooperation among European States in space research and technology and their space applications, with a view to their being used for scientific purposes and operational space applications systems."[61] While individual members retain some autonomy and nations such as the United Kingdom and Germany have expressed space goals, the true might of the European space effort is expressed through the ESA. Though not a subsidiary of the EU, the EU and the ESA do cooperate closely.

Late in 2000, the EU Research Council and the ESA Ministerial Council met and outlined a new European space strategy. Edelgard Bulmahn, Germany's federal minister of education and research, described the strategy as "aimed at providing Europe with its own access to space."[62] The strategy detailed three lines of action: strengthen the foundations of space activities, enhance scientific knowledge, and reap the benefits for society and seize market opportunities.[63] According to the ESA, the first line of action encompasses broadening space technology and guaranteeing access to space through a family of launch vehicles. The second sees Europe continuing to pursue cutting-edge technology, while the third has the objectives of seizing market opportunities and meeting new societal demands.[64] Whereas lines one and two have significant international implications, with the Ariane family of rockets proving quite reliable and competitive on the commercial market, it is in line three where Europeans see their greatest promise. The European Space Agency puts the case directly: "The challenge is to ensure that Europe can take a fair share of the global market and related jobs."[65]

In a highly competitive market and with an eye toward peaceful space exploitation, where might Europe be headed? In a 1999 article in *The Parliamentary Monitor Magazine*, Ian Taylor, a UK Member of Parliament, observed that economic challenges are "transforming the space industry, with larger, leaner suppliers emerging in both the United States and Europe." In an attempt to define what role Europe might play in space, he went on to say, "Perhaps we [Europeans] could challenge the US dominance by backing dedicated niche applications," such as better, smaller, and cheaper satellites.[66]

Taking further action toward independence from the United States and NATO, the EU, at a 1999 council meeting in Cologne, set a goal of creating a 60,000-person "Rapid Reaction Force" by 2003, able to operate independently with "the necessary means and capabilities to assume its responsibilities regarding a common European policy on security and defense."[67] The November 2000 report to the ESA director general (commonly referred to as the "Wise Men Report") asserted that "without a clear space component, the evolution towards the [European Security and Defense Policy] will be incomplete."[68]

European leaders see space as an arena where it must be actively engaged. Europe is moving ahead with Galileo, a civilian satellite navigation program comparable to the US Global Positioning System (GPS) constellation. Per the ESA to the European Parliament, "Galileo is one of the Union's flagship programmes and the first satellite navigation system in the world designed for civilian use. It will enable the Union to remain independent in a time when reliance on global navigation systems continues to grow."[69]

The European Union and the ESA have both the political drive and the technological ability to implement their goals; the problematic area is funding. By 2012 the ESA budget had reached between $4 and $5 billion annually, slightly more than the Japanese space budget.[70] The challenge ahead facing the ESA is successfully articulating goals to an ever stressed international consortium of independent states. Despite funding limitations and competing national priorities, Europe remains a fierce competitor within the aerospace arena.

THE REST

The remaining space-faring nations include India, Australia, Israel, and potentially North Korea and Iran. Each has demonstrated space access capabilities to varying degrees of success. Looking at their accomplishments and aspirations shows that the future model for international development in space will be proliferation rather than retrenchment.

India entered the brotherhood of space-faring nations on October 15, 1994, with the successful launch of its PSLV-D2 rocket with an 804-kilogram Indian Remote Sensing (IRS)-P2 satellite. The focus of India's space program is in the arena of weather, surveillance, and communications, particularly in light of increased tensions with its Pakistani neighbors. The Indian launch program remains active, with its seventh successful flight of its indigenous Polar Satellite Launch Vehicle in September 2002, which placed its first dedicated weather satellite in orbit.[71] India reached further in 2008 when it launched Chandrayaan-1, an unmanned lunar orbiter on a two-year mission to explore the moon.[72]

Australia has a long history of involvement in space flight, mostly through their cooperation in US and British launches from their

Woomera launch site. Australia has on numerous occasions attempted to join the space-faring nations independent of its old allies. The latest occurred in 1999, when SpaceLift Australia Ltd signed an agreement with Russia to launch payloads under 800 kilograms into low-earth orbit. The agreement remains only a stated goal at this time, as the company has yet to meet its planned test launch of 2001.[73] This agreement opened avenues for continued partnering between the two nations. Alexei Korostelev of the Russian space agency Roskosomos stated that "Australian organizations may also participate in other Russian scientific programs, such as putting Australian materials processing equipment on board the Russian segment of the International Space Station."[74]

The *Israeli* space program also has a long history, dating back to 1961 with the launch of its first solid fueled mini-rocket. Desiring greater independence and self-reliance following the 1986 *Challenger* accident, Israel felt compelled to develop an indigenous space capability and on September 19, 1988, launched its first domestically constructed satellite.[75] Since 1988, Israel has continued domestic satellite launches from its Palmachim site, though it also relies upon US and ESA launch support for surveillance and communications capabilities.

North Korea announced on September 4, 1998, that four days earlier it had placed its first satellite into orbit aboard a Taep'o-dong, or Kwangmyongsong-1, rocket.[76] Again, on April 5, 2009, the North Korean government publically declared the successful launch of a satellite aboard a Kwangmyongsong-2 rocket. While international debate immediately erupted concerning the success and intent of both launches, North Korea certainly exhibited both intercontinental ballistic missile (ICBM) and space launch intent, if short of full capability. Shortly after new North Korean leader Kim Jong-un's ascension to power, a spectacular failure of a rocket meant to put a satellite into orbit was more than a $1 billion humiliation.[77] Despite its failures, the attempts, coupled with an open admission of continued nuclear research with open testing, mark North Korea as a challenge, if not a direct threat, to US policy makers in the areas of both international relations and space development.

On February 4, 2008, *Iran* successfully launched the two stages all-liquid propellant suborbital rocket Kavoshgar-1(Explorer-1) on a maiden suborbital test flight from Sharoud, its newly inaugurated domestic space launch complex. Since then, Iranian state television reported that Iran's first "domestically" made satellite, the Omid (from the Persian meaning "Hope") had been successfully launched into low-earth orbit by a domestically produced Safir-2 rocket on February 2, 2009. The operation was made to coincide with the 30th anniversary of the Iranian Revolution. Almost immediately following the launch, US leadership expressed concern about an overlap between the technology used to launch satellites and the technology necessary for making advanced ballistic missiles. Acting State Department spokesman Robert Wood said in a statement: "Iran's development of a space launch vehicle (SLV) capable of putting a satellite into orbit establishes the technical basis from which Iran could develop long-range ballistic missile systems. Many of the technological building blocks involved in SLVs are the same as those required to develop long-range ballistic missiles."[78]

Iran has also expressed an interest in manned space flight, publically declaring that it would place an Iranian in orbit aboard its own spacecraft by 2021. Scientific research on this program has already begun as Iran considers a manned space program, much like its nuclear program, vital in its technological race. While reality may be different, as with North Korea, the expressed intent and some demonstrated capabilities present a challenge for their neighbors, as well as US policy makers.

This brief review of space-faring nations points to a future where space capability represents not just a nation's pride, but also its strategic interests. US policy makers face many uncertainties, though possibly none is more daunting than intent and direction of international space development. Due to the increased activity over the past decades, the question remains whether the United States should be concerned, and if so, what is the best approach to protect its own national interests. The old paradigm of a single adversary is long past. Definitions like enemy or even adversary may even be obsolete, particularly in an era when cooperation and competition live side by side. The loss of a bipolar military environment rather than simplifying deterrence has added significant complexity to the equation.

THE THREAT: SOME CONSIDERATIONS COMPLICATING DETERRENCE

Every nation with space-faring capability or such aspirations openly advertises its peaceful intentions for space. There is open cooperation on the International Space Station and between the United States, Canada, Japan, Russia, the EU, and the ESA. Furthermore, international agreements and treaties discourage weapons in space. But to fully appreciate the impact of increased international development in space, it is necessary to widen the concept of threat. Threat need not be simply defined as militarily based; policy makers must expand the concept to include economic development, because underlying the openly peaceful aspirations for space that are universally expressed are the realistic expressions concerning national security and self-interests. Three areas that provide some indication of the threat are competition, proliferation, and surveillance.

COMPETITION

Today's space race is active and highly competitive. The European Space Agency's Ariane, China's Long-March, Russia's Soyuz, and the Japanese H-2A boosters have all proven highly reliable, and American industry is positioning itself for the future with continued successful launches of the Delta IV and Atlas V boosters. However, launch competition is only one challenge facing the United States. A greater concern to policy makers might well be competition in areas they consider safe, specifically the high technology sector. The ESA has openly expressed the goal of improving its market share in a number of areas, including the civilian navigational satellite market through the program titled Galileo. The outcome of the first partnership between the ESA and the European Commission, the 30-satellite Galileo navigation system is designed to provide high-quality positioning, navigation, and timing services to users across the whole world as a civil-controlled service offering guaranteed continuity of coverage.[79] Referring to Galileo in a January 2002 statement, Claudio Mastracci, ESA's director of application programs, said, "The stakes here [with Galileo] are commercial. The technical issues can be worked out between us [US and Europe] without much difficulty. They are not a problem."[80] French President Jacques Chirac's comments on the situation can be interpreted from an economic as well as a political perspective when he suggested the failure to go ahead with Galileo would have resulted in Europe becoming a "vassal" of the United States.[81]

In light of potential commercial competition, policy makers must address the state of health of the American space industry. Space infrastructure and support industries, such as satellite manufacturing, now account for the second-largest component of the commercial space sector, reaching 32 percent of global space activity by 2010.[82] Total global and total US space sales continued to increase through the next decade, mostly in services. However, the US share of the global market decreased. For example, the US share of satellite manufacturing decreased 20 percent for all commercial communication satellite (COMMSAT) sales and 10 percent for geosynchronous orbit (GEO) COMMSATs between 1999 and 2007.[83] Defense funding, domestic nondefense services, and ground equipment dominated US space industry sales. Export sales, though, represented less than 10 percent of total US company revenues annually from 2003 to 2006.[84] Then the question is whether the US space commercial sector is healthy enough to sustain competition from European consortiums that have proven quite capable and competitive.

Proliferation: The Greatest Threat to Deterrence

Beyond the challenge exhibited by direct competition, the United States must face the specter of technological proliferation, further complicating the deterrence equation. Commercial space launch enterprises have produced some unexpected consequences for US national space policy. Following a Chinese Long-March-2E vehicle failure in January 1995 with a Hughes Space and Communications satellite payload onboard, China and Hughes immediately commissioned an independent review to determine the cause of the failure. The US State Department concluded in its analysis of the review that "Hughes assistance directly supported the Chinese space program in the areas of anomaly analysis/accident investigation, telemetry analysis, coupled loads analysis, hardware design and manufacturing, testing, and weather analysis. Moreover, the assistance provided by Hughes is likely to improve the standing of the Chinese in the commercial launch market, as they make improvements in spacelift reliability and performance."[85] The report went on to predict, "The long-term effect of increased reliability will be to improve the rate of successful deployment of Chinese satellites and, in turn, to facilitate China's access to space for commercial and military programs."[86] China has not had a failure of its Long-March family of vehicles since the assistance from Hughes.

History has proven that technology is extremely difficult to contain, with proliferation appearing as the natural order of things. Accordingly, America is faced with enhanced Chinese spacelift capabilities, increased commercial launch competition, and the potential transfer of technology from the civilian to a more hostile military sector. Policy makers must rapidly determine the most appropriate response to deter potential hostile actions in space, particularly when faced with technological proliferation driven by almost universal access to the Internet and ready entrée by the international community to American colleges and universities.

Intelligence, Surveillance, and Reconnaissance (ISR)

Beyond the arena of increased ISR threat posed by nation-states, US policy makers must also concern themselves with commercially available imagery. Over the past decade, numerous companies have begun providing high-resolution satellite imagery to those willing to purchase their product. One example is the SPOT Image Corporation of France that has been commercially offering high-resolution imagery since the early 1990s. SPOT provides earth observation products for such diverse applications as agriculture, cartography, cadastral mapping, environmental studies, urban planning, telecommunications, surveillance, forestry, land use/land-cover mapping, natural hazard assessments, flood risk management, oil and gas exploration, geology, and civil engineering.[87]

The concern over commercially available imagery became so great during the 2002 Afghanistan campaign that the US National Imagery and Mapping Agency (NIMA) purchased exclusive rights to pictures taken of the war zone by Space Imaging's IKONOS satellite, which has 1-meter black-and-white resolution and 4-meter color resolution. According to Charles Pena of the Cato Institute, this "buy to deny" policy is an example that demonstrates the importance of and demand for commercial space assets.[88] While such arrangements augment government-owned resources, they also preclude others from obtaining like intelligence data. Commercial imagery is rapidly improving, with less than 1-meter resolution available. Further, as providing commercial imagery becomes more profitable, new companies will certainly be enticed to enter the marketplace. For the United States, will "buy to deny" continue to be a successful deterrence strategy to restrict space access? If not, what might be an alternative?

SPACE DEFENSE-IN-DEPTH: A VIABLE DETERRENCE STRATEGY

As more nations field systems, to include such technologies as antisatellites and ground-based jammers and lasers, space superiority cannot be assured. Space control, a concept little different from that of air and potentially cyberspace control, is problematic. The United States does not have the ability to either protect its space assets or deter the actions of others in space. As more nations field space systems, space superiority becomes an illusion. The challenge is to establish a strategy that furthers US national interests and creates a realistic space control architecture. Existing US vulnerabilities in space could drive a strategy that would lead to space weaponization. Space professionals have for years discussed the potential of weapons in space. The imagination of science fiction depicted in such television series as *Star Trek* and movies like *Star Wars* excite the imagination of the possible. To many, space weaponization seems inevitable. As weapons moved from land to sea to air, logically, space appears to be the next domain. The United States' placing weapons in space could potentially spark a space arms race.

A less volatile, less expensive, and potentially more successful strategy to deter hostile actions and obtain space superiority would be to use the entire spectrum of diplomatic, information, military, and economic capabilities to develop a *defense-in-depth* construct for US space operations. By a multilayered approach, space defense-in-depth takes advantage of the nation's strength. It, in fact, places the adversary in a defensive position by not knowing what asset to attack to reach the US space center of gravity. This might also be known as the "make my day" approach. By instilling doubt in the adversary's decision-making process, the US forces any foe to face the question Clint Eastwood posed in his movie *Dirty Harry*, "You've got to ask yourself one question: 'Do I feel lucky?' Well, do ya punk?"[89]

Space defense-in-depth should not begin with a military solution. It starts with the United States taking the lead in engaging the international community to the fullest extent to create a system of protocols and relationships that encourages beneficial and benign behavior in space. Through economic and technical cooperation, nations become interdependent and much less likely to act against their own interests. America already partners widely with the international community in space operations. The United States is engaged with Russia, Japan, Canada, Brazil, and eleven European nations in the ISS. Russia, China, and the ESA have launched satellites for US-based corporations. Further, the United States and Europe are cooperating to avoid frequency overlap in the deployment of Galileo, a European version of GPS. The hope is that through economic and technical cooperation nations become interdependent and less likely to act against their own interests.

Partnering also lays the foundation for international negotiation, regulation, and governance by the rule of law, powerful concepts appreciated by our allies. Currently, the United States is party to a series of international regulations across land, sea, air, and space. A new round of international agreements could call for eliminating all weapons in space, which many nations may well find attractive. Precedents exist to regulate space activity through international negotiation and regulation. Following a successful US space-based nuclear weapons test during the early 1960s, the international arena—with US support—moved to ban such weapons in space.

Such an opportunity exists in relation to anti-satellite (ASAT) weapons. One side effect of the successful Chinese ASAT launch in 2007 was a massive debris field that extends from less than 125 miles to more than 2,292 miles—this range encompasses much of low-earth orbit. Nicholas Johnson, NASA's chief scientist for Orbital Debris, stated, "This satellite breakup represents the most prolific and serious fragmentation in the course of 50 years of space operations."[90] The resulting clutter will affect all nations, including the Chinese, who desire to place satellites in low-earth orbit. However, as the Chinese discovered with their ASAT launch, unintended consequences often outweigh the advantage.

Through global partnering, or rather building partnership capacity, the United States could also gain access to more economical lift. Nations, like Brazil, offer the potential for modern launch facilities where decreased lift is required to place an object in orbit. Further, combining on-site fabrication facilities for satellites and lifters could reduce cost and enhance responsiveness. The United States will continue to need its continental US launch ranges, such as Vandenberg Air Force Base and Kennedy Space Center, particularly for sensitive payloads, but it must move to a lower-cost, more capable alternative for routine lift.

President Ronald Reagan once said, "Trust, but verify." In space this is problematic, for without situational awareness it is difficult to do either. While deterrence is not directly connected to knowing where the aggressor lies, it is certainly enhanced when the deterrer possesses that information. The United States must be prepared to act unilaterally when required to ensure space control and deter hostile activities. Unilateral action, however, requires enhanced situational awareness. Currently, adversaries could alter a satellite's orbit by a few degrees and requisitions may take days or weeks. Additionally, micro-satellites are becoming an increasing reality and the United States has little or no ability to track objects that small. Many of our land-based radar systems were originally designed for ICBM early warning, not objects in low-earth or geosynchronous orbit.

The Air Force has taken positive steps to correct the deficiency with the launch of the Pathfinder, the first Space Based Surveillance System (SBSS), in an attempt to improve space situational awareness (SSA) of geosynchronous orbit. However, the Air Force must also field a capability designed to detect objects in low-earth orbit and integrate space, ground, and maritime systems into a coherent detection architecture. Only with a robust system observing both low- and high-earth orbits will the United States be able to provide comprehensive space situational awareness—an essential element for ensuring true space superiority.

Another essential element to space control, and ultimately space superiority, is guaranteed access to the domain. The Air Force has a rich history of being involved in the nation's race to space. It does not, however, have a record of responsive launch. Special handling requirements for lift vehicles and satellites require months, or years, of planning for any on-time launch. Space systems must become more responsive *and* less vulnerable to meet the warfighter's needs as warfare continues to evolve. The

DOD has long relied on large, expensive satellite systems to meet its needs. However, the launch of the Defense Satellite Communication System (DSCS) follow-on, Wideband Global System (WGS), is an example of this good news and bad news story. While each WGS satellite is more capable than the entire nine-DSCS-satellite constellation, the planned six-satellite-WGS constellation increases US space vulnerabilities by placing greater reliance on a reduced number of satellites.

OPERATIONALLY RESPONSIVE SPACE (ORS): A NECESSARY CONCEPT FOR DETERRENCE

Operationally Responsive Space (ORS), while not a cure-all, must become an element of US national space policy. Over the years the term ORS has become synonymous with what in one era was termed "cheap sat," systems less capable and potentially less effective than the current family of space assets. Under Secretary of the Air Force Peter B. Teets defined ORS in a much broader sense when he identified it as a means "to create a more responsive, reliable, and affordable lift family capable of fulfilling both current and future launch requirements, and the corresponding responsive and affordable satellites."[91]

Spacelift is possibly the most critical element of space control. Without the ability to place satellites in orbit, the United States regresses to the 1950s—totally reliant upon air breathing and terrestrial-based capabilities. The primary space launch vehicles in use by the US Air Force today are known as the Evolved Expendable Launch Vehicle (EELV)—Boeing's Delta IV family and Lockheed Martin's Atlas V family, launched under the joint United Launch Alliance venture. These two lift families are designed to be the primary medium and heavy lifters well into the next decade. Becoming operational in 2002 and at about $100 million per vehicle, the EELV was designed to standardize and improve space launch operability, reduce the government's traditional involvement in launch processing, and save a projected $6 billion in launch cost between 2002 and 2020.

In 2006, a congressionally mandated *National Security Space Launch Requirements Panel* addressing DOD lift concluded that "ample evidence suggests that these rockets [Delta IV and Atlas V] can meet the NSS [National Security Strategy] launch needs of the United States through 2020 (the end of the [panel's] study period), barring the emergence of payload requirements that exceed their design lift capability." The report noted, however, that the two launch families were "largely uncompetitive in today's commercial market," and that because ORS concepts were in the formative stages, "it was premature to specify launcher requirements."[92] The Air Force objective must be to achieve lower cost with responsiveness marked by days and weeks rather than months and years. Less expensive lifters and satellites, which are also operationally responsive, must become commonplace in the Air Force inventory.

To further mitigate vulnerability in space and enhance deterrence capabilities, the United States must establish greater resiliency in its satellite constellations. Accordingly, deterrence need not be through offensive actions alone. It can be dramatically enhanced by robust, resilient defensive capabilities. This can be accomplished by numerous means, some of which include networking a larger number of satellites, having spares on orbit, or being able to replace lost assets rapidly. The basic idea is to eliminate any incentive for an adversary to destroy US space-based assets. If an adversary neutralizes one or more satellites, the nation could recover through networking potentially less complex satellites together, as is done today with computers. Additionally, operational capability can be enhanced through responsive launch and the ability to reconstitute capabilities rapidly.

The US Air Force has a rich history of being involved in the nation's space efforts. It does not, however, have a record of responsive launch. Special handling requirements for the lift vehicle and the satellites dictate months of planning for an on-time launch. Responsive launch has traditionally been viewed in months rather than days or weeks. Further, the space operations process remains mired in a slow, highly expensive acquisition cycle. A stressed national budget will eventually drive a new paradigm for space operations. Smaller, less expensive lifters and satellites must become commonplace. The nation will always require large and corresponding more expensive satellites, especially in geostationary orbit. However, what is needed is a mix of both systems to increase capability and simultaneously reduce vulnerability.

Space systems must become more responsive and less vulnerable at the same time. The Air Force is moving in the right direction with the Minotaur IV, a modified Peacekeeper ICBM, which reduces cost with a smaller lifter for smaller payloads. Additionally, Congress has appropriated funds for continued research and development of ORS systems. With the nation depending to even a greater degree on commercial industry, partnering will be necessary to reach the goal set out by Secretary Teets. Commercial companies like SpaceX and Virgin Galactic may hold the key to rapid and reliable space access, particularly if costs can be driven to single digits when compared with over $30 million per Minotaur.

The US Air Force has for decades attempted to improve its space acquisition process. Historically, it has not been uncommon for a ten- to fifteen-year period to occur from system requirement to launch. Reducing the acquisition cycle reduces US vulnerabilities, enhances deterrence through resiliency, and allows for greater use of current technologies while avoiding the potential for launching satellites designed a decade earlier. Space systems acquisition lives with the heritage of exploring the new frontier. US satellites have been essentially one of a kind, handmade marvels that often push the technological envelope. Cost overruns in the Space Based Infrared Radar System (SBIRS) and the cancellation of the Space Radar program point to an obvious conclusion that Congress has little confidence in the Air Force's ability to acquire and field new space systems. It may take a decade or longer to right the ship, so the programs the Air Force fields in the future must come in on time, on budget, and on message—the Air Force cannot over promise. Accordingly, the next major space program must be well conceived, ruthlessly managed, and delivered as promised.

Space systems have long fallen prey to the approach that the enemy of good is not just better, but best. Stability must be the watchword for all future space systems. Stability in relation to ensuring the right people are in charge and stay associated with the programs they manage over longer periods of time. Stability within the requirements process—just say no to the C model when you need the system sooner and the A version will do. Spiral development is a strategy long used in aircraft acquisition where production of A, B, and C variants is commonplace. The military industrial complex provides exceptional capabilities and it is often difficult for the Air Force to say no to enhancements when offered up by industry. Stability when combined with standardization, from the bus to the subsystems, can make a significant impact on reducing cost and potentially shorten production times.

CONCLUSION

Deterrence is seldom a simple proposition. The US nuclear deterrence strategy of Mutually Assured Destruction took decades to mature. A comparable deterrence strategy for space will also likely take decades. In the interim, the United States enjoys a significant amount of freedom of action in space. As with air superiority, which the United States has enjoyed since the Korean Conflict, the nation can never take space superiority for granted. The approach of defense-in-depth offers a way ahead—a strategy that the nation, and more specifically the Department of Defense, can implement, even in a resource-constrained environment. It is not a panacea, nor does it pretend to satisfy those who would call for immediate weaponization of space. What the strategy attempts to do is to provide an alternative that protects US vital national interests, is less costly, garners international support, and, at minimum, slows the march toward a weapons race in space. Reasonable men may disagree, but only the most foolhardy would discount the concept and ignore its potential benefits.

NOTES

1. Walter A. McDougall, *The Heavens and the Earth: A Political History of the Space Age* (Baltimore, MD: The Johns Hopkins University Press, reprinted 1997), 320.
2. Gordon Adams, forward, paper by Laurence Nardon, "Satellite Imagery Control: An American Dilemma," The French Center on the United States (CFE), Paris, France, March 2002.
3. "The Space Report," Space Foundation, 2011, p. 6.
4. Lt Col Peter L. Hays, "United States Military Space: Into the Twenty-First Century," US Air Force Institute for National Security Studies, US Air Force Academy, INSS Occasional Paper 42, September 2002, 22.
5. EUROPA, "Space: European Space Policy," June 28, 2012, http://ec.europa.eu/enterprise/policies/space/esp/index_en.htm.
6. Cristina T. Chaplain, Director Acquisition and Sourcing Management, "Global Positioning System: Significant Challenges in Sustaining and Upgrading Widely Used Capabilities," testimony before Congress, May 7, 2009, p. 1.
7. The Commission to Assess United States National Security Space Management and Organization, "The Report of the Commission to Assess United States National Security, Space Management and Organization," May 2001, 9.
8. Tech Sgt Scott Elliott, "SECAF: Space Forces Have Become Indispensable," *Air Force News Link*, September 24, 2002, http://www.af.mil/news/Sep2002/92402411.shtml.
9. Tech Sgt Scott Elliott, "Partnership Will Guide Military, Civilian Space Activities," *Air Force News Link*, October 17, 2002, 13, http://www.af.mil/news/Oct2002/101702364.shtml.
10. Gerry J. Gilmore, "Space Must Be Top National Priority, Says SPACECOM Chief," *Air Force News Link*, September 18, 2002, http://www.af.mil/news/Apr20010406_0480.shtml.
11. Norman Schwartz, General, USAF, 28th National Space Symposium, Colorado Springs, Colorado, April 9, 2012, p. 2.
12. Mathew J. Mowthorpe, "The United States Approach to Military Space During the Cold War," *Air and Space Power Chronicles* (March 8, 2001), 2.
13. William A. Davidson, SAF/AA, Letter Subject: Organizational Stand-Up of Executive Agent for Space, April 12, 2002, Department of the Air Force.
14. The Commission to Assess United States National Security Space Management and Organization, "The Report of the Commission to Assess United States National Security, Space Management and Organization," 80.

15. United States Congress, Senate Armed Services Committee, National Defense Authorization Act for FY 2003 Report, SpaceRef, http://www.spaceref.com/news/viewsr.html?pid=5539, June 27, 2012.
16. Mowthorpe, "The United States Approach to Military Space During the Cold War," 11.
17. Ibid., 4.
18. The White House, "Presidential Directive on National Space Policy," February 11, 1988, 1.
19. The White House, "Fact Sheet National Space Policy," National Science and Technology Council, September 19, 1996, 1.
20. William Cohen, Secretary of Defense, letter to all military departments, regarding "Department of Defense Space Policy," Department of Defense, July 9, 1999, 2.
21. US National Security Council, *The National Security Strategy for a New Century* (Washington, DC: National Security Council, December 1999), 12.
22. The Commission to Assess United States National Security Space Management and Organization, "The Report of the Commission to Assess United States National Security, Space Management and Organization," 99–100.
23. US National Security Council, *The National Security Strategy of the United States of America* (Washington, DC: National Security Council, September 2002), 29–30.
24. The White House, *Presidential Directive re. National Space Policy Review*, NSPD-15, June 28, 2002.
25. The White House, US National Space Policy, August 31, 2006, http://space.au.af.mil/doctrine.htm.
26. Kenneth Chang, "Obama Calls for End to NASA's Moon Program," *The New York Times*, February 1, 2010.
27. Nations with space-faring capability: United States, Russia, China, Japan, India, Australia, Iran, and Israel.
28. Charles V. Pena, "US Commercial Space Programs: Future Priorities and Implications for National Security," in *Future Security in Space: Commercial, Military, and Arms Control Trade-Offs*, ed. James Clay Moltz, Center for Nonproliferation Studies, Mountbatten Centre for International Studies, University of Southampton, July 2002, 10.
29. Christopher Myers and Jonathan Ball, "Space Transportation," *Space Web*, 2, http://home.att.net/-SpaceWeb/SPSM5900/Nat_Pol.htm.
30. Ibid.
31. Charles Bolden, "NASA Administrator Bolden Defends Future Manned Space Flight Program," July 1, 2011, http://blogs.orlandosentinel.com/news_space_thewritestuff/2011/07/nasa-administrator-bolden-defends-future-manned-space-flight-plans.html, September 19, 2012.
32. Richard Stenger, "Armadillo, Romanians Join $10 Million Space Race," CNN.com, October 17, 2002, http://www.cnn.com/2002/TECH/space/10/17/xprize.contest/indes.html.

33. Richard Stenger, "Science & Space, Amateur Rocket Fizzles in Record Attempt," CNN.com, September 27, 2002, http://www.cnn.com/2002/TECH/space/09/27/rocket.failure/index.html.
34. Siemens Case Study, Space Exploration Technologies, "SpaceX Delivers Outer Space at Bargain Rates," September 2010, 15, http://www.plm.automation.siemens.com/en_us/about_us/success/case_study.cfm?Component=30328&ComponentTemplate=1481.
35. Space Exploration Technologies Corporation webpage, http://www.spacex.com/dragon.php.
36. Samuel P. Huntington, *The Clash of Civilizations and the Remaking of World Order* (New York: Simon & Schuster, 1996), 28.
37. FAS Space Policy Project, "Russian and Soviet Space Agencies," *World Space Guide*, http://ww.fas.org/spp/guide/russia/agency/indes.html.
38. "Russian Soyuz Blow Up, Killing One," CNN.com, October 16, 2002, http://www.cnn.com/2002/TECH/space/10/16/.soyuq.explosion.reut/index.html.
39. Clara Moskowitz, "Are Russian's Recent Space Woes a Sign of Larger Problems?" SPACE.com, February 15, 2012, http://www.space.com/14588-russian-space-failures-larger-problems.html.
40. "Bodies Found in Cosmodrome Debris," BBC News, May 13, 2002, http://news.bbc.co.uk/2/hi/europe/1983638.stm.
41. "Russian Soyuz Blow Up, Killing One," CNN.com.
42. People's Republic of China, The Information Office of the State Council, "China's Space Activities," November 22, 2000, http://www.fas.org/spp/guide/china/wp112200.html.
43. People's Republic of China, The Information Office of the State Council, "The Day of Carrier Space Flight of China is not Far Off," November 21, 1999, http://www.cnsa.gov.cn/news/20021112002e.htm.
44. Robert Windrem and Alan Boyle, "China Space Shot Has Military Implications," MSNBC, November 23, 1999, http://www.msnbc.com/news/211770.asp?cp1=1.
45. Luan Enjie, "Chinese Space Undertakings toward the 21st Century," *World Space Week News*, October 4, 2000, http://www.cnsa/gov.cn/wsw/read-news_e.asp?mc=News&tmjz=24&xsyh=01.
46. People's Republic of China, The Information Office of the State Council, "Development of China's Aerospace Industry during the 10th Five Year Plan," March 12, 2001, http://www.fas.org/spp/guide/china/bjb031201.html.
47. Morris Jones, "China's Space Program Accelerates," *SpaceDaily* (Sydney, Australia), June 29, 2012.
48. National Aeronautics Space Development Association, "To A New Phase of Japanese Rocket Development," NASDA Report No. 51, September 1996, http://www.nasda.go.jp/lib/nasda-news/1996/09/series_e.html.
49. "Japanese rocket blasts off," BBC NEWS, August 29, 2001, http://news.bbc.co.uk/2/hi/science/nature/1514468.stm.

50. David Whitehouse, "Japan's Uncertain Space Future," BBC NEWS, August 29, 2001, http://news.bbc.co.uk/2/hi/science/nature/1515095.stm.
51. "Japan Sets Space Program Thrust," *AOARD Asia Science Letter*, Vol. 5, January 1995, http://www.nmjc.org/aoard/ASL.5.www.html.
52. Ibid.
53. JAXA Vision-JAXA 2025, http://www.jaxa.jp/about/2025/index_e.html, July 18, 2012.
54. Ibid.
55. Chester Dawson, "Japan Launches Space Cargo Push," *The Wall Street Journal*, May 17, 2012.
56. Kate Wilkinson, "Japan's Evolving Space Program," The National Bureau of Asian Research, http://www.nbr.org/research/activity.aspx?id=173, September 9, 2012.
57. Ibid.
58. Whitehouse, "Japan's Uncertain Space Future."
59. Keiko Chino, "Need for Japanese Manned Spacecraft Suddenly Argued," *The Yomiuri Shinbun*, The Planetary Society of Japan, Column, January 23, 2002, http://www.planetary.or.jp/en/colum/20020123.html.
60. European Space Agency, "About UNEP's Partner," December 2, 1997, http://www.unep.org/unep/partners/regional/esa/.
61. Ibid.
62. Erkki Likanen, "Aerospace and the Evolution of Europe," European Union Press Release, on-line, Internet, October 4, 2002, available from http:europa.eu.int/rapid/start/cgi/guesten.ksh?p_action.gettxt=gt&doc=SPEECH/02/456.
63. European Space Agency, "ESA and the European Union Adopt a Common Strategy for Space," European Space Agency Press Release, November 16, 2000, http://www.esa.int/export/csaCP/Pr_74_2000_p_EN.html.
64. Ibid.
65. European Space Agency, "Shaping the Future of Europe in Space: Which Programmes, Which Needs?," European Space Agency Press Release, April 21, 1999, http://www.esa.int/export/csaCP/Pr_6_1999_i_EN.html.
66. Ian Taylor, "A Competitive Space," *The Parliamentary Monitor Magazine*, August 1999, http://www.political.co.uk/iantaylor/articles%200899.htm.
67. John M. Logsdon, "A Security Space Capability for Europe? Implications for US Policy," *Security Space Forum*, Space Policy Institute, Elliott School of International Affairs, George Washington University, Summer 2002, 1.
68. Carl Bildt, Jean Peyrelevade, and Lothar Spath, "Towards a Space Agency for the European Union (aka Wise Men Report)," *Report to the ESA Director General*, November 2000, 9.
69. Communication From the Commission to the Council, the European Parliament, the European Economic and Social Committee of the Regions Toward a Space Strategy for the European Union that Benefits Its Citizens, Sec (2011), European Commission, April 4, 2011, p. 4.

70. European Space Agency, "All About ESA Funding," January 10, 2012, http://www.esa.int/esaMI/About_ESA/SEMNQ4FVL2F_0.html, September 18, 2012.
71. "India Launches Its First Weather Satellite," CNN.com, September 12, 2002, http://www.cnn.com/2002/TECH/space/09/12/india.satellite.reut/index.html.
72. Somini Sengupta, "India Launches Unmanned Orbiter to Moon," *The New York Times*, October 21, 2008.
73. "Spacelift: Spacelift Australia—SS-25 Missile" *SpaceDaily*, August 1999, http://www.spacedaily.com/news/aust-99e.html.
74. Spatial Source, "Russia and Australia Working Toward Space," http://www.spatialsource.com.au/2011/03/15/article/PDFHLZULDP.html, June 26, 2012.
75. Israeli Space Agency, "Israel Space Agency History: ISA Foundation and The Israeli Space Age," http://www.geocities.com/CapeCanaveral/5150/isahist.htm.
76. Monterey Institute of International Studies, "North Korea's Ballistic Missile Program," *CNS-The 31 August 1998 North Korean Satellite Launch: Factsheet*, http://cns.miis.edu/research/korea/factsht.htm.
77. Choe Sang-Hun and David E. Sanger, "Rocket Failure May Be Test of North Korean Leader's Power," *The New York Times*, April 13, 2012.
78. Eli Lake, "Iran's Space Launch Turns Clock Back," *The Washington Times*, June 25, 2009, http://www.washingtontimes.com/news/2009/feb/04/iran-hails-30-year-old-regime-50-year-old-space-te/.
79. European Space Agency, "Galileo IOV at a Glance: Objectives," http://www.esa.int/SPECIALS/Galileo_IOV/SEMNDEITPQG_0.html, June 29, 2012.
80. Peter B. de Selding, "Europeans Blame US Government for Galileo Delay," *SPACENEWS International*, 13, no. 3 (January 21, 2002): 6.
81. John M. Logsdon, "A Security Space Capability for Europe? Implications for US Policy," Remarks at a symposium on the occasion of the 40th anniversary of the French Space Agency CNES, December 18, 2001, Space Policy Institute, Elliott School of International Affairs, George Washington University.
82. Space Foundation, "The Space Report," 2011, p. 6.
83. Department of the Air Force, *Defense Industrial Base Assessment: US Space Industry, Final Report* (Dayton, OH, August 31, 2007), xi.
84. Ibid.
85. United States State Department, "Satellite Launches in the PRC: Hughes," *State Department Assessment of Damage to National Security* (Washington, D.C., December 18, 1998), 8.
86. Ibid., 9.
87. SPOT Image Corporation, http://www.spot.com/.
88. Charles V. Pena, "US Commercial Space Programs: Future Priorities and Implications for National Security," in *Future Security in Space: Commercial, Military, and Arms Control Trade-Offs*, ed. James Clay Moltz, Center

for Nonproliferation Studies, Mountbatten Centre for International Studies, University of Southampton, July 2002, 10.
89. Harry J. Fink and Rita M. Fink, screenplay, *Dirty Harry*, 1971.
90. Leonard David, *China's Anti-Satellite Test: Worrisome Debris Cloud Circles Earth*, space.com, February 2007, 2, http://www.space.com/news/070202_china_spacedebris.html.
91. Peter B. Teets, Congressional testimony, February 25, 2004, www.nro.gov/speeches/fy04nss_posture_statement.pdf.
92. The Congressionally Mandated National Security Space Launch Requirements Panel, *National Security Space Launch Report*, RAND, 2006, xvi.

CHAPTER 11

CAN UNMANNED AERIAL SYSTEMS CONTRIBUTE TO DETERRENCE?

JAMES D. PERRY

This chapter examines the role of Unmanned Air Systems (UAS) in deterrence and argues that potential adversaries will increasingly adopt "anti-access" strategies in order to deter the United States from projecting power within their geographic regions. If the United States can overcome these anti-access strategies, then such strategies no longer have any deterrent value. Furthermore, the US ability to project power, to deny the adversaries military victory, and to hold their most valuable assets at risk would likely exert a strong deterrent effect. This chapter argues that UAS are the most efficient way—and in some cases, the only way—to overcome anti-access challenges and thus should have a significant deterrent effect if they are acquired in sufficient numbers. Also, the ways in which UAS provide deterrent effects that are *qualitatively* different from manned airborne platforms, rather than simply providing "more of the same" due to greater endurance, are examined. Lastly, the pros and cons of UAS in "strategic deterrence" (i.e., nuclear delivery) and the role of UAS in deterring terrorists and insurgent movements are briefly considered.

Classic deterrence theory holds that deterrence results from effective threats of punishment or denial. "Deterrence through punishment" entails a threat to inflict unacceptable damage on something an adversary values. "Deterrence through denial" involves an effort to convince an enemy that an attack will fail or only succeed at unacceptable cost. Both types of deterrence require accurate knowledge of adversaries—what they value, their capabilities and intentions, and their willingness to take risks and accept costs in order to achieve a particular objective. Both types of deterrence require the United States to communicate threats to its adversaries in a timely and credible manner. The historical record contains numerous examples of the United States failing to understand what its enemies value (and do not value), to appreciate the costs and risks that adversaries are prepared to accept, and to communicate threats effectively. Therefore, the United States should plan for deterrence to fail from time to time, and should prepare to defeat its adversaries rather than simply punish them after the fact. Of course, preparations to defeat the adversaries are required in any case in order to make the threat of "deterrence through denial" credible.

DETERRENCE AND THE ANTI-ACCESS THREAT

For the past twelve years, the Defense Department has described the anti-access threat as a major challenge to American power projection, particularly in Asia. The 1997 National Defense Panel observed that the ability to project power is the "cornerstone of America's continued military preeminence," and that "much of our power projection capability depends on sustained access to regions of concern."[1]

Using the threat of punitive strikes, perhaps involving weapons of mass destruction (WMD), adversaries could coerce US allies into refusing access to forward ports and bases. Adversaries could also attack forward ports and bases with WMD, cruise missiles, or ballistic missiles to deny access.[2] The 2001 Quadrennial Defense Review (QDR) emphasized the need to "overcome anti-access or area-denial threats," and set as a critical goal for the Defense Department "projecting and sustaining US forces in distant anti-access or area-denial environments and defeating anti-access and area-denial threats."[3] The 2006 QDR noted the Defense Department's continued efforts to "mitigate anti-access threats and offset potential political coercion designed to limit US access to any region," and repeatedly emphasized the need for the capability to operate "at great distances into denied areas."[4]

Adversaries understand the central importance of airpower to American military operations and thus particularly strive to reduce the effectiveness of US joint air forces. As US airpower principally consists of relatively short-ranged aircraft, one objective of an anti-access strategy is to deny these aircraft the use of the bases they need to operate. To this end, an enemy could employ ballistic and cruise missiles with precision guidance and submunitions.[5] An enemy could also attack theater airbases with WMD, terrorists, or Special Operations Forces.[6] To deny access to sea-based airpower, an adversary could employ anti-ship ballistic missiles, or launch anti-ship cruise missiles from air, surface, and subsurface platforms. An adversary could also employ advanced submarines, surface vessels, and sea mines. Larger adversaries would have integrated air defense systems that included so-called triple-digit SAMs and advanced fighter aircraft with long-range air-to-air missiles. Non-stealthy platforms could penetrate enemy airspace only with great difficulty in the face of such defenses.

Any US aircraft that did penetrate enemy defenses would face a severe problem with mobile targets. Many of an adversary's missile launchers would be mobile to complicate tracking and targeting, and long-range missile systems and space-denial capabilities would be located deep within the enemy homeland beyond the reach of manned tactical aircraft.[7] Adversary command and control, fielded military forces, and possibly also irregular forces would constitute another large set of mobile or non-preplanned targets.

A large, powerful adversary would probably have a "dense" anti-access network consisting of many of the above capabilities deployed in large numbers.[8] Lesser powers, however, could develop a meaningful anti-access capability relatively cheaply even without a major power sponsor. In the 1990s, the Defense Science Board estimated that

> [p]otential US regional adversaries spending on the order of only $15–20 billion over a decade in the global marketplace could develop robust theater-denial/disruption capabilities. These include conventional anti-naval forces (e.g., ultra-quiet diesel submarines, advanced anti-ship cruise missiles, and sophisticated sea mines); theater-range ballistic and land-attack cruise missiles (with the latter expected to be available in the thousands, and, increasingly, with low-observable characteristics); and nuclear, chemical and biological weapons.[9]

Notably, combat against relatively primitive opponents in Iraq and Afghanistan required US joint air forces to find and track a large number of mobile targets, such as insurgents and foreign volunteers intermingled with the civilian population. This difficult challenge continues today.

Anti-access strategies have a political as well as military dimension. For example, in Operations Enduring Freedom and Iraqi Freedom the access constraints were almost entirely political in nature. Neighboring countries either denied the US access outright or severely restricted what US forces could and could not do from their territory and airspace. Basing options in Central Asia were difficult to exploit because the region was remote and the infrastructure was not well developed.[10]

The fundamental purpose of an anti-access strategy is deterrence. Potential adversaries seek to convince the United States that in the event of conflict, they can defeat US intervention and inflict unacceptable losses on critical national assets, such as aircraft carriers and advanced combat aircraft. Adversaries hope that this prospect of denial and punishment will deter the United States from intervening in disputes within their spheres of influence and that America's regional allies will be politically neutralized or may even join our adversaries' side. The adversaries would then enjoy freedom of political and military action wherever the United States was unable to operate. Clearly, if the United States can project power effectively without suffering excessive losses, then an adversary's anti-access capabilities no longer have any deterrent value. Moreover, the American ability to project power, to deny adversaries military victory, and to hold their most valuable assets at risk would likely exert a strong deterrent effect on them. Therefore, if UAS provide an efficient way to overcome anti-access challenges, they should have a significant deterrent effect if they are acquired in adequate numbers.

Anti-access strategies have multiple dimensions, and overcoming them will require a multidimensional approach that includes air, surface, and subsurface elements. However, this paper focuses on the air dimension. What attributes do airborne platforms need in order to defeat anti-access strategies? In general, they require long organic (unrefueled) range, organic sensing/targeting, deep weapons magazines, and broadband, all-aspect low observability (stealth). The 2006 QDR describes these attributes as follows:

> Joint air capabilities must be reoriented to favor, where appropriate, systems that have far greater range and persistence; larger and more flexible payloads for surveillance or strike; and the ability to penetrate and sustain operations in denied areas. The future force will place a premium on capabilities that are responsive and survivable. It will be able to destroy moving targets in all weather conditions, exploit nontraditional intelligence and conduct next-generation electronic warfare. Joint air forces will be capable of rapidly and simultaneously locating and attacking thousands of fixed and mobile targets at global ranges. The future force will exploit stealth and advanced electronic warfare capabilities when and where they are needed.[11]

If adversaries can deny the United States access to airbases within a certain distance of their territory, but US aircraft have sufficient range to operate effectively from beyond that distance, then adversaries' anti-access strategy is defeated. Long organic range combined with aerial refueling capability permits aircraft to refuel from tankers orbiting beyond the range of enemy air defenses, penetrate deep into enemy territory, and persist long enough to find and attack mobile targets.[12] One analyst notes that current tactical aircraft cannot attack targets "much deeper inside defended airspace than 500–750 [nautical miles] (nm)," but "a number of potential adversaries could locate key facilities deeper inside their borders than 500–750nm."[13] The same analyst advocates the acquisition of aircraft with an unrefueled combat radius of 3,000 nm. Very likely, 1,500 nm should be considered the minimum acceptable unrefueled combat radius needed to deny the sanctuary of strategic depth to a continent-sized adversary or even a lesser adversary located far from friendly bases.[14] An aircraft with shorter range would be inadequate if close-in basing were denied through some combination of geography, diplomatic pressure, and enemy military capability. Long organic range, of course, also increases persistence at depth—the amount of time an aircraft can spend on station over the area of interest—and reduces the burden on the tanker force.

Airborne platforms not only need the range to reach the target area, but also need the "multi-INT" sensor capability (meaning a combination of communications intelligence, electronic intelligence, Moving Target Indication radar, and electro-optic/infrared sensors on a single aircraft) to identify and track mobile or emergent targets. To reduce communications requirements and compress the kill chain, the aircraft should ideally have the onboard capability to process sensor information and generate targeting solutions.[15] Networking allows the aircraft to benefit from, and contribute to, joint battlespace awareness. Organic targeting capability compensates when enemy action disrupts communications links, as a competent enemy will certainly attempt to do.

A deep weapons magazine ensures that the aircraft can remain on station longer before needing to return to base to rearm. Analysts have noted the evolving trend toward payload fractionation.[16] Precision guidance enables aircraft to carry a larger number of smaller weapons per sortie, rather than the smaller number of larger weapons that aircraft typically carried in the unguided weapons era. One implication of this trend is that aircraft can be smaller, possibly cheaper, and stealthier than was previously the case. Ultimately, airborne directed-energy weapons may provide deep magazines with a lower life-cycle cost and a smaller, simpler logistics tail than conventional munitions.

Low observability is essential for survivability in high-threat, anti-access environments.[17] To survive, aircraft must break the air defense kill chain at some point during detection, tracking, and engagement. Common strategies involve some form of concealment, suppression, or destruction of enemy air defenses and electronic warfare and other countermeasures. Low observability seeks to reduce the range at which early warning and fire control radars can detect the aircraft, track it, and guide a surface-to-air missile (SAM) or air-to-air missile interceptor. This allows the aircraft to escape engagement altogether, to destroy SAM sites and radars from outside SAM engagement range, or to destroy enemy fighters before they can launch their missiles. Stealth aircraft have thus far generally flown carefully preplanned routes in order to execute strikes against fixed targets. During such missions, the aircraft seeks to ingress and egress as rapidly as possible and does not attempt to persist in enemy airspace. An effort to persist in enemy airspace in order to find, track, and engage mobile targets is a far more difficult problem, requiring an organic, in-flight capability to replan the optimally survivable route in real time in response to evolving threats while still completing the mission. From the standpoint of aircraft design, aircraft that do not intend to persist in enemy airspace or go deep inland may be optimized for low observability from certain aspects—most importantly, the front—but need not be optimized in all aspects.[18] An aircraft whose radar signature is reduced from the frontal aspect can succeed against less dense threat environments through such tactics as flying around anticipated radar coverage areas. However, in heavily defended airspace, with overlapping radar coverage, such aircraft unavoidably expose their non-stealthy side and rear aspects to enemy radars, and are thus detected and fired upon.[19] Persistent operations at depth, and in heavily defended airspace, demand minimizing observability from all aspects, and in all radio frequency threat bands.[20] This design reduces the number of total air defense engagements and allows the aircraft to follow a route that enables it rapidly to detect, track, and kill time-sensitive targets. True broadband, all-aspect low observability requires a tailless flying wing design, and most optimally, an unmanned design, since incorporating a cockpit compromises stealth.[21] Subsonic aircraft are generally better suited to persistent operations than supersonic aircraft. Supersonic flight greatly increases an aircraft's infrared signature, compromising stealth, and also significantly increases an aircraft's weight and fuel consumption, thus decreasing persistence.

Why do unmanned, tailless aircraft combine the above attributes more effectively than manned platforms? As already noted, unmanned aircraft will have an advantage in low observability relative to manned aircraft, but the most important advantage of unmanned systems is persistence. The persistence advantage of unmanned systems emerges from the limitations that human physiology imposes on manned aircraft. Generally speaking, pilots of single-seat aircraft cannot sustain operations in a combat environment for more than about five hours before fatigue levels rise and the aircraft is forced to return to base.[22] In addition, pilots are limited in the number of hours they can fly per month due to the effects of cumulative fatigue.[23] These factors create a range limit beyond which manned fighter-sized aircraft simply cannot operate effectively because of human physiology; one analyst puts this limit at 1,000 to 1,500 nm.[24] On the other hand, unmanned aircraft are not subject to these limitations and thus have a superior ability to generate the persistent coverage needed to find and attack mobile targets at long range. If an adversary denied the United States access to bases within 1,500 nm of his or her territory, then unmanned air systems able to generate persistent coverage from outside this range might be the best way to overcome this anti-access challenge. Other methods such as submarine-launched cruise missiles or conventional ballistic missiles might be contemplated, but how would these weapons be targeted? Most likely, in combination with space-based sensors, UAS would provide targeting data to enable these weapons to strike mobile targets, and if the UAS is in the target area anyway, then why not simply arm the UAS? Cruise and ballistic missiles are much more expensive than bombs dropped from UAS, and they have time-of-flight issues that bombs from an on-station UAS do not.[25]

To illustrate the persistence advantage of unmanned over manned aircraft, let us compare two aircraft that are otherwise identical, except one is unmanned and the other is manned. Both are low observable tailless designs, and both can be refueled in flight. Each cruises at 460 knots true airspeed (ktas) and has an unrefueled range of 3,000 nm. Assume that the sustained combat endurance of the manned aircraft is 10 hours, owing chiefly to human physiological constraints.[26] Assume that the refueled system endurance of the unmanned aircraft is 50 hours, limited primarily by the expenditure of consumables and equipment with periodic maintenance requirements[27] and that aerial refueling is available and requires 30 minutes per refueling (table 11.1).

Now let us take three scenarios: a short-range scenario, in which the aircraft are based 600 nm from their targets; a medium-range scenario,

Table 11.1 Manned vs. unmanned aircraft

	Notional manned aircraft	Notional unmanned aircraft
Organic range (nm)	3,000	3,000
Cruise speed (ktas)	460	460
Aircrew max combat endurance (hours)	10	50

Table 11.2 Hours on station per sortie for manned and unmanned aircraft at a given range

	Short range (600 nm with 200 nm tanker standoff)	Medium range (1,200 nm with 300 nm tanker standoff)	Long range (2,000 nm with 600 nm tanker standoff)
Unmanned aircraft	37.3	29.4	21.5
Manned aircraft	5.3	3.8	0.3

in which the aircraft are based 1,200 nm from their targets; and a long-range scenario, in which the aircraft are based 2,000 nm from their targets (table 11.2). In the first scenario, the aircraft refuel is at a Tanker Safe Line (TSL) 200 nm from the target area; in the second scenario, the aircraft refuel is at a TSL 300 nm from the target area; in the final scenario, the aircraft refuel is at a TSL 600 nm from the target area. How many hours on combat station per sortie does each aircraft generate in each scenario?

The reason for the dramatic difference in time-on-station is that the manned aircraft can usually only make a single ingress from the tanker safe line before the aircrew endurance limit forces the aircraft to return to base. In contrast, the unmanned aircraft can perform multiple ingress/egress cycles from the tanker safe line before the overall mission endurance limit forces the aircraft to return to base.

Another measure of effectiveness is how many persistent orbits a given force of aircraft can generate (table 11.3). A persistent orbit is defined as one aircraft constantly on station at a given distance from base. Using the same aircraft as above, and using the same scenarios, how many persistent orbits can a force of 100 manned aircraft generate? And a force of 100 unmanned aircraft?

Clearly, UAS are vastly more efficient at generating the persistent coverage at long range necessary to find and attack mobile targets. In the

Table 11.3 Number of persistent orbits a force of 100 aircraft generates at a given range

	Short range (600 nm with 200 nm tanker standoff)	Medium range (1,200 nm with 300 nm tanker standoff)	Long range (2,000 nm with 600 nm tanker standoff)
Unmanned aircraft	55	46.7	33
Manned aircraft	23	15.5	1.25

short-range scenario the unmanned force puts more than twice as many aircraft on station than the manned force, and in the long-range scenario the unmanned force puts more than twenty times as many aircraft on station as the manned force. Looked at another way, the number of aircraft required to generate a persistent orbit increases much more steeply for manned aircraft than for unmanned aircraft at the given ranges. This efficiency translates into a smaller force size needed to sustain the same number of aircraft on station. The Defense Department could either spend less money on an unmanned force while maintaining the same military capability as a manned force or achieve far greater military capability for the same amount of money with an unmanned force relative to a manned force.

Unmanned air systems have a superior capability to overcome anti-access strategies and thus present an adversary with a credible prospect that the United States could defeat any aggression and reverse any gains the aggressor had made. In principle, this should deter a rational adversary from undertaking an aggressive act, at least insofar as aerial weapons could defeat aggression. UAS may also have deterrent effects that emerge from the mere fact that they are unmanned. If adversaries perceive that the United States can act against them without risking the capture or death of aircrew, or political embarrassment, then US airpower may be more "usable" and have a greater deterrent effect when unmanned rather than manned aircraft are employed.

Moving beyond deterrence, the Defense Department has argued that American strategic forces must not merely deter and defeat potential aggressors, but must assure allies and dissuade potential competitors from initiating military competition with the United States.[28] To this end, the Nuclear Posture Review recommended the acquisition of nonnuclear strategic strike forces to complement US nuclear forces. A full discussion of assurance and dissuasion is beyond the scope of this chapter. However, one should note that anti-access strategies, if not countered, would, over time, increasingly convince America's allies that America could not protect them because American forces could not operate effectively from regional bases and waters in the event of conflict. A force of stealthy, refuelable UAS able to operate effectively from extended ranges would provide a powerful and credible means to assure allies in peacetime that the United States could protect them in the event of war.

Dissuasion strategies seek to increase the perceived costs and decrease the perceived benefits of competing militarily with America.[29] Stealthy, long-range UAS provide a means to conduct persistent surveillance and high-volume strikes against all classes of targets, even at extended range.[30] Therefore, they enhance the military component of dissuasion because they diminish the perceived benefits of acquiring threatening military capabilities.[31] The 2006 QDR states that "to dissuade major and emerging powers from developing capabilities that could threaten regional stability, to deter conflict, and to defeat aggression should deterrence fail," the United States needs the capability to "mitigate anti-access threats and offset potential political coercion designed to limit US access to any region."[32] To this end, the United States requires "persistent surveillance, including systems that can penetrate and loiter in denied or contested areas" and "prompt and high-volume global strike to deter aggression or coercion."[33] Stealthy, refuelable unmanned combat air vehicles clearly provide such capabilities and can mitigate anti-access threats. In sum, a force of UAS able to overcome anti-access threats and to deter and defeat an adversary would also be highly effective at assuring America's allies and dissuading adversaries from competing with the United States.

UAS AND NUCLEAR DETERRENCE

The self-evident need to recapitalize the nation's aging nuclear weapons and delivery systems raises the question of whether some, or all, of the air-breathing component of the triad should be unmanned. The case for nuclear-armed UAS depends to a great degree on what one assumes about the nature of nuclear deterrence, defense, and warfare in the "Second Nuclear Age;" that is, whether nuclear weapons will be "usable" in certain scenarios. For example, one analyst advocates acquiring a stealthy, manned bomber in case it is necessary to conduct limited nuclear strikes "against authoritarian regimes with small atomic arsenals and less than intercontinental reach."[34] In my view, if we choose to build a new nuclear-capable bomber, the unmanned option should not be rejected out of hand, because the arguments that a nuclear-capable bomber *must* be manned are weak. The most plausible role for UAS in nuclear operations, however, is not to deliver nuclear weapons, but to provide intelligence, surveillance, and reconnaissance (ISR) and targeting for other nuclear delivery systems, such as ballistic missiles.[35] UAS can also conduct conventional precision strikes on enemy strategic systems and provide a launch platform for boost-phase ballistic missile defense interceptors.

The United States has operated "unmanned" nuclear systems for a long time, in the form of ICBMs, SLBMs, and cruise missiles, but a nuclear-capable UAS would still have to surmount strong cultural and psychological resistance. The chief difference between a UAS and a cruise missile in flight is that in the past, cruise missiles operated "autonomously" after launch and could not land after launch, while UAS accepted operator control and direction and could land after launch. The trend in cruise missiles, however, is increasingly to permit operator intervention and dynamic re-tasking in order to engage mobile targets. In effect, the cruise missile becomes an air-launched UAS controlled from the launch platform. The Air Force, if it developed a successor to the AGM-129, could require the new missile to accept in-flight re-tasking from the launch platform. If so, the resulting missile would differ from a stealthy UAS only in that it would not have the ability to land, though this, too, could be incorporated if desired in order to recover the weapon if it is not used.

The safe recovery of a nuclear-armed unmanned aircraft would be a concern, but unmanned bombers need only fly with nuclear weapons aboard during a fully generated alert. Such alerts were exceedingly rare events even during the Cold War. UAS would not need to fly training flights with nuclear weapons onboard.[36] An advantage of unmanned aircraft is that operator training can occur almost entirely through simulation, reducing the costs and risks of flying the aircraft itself for training purposes. While "low end" UAS have, historically, been crash-prone, there is no technical reason that UAS cannot have a level of reliability equal to manned systems, and in fact UAS reliability is already approaching manned levels.[37] Smaller UAS are more crash-prone because they are cheap and disposable by design, but a nuclear-capable UAS would be designed to the highest levels of reliability. Even a nonnuclear-capable unmanned bomber would require extremely high levels of reliability, and the same technology path would assure the reliability of an unmanned nuclear-capable bomber.[38]

Nuclear-capable UAS would unquestionably require secure, reliable, and survivable communications. This requirement is not, however, specific to unmanned aircraft. Any communications system secure, reliable, and survivable enough for manned aircraft to conduct nuclear operations should be secure, reliable, and survivable enough for unmanned aircraft, too. Some analysts argue that manned bombers are preferable to unmanned aircraft or ballistic missiles "because they permit more time for second thoughts or last-minute changes of the President's mind."[39] The thought of the president making decisions on this timescale and micromanaging a nuclear operation up to the moment of weapons release scarcely seems plausible. Nevertheless, if we assume that a communications system exists that can recall a manned bomber up to the very moment of weapons release, then that same system could also recall an unmanned aircraft in the same circumstances. (Either the communications system can support nuclear micromanagement or it cannot!) A manned bomber on a nuclear mission that lost connectivity would either attack the preplanned target or return to base without using its weapon. An unmanned bomber could certainly be programmed to perform the same tasks (attack preplanned targets or return to base) in the same situation. Moreover, the "recall" capability simply reduces the amount of time in which no recall is possible from the 15- to 30-minute transit time of a ballistic missile to the minute or two it takes for a bomb to detonate after it leaves an aircraft. Providing the president with an extra 13 to 28 minutes of "dither time" is not a compelling capability for the nation to spend tens of billions of dollars to acquire.

If we assume that the cultural and communications issues are surmounted, what utility would an unmanned nuclear-capable bomber enjoy versus major powers and lesser adversaries? The Air Force states that nuclear operations against major powers "usually strike fixed, high-value targets."[40] In such a scenario, presidential micromanagement of individual aircraft is hardly possible, and the ability to recall aircraft is essentially irrelevant, if not actually harmful. (The ability to recall a nuclear attack after it is launched undermines deterrence, because the possibility that you can change your mind allows the enemy to think you might actually do so.) An unmanned aircraft could certainly be programmed to attack specific, previously identified fixed targets with nuclear weapons just like a manned bomber could. UAS would provide the critical persistent surveillance needed to find enemy mobile ballistic missiles, but attacking such targets would not necessarily require arming the UAS with nuclear weapons. The UAS could attack with conventional munitions or cue an attack from a manned nuclear-armed bomber. An unmanned bomber would force the adversary to devote considerable effort to air defense, but manned bombers, cruise missiles, and even unmanned nonnuclear-capable aircraft also achieve this effect.

Against regional adversaries, most strategic target classes would require conventional attack. Those that required nuclear attack, such as hardened, deeply buried facilities, would generally not be mobile or time-critical. Nuclear-armed UAS would only be useful against the very small number of targets that were mobile, not vulnerable to conventional munitions, important enough to require nuclear attack, and urgent enough to require immediate attack with nuclear gravity bombs rather than waiting 15 to 30 minutes for a ballistic missile warhead to arrive. The only mission that likely qualifies is preemption of a nuclear missile or certain other classes of WMD attacks, and arguably conventional precision strike may even suffice for this mission. Such conventional strikes would destroy the delivery systems, even if they did not destroy the weapon itself. A 2009 Defense Science Board study considered a scenario in which a regional power with a limited number of ICBMs threatened to strike the United

States or one of its allies. The study argued that conventional SLBM and cruise missile attacks could defeat this threat and noted that stealthy cruise missiles offered "both penetrability without detection and hard target disruption capability." Curiously, this study did not focus on UAS as strike platforms in any detail, even though time-critical conventional strike is what stealthy UAS do best. The study did, however, recommend that the "USD (ATL) [Under Secretary of Defense for Acquisition, Technology and Logistics], with support from the Air Force and DARPA [Defense Advanced Research Projects Agency], perform a study to evaluate the relative performance, cost and risk for a next generation remote, time critical, conventional strike capability based on loitering or penetrating unmanned air breathing weapons."[41]

UAS could support a largely if not entirely nonnuclear damage-limitation strategy in order to deter or defeat nuclear-armed regional adversaries with relatively limited geographic territories and missile arsenals. This would be consistent with the 2002 Nuclear Posture Review's goals of employing advanced conventional strike capabilities to assure allies and dissuade, deter, and defeat adversaries:

> Systems capable of striking a wide range of targets throughout an adversary's territory may dissuade a potential adversary from pursuing threatening capabilities....
>
> Defenses can make it more arduous and costly for an adversary to compete militarily with or wage war against the United States. The demonstration of a range of technologies and systems for missile defense can have a dissuasive effect on potential adversaries. The problem of countering missile defenses, especially defensive systems with multiple layers, presents a potential adversary with the prospect of a difficult, time-consuming and expensive undertaking....
>
> [Missile] defense of U.S. territory and power projection forces, including U.S. forces abroad, combined with the certainty of U.S. ability to strike in response, can bring into better balance U.S. stakes and risks in a regional confrontation and thus reinforce the credibility of U.S. guarantees designed to deter attacks on allies and friends....
>
> Composed of both non-nuclear systems and nuclear weapons, the strike element of the New Triad can provide greater flexibility in the design and conduct of military campaigns to defeat opponents decisively. Non-nuclear strike capabilities may be particularly useful to limit collateral damage and conflict escalation.[42]

The 2010 Nuclear Posture Review notes the importance of "strengthening regional deterrence while reducing the role and numbers of nuclear weapons."[43] Conventionally armed UAS acquired in sufficient numbers would support a strategy of strengthening the nonnuclear elements of regional security, particularly because they would be "capable of fighting limited and large-scale conflicts in anti-access environments," which the report considers critical to credible deterrence.[44] Conventionally armed UAS would also support two of the "key initiatives" for strengthening regional deterrence mentioned in the report:

> Develop non-nuclear prompt global strike capabilities. These capabilities may be particularly valuable for the defeat of time-urgent regional threats.
>
> Develop and deploy, over the next decade, more effective capabilities for real-time intelligence, surveillance, and reconnaissance capabilities.[45]

In sum, the technical arguments against nuclear-capable UAS are not compelling. Nuclear-capable UAS could, contrary to the opinions of some authors, conduct limited nuclear strikes against authoritarian regimes with small WMD arsenals if that capability was desired. Nuclear-capable UAS could, in a war with a major power, strike high-value fixed targets just like manned aircraft could. Of course, cruise missiles are a relatively cheap, accurate, difficult-to-defend against, and politically accepted way to conduct nuclear strikes on fixed targets.

The Air Force currently does not intend to permit UAS to carry nuclear weapons. However, UAS can support all types of strategic strikes by providing persistent surveillance to cue other systems, including nuclear delivery systems, and by conducting conventional precision attacks. The shortfall in penetrating, persistent surveillance and high-volume global strike capability amply justifies the development of a stealthy, unmanned bomber.[46] Unmanned bombers should be hardened for operations in nuclear environments in order to prevent adversaries from using electromagnetic pulse attacks to defeat the system.[47]

UAS AND THE DETERRENCE OF NONSTATE ACTORS

Whether or not UAS can "deter" people from joining an insurgency or terrorist group remains an open question. The question of deterring terrorism is larger than simply deterring terrorist groups themselves. If one could not deter terrorist "frontline" leaders or fighters directly, one might nevertheless seek to apply the principles of deterrence to the "less motivated" elements of the terrorist network, such as financiers, state sponsors, or the supporting population.[48] Broadly speaking, while there is no technological "quick fix" to the problems of terrorism and insurgency, unmanned aircraft could provide the persistent surveillance and attack capability needed as part of any comprehensive strategy to counter these nonstate challenges.

Some analysts argue that forcing enemies to risk their lives to fight machines, with no hope of killing a human enemy in return, and covering the battlespace with seemingly omnipresent UAS that can strike without warning, demoralizes the enemies and deters people from joining an insurgency.[49] Others claim that enemies regard the employment of UAS with contempt, because UAS show that the United States is afraid to put its soldiers in harm's way.[50] In a recent controversy over the ongoing "drone war" in Pakistan and Afghanistan, some observers contended that the employment of UAS was positively counterproductive, because the unmanned strikes generated outrage and provoked people to join the insurgency.[51] Former CIA director, General Michael Hayden, took a contrary view:

> By making a safe haven feel less safe, we keep al Qaeda guessing. We make them doubt their allies, question their methods, their plans, even their priorities. Most importantly, we force them to spend more time and resources on self-preservation. And that distracts them, at least partially and at least for a time, from laying the groundwork for the next attack.[52]

His successor, Leon Panetta, argued that UAS strikes were not only "very effective" but were also "the only game in town in terms of confronting or trying to disrupt the al Qaeda leadership."[53] This is inarguably true, and thus UAS strikes will likely continue on the grounds that they are the "least bad" option, whether or not they deter people from joining al Qaeda or encourage them to do so.

One author argues that the United States should form, in conjunction with partner nations, a global counterterrorism network to deter and defeat terrorist groups. Over time,

> [t]his network will become so expansive and dense that transnational terrorist groups will no longer be able to operate effectively. The underlying goal is to increase dramatically the anticipated costs of conducting terrorist acts, convincing would-be terrorists that the probability of successfully orchestrating a major plot is very low, while punishment would be painful, swift, and certain. In theory, by influencing the cost-benefit calculus associated with terrorist, the [network] will deter terrorists from acting—and in the event deterrence fails, it will effectively disrupt terrorist plots before they are hatched.[54]

The backbone of such a network would be human intelligence. Nevertheless, the 2006 QDR notes that "persistent surveillance to find and precisely target enemy capabilities in denied areas" and "prompt global strike to attack fleeting enemy targets rapidly" are critical capabilities for defeating terrorist networks.[55] Unmanned combat air systems provide these capabilities, and complement manned aircraft and troops on the ground. For example, Predator UAS watched terrorist leader Abu Musab al-Zarqawi for 600 hours before an F-16 attack killed him.[56] The United States should therefore increase the capability and capacity of its fleet of UAS employed in irregular warfare. The United States needs not only non-stealthy, "low end," and relatively short-legged UAS such as the Predator and Reaper, but also stealthy UAS suitable for operations in denied areas:

> A major capability shortfall of the proposed hunter-killer fleet is that neither the Predator nor the Reaper is stealthy. For conducting surveillance and, in some cases, strike missions in denied areas (e.g., Iran) and sensitive areas (e.g., countries with which the United States is not at war, and which possess modern air surveillance systems), it would be highly desirable to have a stealthy, long-endurance [unmanned combat air systems]. While this is admittedly a niche capability in the war against transnational terrorist groups, it could be a critical one in many plausible contingencies. As air defense systems proliferate and become more capable over the course of the coming decade, the need for stealthy [unmanned combat air systems] will grow more pressing. This requirement, moreover, overlaps with the need to develop and field a stealthy, persistent surveillance-strike capability to hedge against the rise of China as a military competitor.[57]

Stealthy, long-range UAS could have a particularly important role in preventing states and terrorist groups from acquiring or using WMD. States seeking to acquire WMD might not have the anti-access capabilities described earlier in this chapter, but still might have sufficiently capable air defenses to deny their airspace to non-stealthy airborne platforms. Moreover, the United States might be reluctant to risk the death or capture of aircrew in order to conduct surveillance of such a state's WMD programs on a routine basis. Stealthy UAS could provide a means to "detect, identify, locate, tag and track key WMD assets and development infrastructure in hostile or denied areas and to interdict WMD, their delivery systems, and related materials in transit" without risking aircrew loss.[58] Stealthy UAS could also support Special Operations Forces in their efforts to collect intelligence on WMD programs, interdict WMD movements, and "render safe" loose weapons or materials.[59] Similar considerations would prevail if a time-critical target (such as a terrorist meeting or a terrorist team with WMD) emerged on the territory "neutral" state. In such scenarios, stealthy UAS would provide persistent, covert surveillance and attack capability that could support other forms of strategic strike or execute strikes themselves.[60]

CONCLUSION

Stealthy, long-range UAS offer a cost-effective means to provide the persistent surveillance and attack needed to find and attack mobile targets at long range in the face of enemy anti-access capabilities. The ability of stealthy, long-range UAS to counter anti-access strategies should deter rational adversaries and dissuade them from acquiring threatening military capabilities. Furthermore, such UAS should help to assure America's regional allies that we can protect them in the event of conflict. Stealthy, long-range UAS can contribute to nuclear deterrence principally by providing targeting information to other strike systems. UAS could also conduct conventional strikes against enemy strategic systems and defend against enemy ballistic missile launches with air-launched interceptors. UAS can provide persistent surveillance and attack capability that may deter terrorists and insurgents from acting, and defeat them if they do. Of course, UAS are not a "stand-alone" solution to the problems of terrorism and insurgency, but must be part of a comprehensive strategy for the defeat of nonstate challenges.

NOTES

1. National Defense Panel, *Transforming Defense: National Security in the 21st Century*, December 1997, 12–13.
2. Ibid.
3. Office of the Secretary of Defense, *Quadrennial Defense Review Report*, September 30, 2001, 30.
4. Office of the Secretary of Defense, *Quadrennial Defense Review Report*, February 6, 2006, 30, 31, 34, 45.
5. John Stillion and David Orletsky, *Airbase Vulnerability to Conventional Cruise-Missile and Ballistic-Missile Attacks: Technology, Scenarios, and US Air Force Responses* (Santa Monica, CA: RAND Corporation, 1999).
6. Robert W. Chandler, *Tomorrow's War, Today's Decisions* (McLean, VA: Amcoda Press, 1996) discusses WMD attacks on theater ports and airbases. Regarding ground attacks on airbases, see Alan J. Vick, *Snakes in the Eagle's Nest* (Santa Monica, CA: RAND Corporation, 1995).
7. Office of the Secretary of Defense, *Quadrennial Defense Review Report*, September 30, 2001, 31.
8. For example, Office of the Secretary of Defense, *Military Power of the People's Republic of China*, 2009, 20–25.

9. Department of Defense, *Final Report of the Defense Science Board Task Force on Globalization and Security*, December 1999, 25.
10. See Benjamin S. Lambeth, *Air Power Against Terror* (Santa Monica, CA: RAND Corporation, 2005) for a discussion of political constraints on access during OEF.
11. Office of the Secretary of Defense, *Quadrennial Defense Review Report*, February 6, 2006, p. 45.
12. The ability to refuel in flight is critical to achieving the full persistence benefits of the unmanned revolution. Achieving long organic range *without* aerial refueling capability requires a much larger aircraft that is more expensive and—in the case of naval unmanned aircraft—is not carrier-suitable. Aerial refueling of an unmanned aircraft with a short organic range would still be useful, but the tankers would have to fly closer to enemy territory and would thus be more vulnerable. More importantly, the unmanned aircraft's ability to persist over enemy territory would be reduced.
13. Barry D. Watts, *Moving Forward On Long-Range Strike* (Center for Strategic and Budgetary Assessments, September 27, 2004), 21.
14. Xinjiang, the point on Earth farthest from any ocean, is about 1,500 nm from the nearest ocean.
15. The "kill chain" is the colloquial term for the process used to prosecute "dynamic" targets, i.e., targets outside the normal tasking cycle. The kill chain has six phases: Find, Fix, Track, Target, Engage, and Assess (F2T2EA). See Air Force Doctrine Document 3–60, *Targeting*, June 8, 2006, 49, http://www.e-publishing.af.mil/shared/media/epubs/AFDD3-60.pdf.
16. Barry D. Watts, *Long Range Strike: Imperatives, Urgency, and Options* (Center for Strategic and Budgetary Assessments, April 2005), 68–70.
17. Rebecca Grant, *The Radar Game* (Arlington, VA: IRIS Research, 1998), is the basis for this discussion of stealth.
18. These aircraft have what Grant calls the "Pacman" or "Bowtie" signature, 31.
19. See the discussion in Grant, 40–46.
20. These aircraft have the closest real-world approximation to what Grant calls the "Fuzzball" signature (Grant, 30). See also Grant's discussion of survivability in heavily defended airspace on 40–42.
21. Cockpits are transparent to radar energy and are filled with radar-reflecting surfaces like the ejection seat and the pilot's helmet. Cockpits thus greatly increase the radar signature of an aircraft, and mitigating this problem is a critical issue in stealth aircraft design. See Doug Richardson, *Stealth Warplanes* (Minneapolis, MN: Zenith Press, 2001), 38–39. While the F-117, B-2, F-22, and other manned platforms are stealthy, unmanned platforms of equivalent size and shape to these aircraft, but without a cockpit, would be much stealthier than the manned version. This was understood even in the late 1970s. See Ben Rich, *Skunk Works* (Boston: Little, Brown & Co., 1994), 65.
22. Christopher J. Bowie, *The Anti-Access Threat and Theater Air Bases* (Center for Strategic and Budgetary Assessments, 2002), 11–13.

23. Ibid., 14.
24. Ibid., 15. Keep in mind that manned aircraft would have to be based far closer to the target area in order to conduct persistent operations against mobile targets than they would to conduct "in and out" strikes on fixed targets.
25. Cruise missiles are about 100 times more expensive than direct-attack munitions like JDAM. Watts, *Long Range Strike: Imperatives, Urgency, and Options*, 71.
26. Ten hours is a very generous assumption. See Bowie, *The Anti-Access Threat and Theater Air Bases*, 11–13, for a good discussion of this point.
27. This number was arbitrarily selected and is conservative. Other complex variables have been simplified, such as mission planning and management, mission survivability, and mission availability. No crew ratio limits are assumed for manned aircraft, and maintenance turnaround time is 2 hours for both types of aircraft.
28. Department of Defense, *Findings of the Nuclear Posture Review*, January 9, 2002, slide 12, http://www.defenselink.mil/dodcmsshare/briefingslide/120/020109-D-6570C-001.pdf.
29. See Office of the Secretary of Defense, *Quadrennial Defense Review Report*, February 6, 2006, 27–32, and Bob Martinage, *Dissuasion Strategy*, Center for Strategic and Budgetary Assessments (May 6, 2008), slide 5, http://www.csbaonline.org/4Publications/PubLibrary/S.20080506.Dissuasion_Strateg/S.20080506.Dissuasion_Strateg.pdf.
30. In principle, a sufficiently large land-based UAS could carry penetrating weapons capable of defeating even hardened and deeply buried targets.
31. See Martinage, *Dissuasion Strategy*, slides 9 and 16.
32. Office of the Secretary of Defense, *Quadrennial Defense Review Report*, February 6, 2006, 30.
33. Ibid., 31.
34. Barry D. Watts, *The Case for Long-Range Strike: 21st Century Scenarios* (Center for Strategic and Budgetary Assessments, 2008), 44.
35. As noted above, because of the time-of-flight problem, armed UASs are a superior alternative to ballistic missiles for prompt *conventional* strikes against mobile targets. Time-of-flight is a less compelling argument against ballistic missiles for *nuclear* strikes. A mobile target is unlikely to get outside the envelope of lethal nuclear effects before the ballistic missile warhead arrives. More importantly, nuclear strikes are most likely to be directed against fixed targets, and against such targets the 15- to 30-minute time-of-flight of a ballistic missile is probably acceptable.
36. A study of accidents involving US nuclear weapons from 1950 to 1980 notes that most accidents occurred during logistic/ferry missions and during the airborne alerts that were discontinued in 1968. Hypothetical nuclear-armed UASs need not fly such missions. See http://nsarchive.files.wordpress.com/2010/04/635.pdf.

37. Department of Defense, *FY2009–2034 Unmanned Systems Integrated Roadmap*, 92–93. See also Department of Defense, *Unmanned Aircraft Systems Roadmap 2005–2030*, Appendices F and H.
38. The 2005 UAS Roadmap shows that UAS cost is linearly related to weight (57). If deemed desirable, an unmanned nonnuclear bomber would be large, and thus would not be cheap. This point is often lost on those who think UASs should be "cheap" simply because small, disposable UASs are relatively inexpensive. An unmanned bomber would have to be sufficiently reliable to preserve an asset bought in limited numbers and used for critical missions.
39. Watts, *The Case for Long-Range Strike: 21st Century Scenarios*, 49.
40. *US Air Force White Paper on Long Range Bombers*, March 1, 1999, 17.
41. Defense Science Board, *Time Critical Conventional Strike from Strategic Standoff*, March 2009, 5–6, 81–84.
42. http://www.fas.org/blog/ssp/united_states/NPR2001re.pdf.
43. Department of Defense, *Nuclear Posture Review Report*, April 2010, 32, http://www.defense.gov/npr/docs/2010%20nuclear%20posture%20review%20report.pdf.
44. Ibid., 33.
45. Ibid., 34.
46. One DSB study noted that "using persistent surveillance and strike to deny sanctuary is a key objective of US forces. Current and planned forces cannot achieve this in the presence of modern air defenses. A near-term approach for achieving persistent surveillance/strike throughout moderately defended battlespace is to develop and deploy a family of stealthy, refuelable, subsonic, unmanned, global surveillance/strike systems (UGSSS)." UGSSSs would have a 6,000 nm range, advanced stealth, aerial refueling capability for 100-hour sorties, multi-INT sensors, and a 20,000 lb payload. In the author's view, the case for such a system remains strong. Defense Science Board, *Future Strategic Strike Forces*, February 2004, 5–12, 5–13.
47. On electromagnetic pulse, see Commission to Assess the Threat to the United States from Electromagnetic Pulse (EMP) Attack, http://www.empcommission.org/.
48. Robert F. Trager and Dessislava P. Zagorcheva, "Deterring Terrorism: It Can Be Done," *International Security* (Winter 2005/2006): 96–98. In particular, states that sponsor or host terrorists have assets that airpower can hold at risk. Deterrence should, in principle, function against these states.
49. Jeremy Hsu, "Real Soldiers Love Their Robot Brethren," *LiveScience*, May 21, 2009.
50. Mark Mazetti, "The Downside of Letting Robots Do the Bombing," *The New York Times*, March 21, 2009.
51. David Kilcullen and Andrew Exum, "Death from Above, Outrage from Below," *The New York Times*, May 17, 2009. See also Steve Coll, "In Search of Success," *The New Yorker*, May 25, 2009.
52. Nick Schifrin, "US Drone Strikes with Deadly Accuracy," ABC News, November 19, 2008, http://a.abcnews.com/print?id=6289748.

53. "US Airstrikes in Pakistan Called 'Very Effective'," CNN, May 18, 2009, http://www.cnn.com/2009/POLITICS/05/18/cia.pakistan.airstrikes/.
54. Robert Martinage, *Special Operations Forces: Future Challenges and Opportunities* (Washington, DC: Center for Strategic and Budgetary Assessments, 2008), 27. See also Adm. Eric T. Olson, "The Terror Threat: What It Will Take To Deter, Disrupt, and Defeat It," Speech to the Center for a New American Security, March 3, 2008, 8–9, http://www.cnas.org/files/multimedia/documents/AdmOlson_CNAS_Transcript.pdf.
55. Office of the Secretary of Defense, *Quadrennial Defense Review Report*, February 6, 2006, 23–24. The 2010 QDR noted the "invaluable" role of long-dwell UASs for counterinsurgency and counterterrorism, and called for an expansion of such systems. Office of the Secretary of Defense, *Quadrennial Defense Review Report*, February 2010, 22.
56. Tom Bowman, "Predator Pilots Engage in Remote Control Combat," National Public Radio, September 4, 2007, http://www.npr.org/templates/story/story.php?storyId=14162045.
57. Martinage, *Dissuasion Strategy*, 70. See also 77–78. A "moderately stealthy" UAS, the RQ-170, has operated in Afghanistan, though its precise role is unclear. David A. Fulghum and Bill Sweetman, "Stealth Over Afghanistan," *Aviation Week and Space Technology*, December 14, 2009, 26–31.
58. Office of the Secretary of Defense, *Quadrennial Defense Review Report*, February 6, 2006, 34. See also 35: "Preventing state or non-state actors from acquiring or using WMD highlights the need for... persistent surveillance over wide areas to locate WMD capabilities or hostile forces." UASs excel at providing persistent surveillance over wide areas.
59. Martinage, *Dissuasion Strategy*, xiii, 37–38.
60. These scenarios are described in Defense Science Board, *Time Critical Conventional Strike from Strategic Standoff*, March 2009, 69–80.

Notes on Contributors

Kevin R. Beeker is a United States Air Force senior A/OA-10 combat pilot and has also completed a joint tour flying F/A-18s with the United States Navy. He currently works in the Combat Targeting Division at United States Cyber Command, Ft. Meade, Maryland. He received his MS in CyberWarfare from the Air Force Institute of Technology, Wright-Patterson AFB, Ohio.

Stephen J. Cimbala is a distinguished professor of Political Science at Penn State University–Brandywine. Dr. Cimbala is the author of numerous works in the fields of national security policy, nuclear arms control, and deterrence theory, among others. He won the campus Distinguished Teaching Award in 2012 and recently published *Nuclear Weapons in the Information Age* (Continuum, 2012).

Elbridge Colby is a principal analyst at the Center for Naval Analysis, where he advises a number of US government entities on deterrence and nuclear weapons issues. He previously served in a number of government positions, including on the New START negotiations and ratification for the Department of Defense and as an expert advisor to the Congressional Strategic Posture Commission. He is a graduate of Harvard College and Yale Law School.

Dr. Anne Fitzpatrick gained her PhD in Science and Technology studies from Virginia Tech in 1998. She has lived and worked in the former Soviet Union, and her research includes high-performance computing and strategic science and technology analyses. She is fluent in Russian.

Dr. Michael R. Grimaila is an associate professor of Systems Engineering at the Air Force Institute of Technology, Wright-Patterson AFB, Ohio. He received his PhD in Electrical Engineering from Texas A&M University. His research interests include mission assurance, network management and security, quantum cryptography, and systems engineering.

Dr. Michael W. Haas is a principal electronics engineer at the 711th Human Performance Wing, Air Force Research Laboratory, Wright-Patterson AFB, Ohio. He received his PhD in Engineering and Applied Science from the University of Southampton, United Kingdom. His research interests include cyberspace operations, information operations, and human interface technology.

Dr. Dale Hayden is the director of research at the Air Force Research Institute (AFRI). He has authored a number of articles on Air Force topics, with a focus on space issues. Colonel Hayden completed a distinguished Air Force career in 2008 after more than 25 years of service as a space and missile officer. He holds a PhD in Administration of Higher Education from the University of Alabama.

Dr. Kamal T. Jabbour, a member of the scientific and technical cadre of senior executives, is senior scientist for information assurance, Information Directorate of the Air Force Research Laboratory, Rome, NY. He began his professional career on the computer engineering faculty at Syracuse University, where he taught and conducted research for two decades, including a three-year term as department chairman. Dr. Jabbour has received one US patent, published more than 60 papers in refereed journals and conference proceedings, and penned 317 articles on running.

Dr. Adam B. Lowther is a research professor at the Air Force Research Institute (AFRI), Maxwell Air Force Base. He is the author of numerous books, chapters, journal articles, and editorials on contemporary defense issues. Before joining AFRI, Dr. Lowther taught International Relations and Security Studies at two universities. He also served in the United States Navy aboard ship and at several shore commands. He holds a PhD in International Relations from the University of Alabama.

Dr. Robert F. Mills is an associate professor of Electrical Engineering at the Air Force Institute of Technology, Wright-Patterson AFB, Ohio. He received his PhD in Electrical Engineering from the University of Kansas. His research interests include network management and security, electronic warfare, and systems engineering.

James D. Perry has an MA in Security Policy studies and a PhD in history from George Washington University. He was a visiting fellow at the Hoover Institution, Stanford University, in 1996 and 1997. After completing his fellowship, he joined Science Applications International Corporation, where he analyzed national security issues for US government and military clients. He is currently a senior analyst for Northrop Grumman Corporation, where he conducts defense policy, operational, and budgetary analysis to support company programs. His particular areas of expertise include long-range strike, unmanned systems, and emerging anti-access threats to power projection.

E. Paul Ratazzi is a principal engineer in the Cyber Assurance Branch of the Air Force Research Laboratory in Rome, NY. His research interests include access control and security for mobile devices and assured cloud computing. He holds a

BSEE and an MS in Management from Rensselaer Polytechnic Institute, as well as an MSEE from Syracuse University, and is currently a PhD candidate (ABD) in Electrical Engineering and Computer Science at Syracuse University.

Dr. Gary Schaub Jr. is a senior researcher at the Centre for Military Studies of the University of Copenhagen, Denmark. He is a former member of the faculty of the Air War College and the School of Advanced and Space Studies, as well as a research fellow at the Air Force Research Institute. He holds a PhD from the University of Pittsburgh.

Jonathan Trexel is an employee of Science Applications International Corporation and is currently program manager of the Strategic Deterrence Assessment Lab. He has over 25 years' experience in deterrence and other national security policy and intelligence analysis. Trexel has a bachelor's degree in Political Science and a master's in Strategic Intelligence and is a PhD candidate from the University of Nebraska specializing in US National Security and Foreign policy.

Index

Advanced Strategic Computing (ASC), 100–2
Advanced Strategic Computing Initiative (ASCI), 100
Afghanistan, 1, 119, 145, 164, 171, 173, 186, 189, 203, 217, 229
airpower, 187, 216, 217, 223
al Qaeda, 5, 7, 151, 164, 167, 168, 169, 171, 172, 177, 229
ambiguity, 7
annihilation, 7
arsenal, xi, xii, xiii, 10, 39, 50, 224, 227, 228
assurance, xii, 10, 19, 25, 26, 30, 34, 35, 36, 37, 88, 89, 91, 223, 238, 239
avoidance, 34, 35, 36, 37, 86, 124, 129

ballistic missile defense (BMD), 118, 150, 184, 224
bin Laden, Osama, 7
bipolar, 58, 165, 166, 200
Brodie, Bernard, 1, 142, 154n3

China, 55, 60, 61, 62, 64, 66, 67, 121, 150, 190, 191, 192, 193–5, 196, 201, 202, 204, 230
  Long-March vehicle, 191, 193, 201, 202
coercion, 52, 64, 66, 67, 79, 139, 151, 170, 172, 216, 224
Cold War, xi, xii, 1, 2, 3, 4, 5, 6, 8, 9, 10, 11, 40, 50, 58, 61, 65, 66, 67, 71n38, 82, 84, 93, 94, 97, 99, 103, 104, 108, 109–10, 119, 121, 122, 135, 140, 141, 142, 153, 163, 171, 176, 184, 188, 189, 190, 192, 193, 225
compellence, 167
Comprehensive Nuclear Test-Ban Treaty (CTBT), 100
conventional ballistic missiles, 221
conventional deterrence, 9, 11, 166
cooperation, 55, 69n13, 78, 86, 119, 124, 130, 141, 146, 177, 180n38, 183, 188, 194, 195, 197, 198, 200, 204
counterinsurgency, 49, 151, 175
counterterrorism, 49, 94, 229
course of action (COA), 80, 81, 83, 85, 87, 89, 90, 91, 96n5, 98, 136, 149
credible threat, 1, 40, 64, 66, 155n6, 165
cyber deterrence, 9, 33, 37, 39–40
cyberspace, 9, 17, 18, 19, 20, 21, 22, 23, 24, 25, 26, 27, 28, 29, 30, 31, 33, 34, 36, 37, 38, 39, 40, 41, 42, 43, 75, 203, 238
  attacks, 5, 19, 26, 27, 31
  infrastructure, 21, 22, 23, 24, 25, 26, 27, 28, 29, 30, 31, 41, 42
  operations, 22, 26, 28, 33, 34–7, 38, 41, 238
  superiority, 17, 18
cyberwarfare, 5, 237

decision calculus, xii, 76, 77, 79, 82, 84, 88, 91
decision makers, 1, 6, 7, 8, 9, 63, 94, 152, 155n13
Defense Science Board Task Force, 103
defensive strategy, 34, 43
democratic governments, 53, 58, 140, 164, 174
democratization, 2, 5, 54
Department of Energy (DOE), 100, 101, 102, 103, 112n25
deterrence by denial, 39, 42, 148, 166–7, 174, 176
deterrence by dissuasion, 166, 172, 174, 175
deterrence by threat, 41, 166–7, 174, 176
deterrence failure, 7, 8, 78, 85
deterrence policies, 4, 5, 6, 7, 8, 30, 177
deterrence strategy, 6, 7, 8, 11, 18–19, 31, 34, 40, 77, 78, 81, 83, 84, 85, 86, 90, 91, 92, 165, 166, 167, 172, 173, 178, 203–6, 208
Deterrence Joint-Operating Concept (DO JOC), 10, 18–19, 76, 83, 95, 136, 139, 149, 151, 152, 166
DIMEFIL (diplomatic, information, military, economic, financial, intelligence, and law enforcement), 78
dominance, 17, 20, 50, 57, 58, 64, 71n36, 192, 197
Dual-Axis Radiographic Hydrodynamic Test (DARHT), 100, 101, 102

economic interdependence, 54, 65
Europe, 54, 56, 57, 58, 59, 60, 61, 62, 64, 65, 66, 71n36, 71n38, 117, 118, 119, 120, 121, 122, 123, 124, 130, 141, 148, 166, 167, 169, 185, 190, 191, 192, 196–8, 201, 202, 204

European Phased Adaptive Approach (EPAA), 117, 118, 119, 120, 130
European Space Agency (ESA), 185, 190, 191, 195, 196–8, 199, 200, 201, 204
European Union (EU), 185, 197, 198, 200

foreign internal defense (FID) programs, 176

Germany, 52, 53, 57, 58, 63, 64, 69n10, 71n38, 92, 147, 169, 196, 197
global commons, 38
Global Information Grid (GIG), 24, 33
globalization, 2, 5, 10, 164, 168, 174
Global Positioning System (GPS), 184, 186, 187, 198, 204
global security environment, 3
great power conflicts, 73n57

hegemon, 51, 52, 57, 58, 66, 67, 121, 144, 145, 164

information technology (IT), 20, 33
intercontinental ballistic missile (ICBM), 125, 126, 127, 128, 199, 205, 207, 224, 226
insurgents, 4, 151, 160n82, 168, 169–70, 171, 175, 176, 177, 215, 217, 231
intelligence, surveillance, and reconnaissance (ISR), 11, 86, 88, 184, 202–3, 224, 228
international criminal organizations, 168, 171
International Space Station (ISS), 183, 192, 193, 196, 199, 200, 204
Iran, 18, 60, 67, 92, 119, 124, 135, 144–8, 150, 153, 158n59, 159n65, 159n68, 198, 199–200, 210n27, 230
space program

INDEX

Iraq, 1, 7, 18, 82, 86, 87, 90, 92, 93, 145, 146, 151, 164, 165, 171, 173, 217
Islamic fundamentalism, 5
Islamic fundamentalists, 4, 167
Israel, 82, 86, 89, 92, 145, 146, 148, 150, 159n77, 191, 198, 199, 210n27

Japan, 7, 8, 52, 54, 69n10, 92, 168, 191, 192, 198, 200, 201, 204, 210n27
  National Space Development Agency (NASDA), 195–6
Joint Chiefs of Staff, 20, 94
Joint Forces Command (JFCOM), 136
joint force commander (JFC), 21, 136, 137

Kennan, George, 141, 142, 143, 144, 157n35
kinetic force, 5, 6

Latin America, 64
low observability, 218, 219, 220

Mediterranean, 60, 61
Middle East, 61, 144, 146, 148, 169, 176, 177
misperception, 8, 28, 155n13
mission-essential functions (MEFs), 36, 42
mutually assured destruction (MAD), 41, 43, 157n42, 208

National Aeronautics and Space Administration (NASA), 187, 188, 190, 192, 204
National Nuclear Security Administration (NNSA), 101, 102, 104, 113n34
National Security Strategy (NSS), xi, xii, 180n38, 188, 189, 206
neorealism, 62, 72n48
Net Force Maneuver, 22, 28, 31

New Look Policy, 163
New START, 118, 119, 120, 124, 130, 132n18, 237
next generation, 29, 227
nonstate actor, xi, 2, 4, 5, 6, 9, 11, 109, 163–82, 228–31
North Atlantic Treaty Organization (NATO), 58, 66, 93, 94, 95, 117, 118, 119, 121, 122, 123, 124, 130, 163, 164, 165, 197
North Korea, 67, 84, 173
  space program, 198, 199, 200
nuclear deterrence, 3, 5, 9, 10, 43, 49–73, 97, 99, 103, 106, 107, 108, 110, 117, 122, 208, 224, 231
  forces, xii, 8, 9, 79, 108, 118, 120, 121, 122, 124, 128, 129, 223
  proliferation, 5, 10, 75–96, 108
  strategy, 1, 9, 66–7
  weapons, xi, xii, xiii, 3, 4, 5, 10, 49, 50, 51, 53, 55, 56, 61, 63–5, 66, 67, 73n62, 75, 76, 78, 80, 82, 83, 84, 85, 87, 88, 89, 90, 91, 92, 93, 96n4, 96n5, 97–115, 117–32, 141, 145, 146, 163, 165, 204, 224, 225, 226, 227, 228, 233n36, 237
Nuclear Posture Review, 104, 122, 223, 227

Obama, President Barack, xi, 20, 29, 49, 117, 118, 119, 120, 122, 124, 165, 190
Operationally Responsive Cyberspace (ORC), 9, 17–32
Operationally Responsive Space (ORS), 17–32, 206–8
Operation Enduring Freedom, 171
Orbit, 21, 183, 184, 188, 191, 193, 194, 195, 198, 199, 200, 201, 204, 205, 206, 207, 219, 222, 223
  geosynchronous, 201, 205

Orbit—*continued*
   high-earth, 183, 205
   low-earth, 183, 184, 188, 194, 199, 204, 205
   near-earth, 183

Peace of Westphalia (1648), 167
peer competitor, 5, 9, 165
Persian Gulf, 145
persistent surveillance, 223, 224, 226, 228, 229, 230, 231, 234n46, 235n58
policy makers, 2, 4, 8, 30, 43, 79, 106, 135, 136, 137, 138, 140, 152, 163, 165, 175, 186, 199, 200, 201, 202
post–Cold War, xi, 3, 50, 82, 94, 97, 109, 121, 122, 188, 189
psychological effect, 165

Quadrennial Defense Review (QDR), 216, 218, 224, 229, 235n55

range of military operations, 137
Rapid Response Space Center (RRSC), 21
realists, 62, 164
Reliable Replacement Warhead (RRW), 104, 113n32, 114n34, 114n35
resiliency, 26, 28, 29, 207, 208
rogue regimes, 5, 9, 10, 11, 135–61
Russia, 55, 57, 60, 67, 117–32

Science Based Stockpile Stewardship Program (SBSS), 100
smart power, 10, 75–96
Soviet Union, 1, 2, 4, 8, 50, 58, 71n36, 93, 135, 141, 142, 144, 153, 157n42, 163, 166, 169, 187, 190, 192, 193, 237
Space Based Infrared Radar System (SBIRS), 208
Space Commission, 186, 187, 189
space deterrence, 11, 183–214

space launch vehicle (SLV), 191, 200, 206
space situational awareness (SSA), 205
Special Operations Forces, 217, 230
Stockpile Stewardship Program (SSP), 10, 100, 101, 102, 107, 111n11
strategic challenges, 1
superiority, 6, 17, 18, 33, 39, 67, 183, 184, 186, 203, 204, 205, 208
surface-to-air missiles (SAM), 220

Tanker Safe Line (TSL), 222
targeting, 66, 129, 174, 184, 217, 218, 219, 221, 224, 231, 237
technological domain, 37, 41
terrorists, 2, 4, 5, 148, 160n82, 167–77, 190, 215, 217, 228, 229, 230, 231, 234n48
theater missile defenses (TMD), 122, 123

United Nations (UN), 163, 194
United States Air Force, 17, 26, 34, 49, 155n6, 184, 186, 187, 188, 205, 206, 207, 208, 216, 217, 218, 225, 226, 227, 228, 232n15, 237, 238, 239
United States Cyber Command (USCYBERCOM), 23, 24, 31, 237
United States Strategic Command (USSTRATCOM), 10, 20, 21, 23, 30, 112n16, 132n18, 136, 152, 166, 179n15, 188
United States tested anti-satellite (ASAT), 184, 204, 205
Unmanned Aerial Systems (UAS), 11, 215–35
Unmanned Air Systems, *see* Unmanned Aerial Systems (UAS)

weapons of mass destruction (WMD), 4, 5, 75, 82, 83, 86, 88, 91, 92, 122, 216, 217, 226, 228, 230, 231n6, 235n58

CPSIA information can be obtained
at www.ICGtesting.com
Printed in the USA
BVHW04*1237091018
529676BV00005B/3/P